REFLECTIONS FROM BOTH SIDES OF THE GLASS CEILING

Foreword by Brian K. Bond, Executive Director, PFLAG National

REFLECTIONS FROM BOTH SIDES OF THE GLASS CEILING

FINDING MY TRUE SELF IN CORPORATE AMERICA

STEPHANIE BATTAGLINO

Follow Your Heart Press
287 Vista Royale Circle West
Palm Desert, CA 92211

www.StephanieBattaglino.com

Reflections From Both Sides of the Glass Ceiling
Battaglino, Stephanie.

Second Edition

ISBN 979-8-2181477-6-1

ENDORSEMENTS

"Stephanie Battaglino has the gifts of a natural storyteller. This is the story of her remarkable life and journey to becoming the full human being, the authentic woman that was always the core of her soul. Today, while Transgender people are making great strides, we have precious few individuals who can tell the story of gender transition from within the elite executive offices of corporate America. Stephanie tells that story with honesty, grace, and wit. And in telling that story, she reinforces the essential values of respect, opportunity and hard work."

Lisa Middleton, Mayor Pro Tem, Palm Springs, California

...

"In a detailed, personal account of metamorphosis, Stephanie Battaglino's story of her internal and external transition from male to female fills you in on the inner turmoil and psychic pain caused by the discovery that you don't align with society's concepts of gender. Her story also gives insight into how transgender people can soar after finding their true self and the courage to live it. Couple that with the realization that her male privilege also ended with her transformation, and the reader receives a wide angled view of how our multiple identities intertwine to create the person we are and the person the world perceives. If you want to understand the people in the transgender community--and find yourself as an ally, too--Stephanie's book is a great guide."

Steve Humerickhouse, Executive Director at The Forum on Workplace Inclusion, a program of Augsburg University

...

"Reflections from Both Sides of the Glass Ceiling sheds light on the private struggles so many trans people have faced in solitude. The book is an insider's guide to being a better LGBTQ+ ally in the workplace and beyond, offering us a unique and necessary look at white privilege and gender bias. By telling it like it is, Stephanie Battaglino debunks the mystery around the trans experience through her authenticity, humility, and humor. She is a trans pioneer who has the courage to wear her heart on her sleeve, calling us to join her on her journey from shame to acceptance."

M. Dru Levasseur, Esq., Director of Diversity, Equity, and Inclusion at National LGBT Bar Association

...

"Stephanie Battaglino speaks from the heart in Reflections from Both Sides of the Glass Ceiling. This book is perfect for those who desire real insight into the complexities of diversity, inclusion and equity. I found this to be a very capable source for improving one's awareness and advancing inclusive behavior skills. I was inspired by this book's courageous authenticity. For all those who desire to make a difference in building effective workplace relationships by being an ally and an advocate, this is a must read!"

May Snowden, Senior Fellow & Program Director, Human Capital Practice, The Conference Board

...

"Reflections is a moving personal account of the challenges that Stephanie faced as a transgender woman seeking to find her place at work and in life as her true self. But it's also a primer on the near-universal struggles that transgender people still face on a daily basis. Reflections is a must-read for anyone seeking to understand these unique challenges and help make workplaces and our society better and more inclusive for everyone."

Michael Silverman, former Executive Director of the Transgender Defense & Legal Education Fund (TLDEF)

...

"This book is a must read to understand corporate culture and how important perspective really is in this world. Stephanie's journey is a great tale of why inclusion ultimately makes the difference in people's lives. I enjoyed this great read and highly recommend it!"

Ashley Brundage, Equity, Inclusion and Belonging Leader, Author of *Empowering Differences*

...

"We hear a lot about trans people in the media, but it's rare that we get such a warm welcome into the up close and personal view of those individuals' real-life experiences. Stephanie's stories of transitioning on the job in corporate America—and the wisdom gained along the way—offer an insightful voice in the gender equity conversation. A must-read for workplace inclusion warriors!"

C. Michael Woodward, MPH, Transgender and LGBTQ+ Inclusion Expert

…

"Stephanie Battaglino has woven a powerful and inspiring story, spanning everything from corporate culture, to self-discovery, to gender politics, to indispensable professional advice. With a unique and relatable voice, Stephanie seamlessly guides readers between humor, honesty, and hope. As a cisgender woman, I found "Reflections from Both Sides of the Glass Ceiling" immensely illuminating and insightful. But make no mistake: this book will universally resonate with anyone who has felt like an outsider in corporate America—regardless of gender identity."

Jennifer Brown, Founder & CEO, Jennifer Brown Consulting

…

"In 'Reflections from Both Sides of the Glass Ceiling,' Stephanie Battaglino gives us a glimpse of the unique experiences of transgender people who transition at work and an understanding of how gender affects workplace experience in tangible and inescapable ways. Warm, funny, and insightful – Stephanie allows us to look at the intersection of gender and power in an approachable way. This book is a must read for leaders seeking to understand how identity shapes workplace experience and their role in creating welcoming, equitable spaces for all.

Beck Bailey, Former Director, Workplace Equality Program, Human Rights Campaign (HRC)

…

"Stephanie Battaglino's lifeline is authenticity. As a proud transgender woman, and as a business leader and storyteller, her passion for authenticity has inspired a full life and a remarkable career. Her memoir is a truly rewarding way to open doors, minds and hearts."

Bob Witeck, President Witeck Communications, Inc.

…

"This most engaging book is a treasure map to an intimate understanding of the challenges, sacrifices, and joyful fulfillment of being a self-affirmed woman who is transgender. Stephanie's honest storytelling is compelling and enlightening. As she makes clear, it's just one person's tale, but her very personal sharing will open hearts and minds and will resonate with anyone who has made the hero's journey to authentic living."

Brian McNaught, author of *Brian McNaught's Guide to LGBTQ Issues in the Workplace,* **"The godfather of gay diversity training" The New York Times**

...

Both Sides of the Glass Ceiling: Finding My True Self in Corporate America is a businesswoman›s memoir about how she transitioned while working as a senior executive at New York Life. Her experience provides a unique perspective on the glass ceiling in business from the viewpoint of a male who became female and unexpectedly confronted the disparity in not just income, but respect between the genders.

Many books are now on the market covering the social impact of transitioning. However, more so than most, Stephanie Battaglino's candid discussion of the business world is striking from the start and will open many eyes to the issues: "I have lived a life on both sides of the glass ceiling. On one side, I came into the world identified by an anatomy that said to society I was male, even though inside I knew I was really female. On the other side of the glass, I lived with the privilege afforded to most white males and did not understand what that privilege really meant until I lost it. When I stepped into my office as Stephanie, a trans woman and a person that most of my colleagues saw as female, I suddenly found myself looking at the glass ceiling from a very uncomfortable perspective—with my nose firmly pressed up against it, thinking, "How far I have fallen!" But that's not even the half of it. What happened at that moment was just the first of many challenges I faced in finding my true self in corporate America.

Stephanie's candid honesty in charting these revelations is part of what sets this memoir apart from others, creating a solid inspection of status quo, class, and gender issues that traces experiences from both sides of the table she sat at.

Readers uncomfortable with issues of gender equality and underlying attitudes and prejudices might find Both Sides of the Glass Ceiling a difficult read because it forces the viewer to confront these in their own approaches to life and business. Battaglino's focus on creating human connections that lead to understanding over confrontation, her contrast between the trans and non-conforming community and the traditional business world, and her stance on cultivating honesty and a complete life pulls no punches; yet delivers its hard-hitting message with a gentle insistence on understanding.

Her words are passionate, clear, and inviting even as they acknowledge the inherent privilege of being white: "...in the grand scheme of things, I have it easy—really I do. To many who see me, I'm just another white woman of privilege, and with that comes a free pass, a "Get Out of Jail Free" card of sorts that society allows me to carry with me every day. The daily reality for many of my trans brothers and sisters, especially those of color, is nothing at all like mine. But I have a responsibility to raise up into your consciousness a different daily reality. The one that the vast majority of trans people live with; the one that involves pain, hardship, and for some, violence."

Between her divorce, handling her son, and her business pursuits, Battaglino's memoir embraces the building blocks of constructing a completely different life.

Few memoirs embrace the mission of fostering ideals of transgender workplace inclusion. Few juxtapose the personal and business impact of these actions in such a candid, revealing manner.

This book's discussions of power, attitude, prejudice, and redemption makes for a powerful read highly recommended not just for trans people navigating a new glass ceiling in the workplace, but for business and workplace readers seeking a better understanding of what inclusion really means.

Its hard-hitting discussions will leave everyone thinking long after the story is finished.

Diane Donovan, *Midwest Book Review*

...

"Stephanie's compelling story of what it was like coming out in corporate America really speaks not only from a transwoman's perspective but from a woman's perspective, as well. Her courage is an inspiration to the trans community and to all women! «Reflections from Both Sides of the Glass Ceiling» speaks of sexism in corporate America as well as the struggles of anyone with a gender identity that does not align with the binary society of America. This book is a must-read and perfect for my library and for everyone fighting for a more equitable and inclusive world for all transgender and non-binary people.»

Dr. Gennifer "Genn" Herley, PhD, Founder & Executive Director, TransNewYork

CONTENTS

To my wife Mari, the yin to my yang and my chief everything officer. Thank you for stumbling through the world with me. I love you. And always remember, life could be boring.

"We travel, some of us forever, to seek other states, other lives, other souls."

~ Anais Nin

AUTHOR'S NOTE

The reflections that appear in these pages are from the memories of my own lived experience in my particular slice of the corporate world and, more broadly, from my life. The stories are based solely on my recollection of how they made me feel and how I processed their impact. My reflections are wholly my own. I have also changed the names of the majority of the people who appear in the book in an effort to retain their anonymity and respect their privacy.

FOREWORD

IT BEGINS WITH KEARNY, NEW JERSEY. IT WILL END with me telling you why I believe this book will change hearts and minds.

But it begins with Kearny, New Jersey.

I met Stephanie Battaglino at my very first meeting of the PFLAG National Board of Directors, shortly after being hired in February 2019 as the new Executive Director of the organization. I was nervous before the meeting. PFLAG had long held a special place in my heart. I didn't know about the organization back when I was a closeted gay kid growing up in conservative, rural Missouri—an anxious kid who was more comfortable with his 2000-pound steer Rufus than with his schoolmates. Later, when I learned about PFLAG, I'd wished I'd known of it sooner, and its mission and members meant the world to me. In fact, during my time in the Obama White House, I often referred to PFLAG members and their stories, knowing that parents, families, and allies sharing their stories could make a huge impact.

And now here I was, in Washington, D.C., preparing to lead this organization, and getting ready to meet the people who were, for all intents and purposes, my bosses. When I was introduced to Stephanie, it was immediately clear that she was a force to be reckoned with. Bright eyes, bold ideas, and a shared passion for the PFLAG mission. And while she was a stranger to me, something about her seemed very familiar. As she shared more about herself—and her journey transitioning while working as a senior executive at New York Life—I realized where the familiarity was coming from: She reminded me (in only the best ways) of my ex-husband's family who, like Stephanie, were raised in Kearny, New Jersey.

You know when they say you can take the person out of New Jersey...? It's absolutely true. And Stephanie is all Jersey. Honest. Real. Strong. Authentic. With a no-holds-barred way of saying what needs to be said, but always in service of support and moving things forward. We connected immediately, and as we worked more closely together—her business acumen a guiding force on PFLAG National's Business Advisory Council—it was clear I'd found a friend and comrade in this work for equality. Don't get me wrong, it hasn't been all work. It isn't too difficult for us to go down memory lane of our mutual connection to Kearny and end up talking about Brother's Bakery, Chicken Galore, or The Thistle Fish and Chips, to name a few of our favorites.

Stephanie's work has been colored by every moment she shares in this book, a book that she is uniquely suited to write, with a story that is foundational to all that she is and does. She has built on this foundation and taken her advocacy to another level, working tirelessly not only for transgender and nonbinary workplace inclusion, but for gender equity everywhere.

Stephanie's story of fighting for fairness in places and spaces that still struggle to be diverse and culturally humble will undoubtedly help anyone who is in need of hope, offered through the personal lens of a journey that proves that things can change for the better, once you are able to bring your whole self into the world, into every facet of your life. When you can show up authentically, as Stephanie did and always does, you will undoubtedly be your best self. Your work, your time with family and friends, your volunteerism—all of it will be impacted for the better, because the fear of being found out disappears. I remember that fear all too well from my rural Missouri childhood. I was reminded of it reading this book, and I was also reminded of the deep relief I felt when I finally opened the closet door.

I've had the opportunity now over the last two years to see Stephanie in action, and my first impressions have only deepened and become colored by the new respect I've grown to have for her as I've learned more about her, about her story, and about the work she is doing to move inclusion in the workplace forward, not just for LGBTQ+ people, but all people.

I am grateful for Stephanie and for the work that she does. She is a powerful example of moving gracefully through struggle. Sharing her story with everyone who is learning to live life deeply, meaningfully and—most significantly—authentically, will indeed change lives. And that's because she will always tell it like it is.

I expect no less from my friend from Kearny, New Jersey.

BRIAN K. BOND
Executive Director, PFLAG National
Former Obama Administration Deputy
Director of the White House Office of
Public Engagement

PROLOGUE

I HAVE LIVED A LIFE ON BOTH SIDES OF THE GLASS ceiling. On one side, I came into the world identified by an anatomy that said to society I was male, even though inside I knew I was really female. On the other side of the glass, I lived with the privilege afforded to most white males, and did not understand what that privilege really meant until I lost it. When I stepped into my office as Stephanie, a trans woman and a person that most of my colleagues saw as female, I suddenly found myself looking at the glass ceiling from a very uncomfortable perspective—with my nose firmly pressed up against it, thinking, "How far I have fallen!" But that's not even the half of it. What happened at that moment was just the first of many challenges I faced in finding my true self in corporate America.

I had arrived rather abruptly at the intersection of my gender identity and gender inequality. I began to see my world through a different set of eyes, taking in a view that was at once terrifying and exhilarating. There was much to assimilate about myself and about this new circle of female colleagues that I now counted myself among. How I navigated that space, and what I learned along the way is what this book is all about.

Woody Allen famously once said, "Eighty percent of success is showing up." Well, I have shown up. And by reading this far, so have you. It's wonderful to meet you. My sole reason for being here is that I want to help move the needle in a positive direction toward a world of workplace equality for all transgender and gender non-conforming individuals. Everyone, regardless of their life's journey, has the right to gainful employment in the United States of America. There should be no exceptions to this, no asterisks, no, "we'll come back and include you later." A vibrant, engaged, and fully functional workplace must include individuals of all stripes. It is precisely this diversity of human experience that can propel workplaces forward, leading to greater levels of innovation and accomplishment. The trans and gender non-conforming community have a vital role to play in this workplace evolution. At its genesis is the richness and depth of our personal stories.

I choose to show up where people have never seen a trans person before. As a wholly human being, I have a right to participate in any aspect of society of my choosing. I should not, and will not, be excluded from those very things that bring me joy, happiness, and completeness. If, for some reason, my participation offends the sensibilities of those around me then I have three words for them: Get. Over. It.

I will not go away and step back into the darkness. By remaining steadfast in this core belief, by pushing the envelope, by showing up— and participating—that is how I contribute to the broadening of the transgender narrative.

But it's also about changing hearts and changing minds. And the only way to accomplish that is by first creating a human connection. I believe I have had success in moving people by creating an understanding of our shared humanity. In a very real sense, it is our greatest common denominator. It creates the foundation upon which we can build a house full of meaningful learning.

My hopes, my dreams, my worries, and my typical day are the same as most everyone else's. I have many of the same issues that you do, plus another very important one. People don't understand who I am. Among other things, they want me to use a different bathroom—one that will make them feel less threatened. They use incorrect pronouns to describe me based upon what they think I am—without asking first. They stare. They snicker. Some even laugh and shake their heads in disbelief. Worse still, many seek to marginalize me and my community as a perceived threat to society.

But in the grand scheme of things, I have it easy—really I do. To many who see me, I'm just another white woman of privilege, and with that comes a free pass, a "Get Out of Jail Free" card of sorts that society allows me to carry with me every day. The daily reality for many of my trans brothers and sisters, especially those of color, is nothing at all like mine. But I have a responsibility to raise up into your consciousness a different daily reality. The one that the vast majority of trans people live with; the one that involves pain, hardship, and for some, violence.

ⅈ

According to the National Center for Transgender Equality, in the years 2018 and 2019 combined, forty-nine transgender people were fatally shot or killed by other violent means. At least thirty-eight transgender people were murdered through November of 2020, which far surpassed the entire total for 2019. Sadly, this horrific epidemic of violence is particularly pronounced for my trans sisters of color. And it is a global crisis that has shown no signs of ending.

No one should ever have to live in fear for their life simply for living their truth. No one should feel so afraid and isolated that the only options they feel they have left are to deny their true self, or worse, take their own life. It is the second decade of the twenty-first century, and we must do better.

Ignorance is no longer an excuse, because the information about the transgender and gender non-conforming community and the issues it faces is out there. It's time to wake up and learn. We must learn to practice tolerance. Through tolerance we can lift ourselves up and those around us. As I once heard Maria Hinojosa, the host of *Latino USA* on National Public Radio (NPR) say during her keynote at *The Forum on Workplace Inclusion*, "Learn to see yourself as the person most unlike yourself."

It's not just about the violence either. Trans people face quality of life issues at every turn. And it all begins and ends with having a job.

The stark reality is if you don't have substantial employment you cannot put a roof over your head, you cannot put food on your table, you cannot clothe yourself, and you cannot have any chance at a meaningful life. Unfortunately, for many trans people, a lack of work can mean a life on the street, homelessness, or possibly selling their bodies just to survive. These are the people of my community who are the most vulnerable to violence. But what's much worse than all of this is that not having a job means not having hope. And no one deserves that.

As a community, trans and gender non-conforming people are arguably more visible now than we have ever been. That is why the timing for this book is now, because shifts in the social, political, and cultural climates are putting us squarely in the middle of the national discourse.

My story may not seem unusual in that the conversation about transgender issues has become more common, but that is the rub. While my community's stories and issues may be more prevalent in today's society, we are still fighting for our rightful place at the broader LGBTQ equality table. We are not there yet. I was among the initial wave of trans persons to come out in corporate America, and I made it through the very small window that existed at that time. But, the truth is, the struggle continues. I want to push that window open even further, not only for transgender people, but for cisgender women struggling for equality in the corporate environment.

Our stories are now more frequently seen throughout popular media. We have become, to quote the vernacular, "the flavor of the month." Some might even go so far as to use the term *trendy* to describe us. Arguably, trans and gender non-conforming people are making themselves more visible and are sharing their own personal journeys more frequently than they ever have, and at younger and younger ages. Taken together, these stories form a powerful and evocative narrative about gender in our society.

Yet there are many who haven't been paying attention, either because they just never saw the need to or because they don't really care. It's for these people that I have written this book. Because an educated populace is the necessary prerequisite to meaningful dialogue on the issues that have dogged the transgender community for decades. My hope is that by adding my voice to the conversation, more momentum will be created and sustained.

Depending on what article or study you read, the total number of transgender Americans numbers somewhere around 1.4 million. That makes up just 0.6 percent of the total U.S. population. It is widely thought that this number is, in reality, somewhat higher as more and more younger people in their teens come out as trans. But one thing is for sure, this is most definitely not a big number.

When you don't have the population numbers that means that your voice is seen as smaller. And a smaller voice means that your issues, your injustices, and your calls for equal treatment go unheard. To put it bluntly, you don't get a seat at the table.

There are only so many of us who advocate on behalf of our community and for ourselves. For our rights. For our piece of whatever the "American Dream" looks like nowadays. We can't do this alone. That's why we need help. We need our allies. We cannot create the change we seek on our own. We need others to stand shoulder-to-shoulder with us in our fight for equality. In our fight to be included with everyone else.

So at this point you might be asking yourself, "where do I start?" That is a question I have fielded more times than I can count from many well-intentioned colleagues and people I have met at companies across the country. And what I always say in reply is: educate yourself. It's where every journey to allyship begins.

And then there are those whose desire to remain uneducated and unwilling to engage in constructive discussion has reached its nadir. In the four years or so that have passed since I first started writing this book, this resistance has metastasized into a wave of governmental actions designed to squeeze the life out of the transgender community.

The worst of these governmental actions aimed directly at the transgender community was the Trump administration's position that gender should be narrowly defined as a biological, immutable condition determined by genitalia at birth. This sent shockwaves throughout the transgender community. The mantra "We will not be erased" was born. #WontBeErased went viral.

This is discrimination, pure and simple. But this isn't your father's brand of discrimination. It is prejudice at its most insidious level. It is bigotry designed with one objective in mind: to eradicate an entire community of human beings from society. These actions aren't undertaken to merely roll back any gains that we have made and shove us back into the margins of society. These have been advocated for, and championed by, individuals who seek to legislate the transgender community completely out of existence.

And just when I thought I had seen and heard all there is to see about the marginalization of an entire group of people, I was thrust into the experience of an entirely different type of discrimination. What many of my cisgender female colleagues were facing was not new to me, but the way I was seeing and feeling it from a new perspective most certainly was. My eyes were opened to inequitable patterns of behavior that had existed for decades throughout corporate America. What I once had only viewed from a distance was suddenly front and center in my work life.

I stand in solidarity with every cisgender female colleague I have ever worked with who has felt the sting of not being recognized for their ideas and achievements, or who has been passed over for advancement in their career because their merits were somehow seen by the men they worked with as not good enough. And while I'm at it, I am here to tell you that this collective "we" that I have the privilege of being a part of will never be silenced.

As for me, and who I am as an out and proud transwoman, I will not disappear. Try as I might, I will never completely understand what it is about being transgender that some people find so threatening. I'm just trying to live my life in the best and most honest way that I can. You know what I'm talking about, the whole "unalienable rights" and "pursuit of happiness" thing that our forefathers wrote about in the Declaration of Independence.

When people stand up and say they are transgender, it is a courageous act, because in doing so, they run the risk of losing everything. Everything! I ran that risk.

Think about that level of risk for a moment. After years, and in some cases decades, of denying what you know in your heart and soul is your truest self, you cast your fears aside and take that first step on your journey to wholeness, to completeness. But instead of finding joy, happiness, and affirmation, you are confronted with hatred and scorn. You are thrown out of your home and onto the street. You are isolated. You could be beaten or even killed. You have seemingly nothing. Your life as you once knew it to be is over. You...are...alone.

It is the ultimate irony: what should be a shining moment in your life is instead overcome by hatred. *Hatred* is such a horrible word. But at its roots you will find fear. Fear of what on the surface seems so foreign, so "out there," so not normal. And for some in our world that's all that's needed to commit acts of violence against trans people. That is precisely why we must educate, must create a dialogue, must tell our stories. Our future depends on it.

At first glance, you might think that telling a story or two about how I arrived at my true self might seem a bit self-indulgent, or even narcissistic. However, our stories are the strongest weapon we possess in our fight against the withering barrage of hate and discrimination in our communities.

Many people have asked me over the years, "how did you know it was time to come out?" The flippant answer, of course, is, "How did I *not* know?" But honestly, it is difficult to describe, no less understand, unless you are a person who has taken a similar journey to mine. It is a deeply personal decision rooted in the essence of one's soul that I believe is best expressed in this quote from Anais Nin:

> *"And the day came when the risk to remain tight in a bud*
> *was more painful than the risk it took to blossom."*

I often tell people that my life is an open book. Trust me, I have a million stories that I could tell you that can answer just about any question you could think of to ask me. To some that may seem like over-sharing, and I get that, but how else are we to learn? How else are we to teach? How else are we to evolve? Since the beginning of time human beings have been telling and sharing stories—on cave walls and in the

Bible, the Koran, the Torah, and the Pali Canon. All in an effort, in one way or another, to do exactly that.

I've learned much along the way, and the time has now come to share it so that others, too, may learn. My experiences are by no means a panacea. But they are uniquely mine, and if sharing what I have learned about myself and those that have arced in and out of my life can change just one heart and one mind then I have achieved what I set out to do.

It is my hope that this book will help others understand and support these flowering buds—or the image of a butterfly emerging from its cocoon comes to mind. It is an apt comparison, because a butterfly has to spend the first part of its life in a body that looks nothing like they truly are. They must hide in their cocoon until they are ready to shed the old caterpillar body and identity, and spread their wings and announce to the world they are ready to fly. For so many of us throughout the transgender and gender non-conforming community, the time to fly is now.

In my experience I have found that we all, to one degree or another, have experienced feelings of pain, hurt, frustration, and anger at various points in our lives. It is what bonds us to one another. But we all cross paths with these emotions in a variety of ways. These emotions may come to us because we did not achieve a personal or professional goal we have set for ourselves, or maybe because we haven't been able to let go of a wrong or injustice—real or perceived—that was done to us, or worse yet, because we have been denied the love of a parent or sibling who felt we somehow didn't deserve it.

It is within this matrix of emotions where our lives intersect. The venue within which you have felt the sting of rejection, for example, may be different than mine was when I realized my brothers could not deal with my coming out as transgender, but that in no way diminishes the effect that feeling has had on each of us.

That is the precise place where our life's arcs intersect. Where our greatest common denominator of humanness fuses us together. On the surface you might say, "I cannot relate at all to you as a transgender person," but if you allow yourself to touch the essence of the emotions that I experienced, you will no doubt connect with a parallel emotion from your own lived experience and—voila—we have found the beginning of our kinship. Our foundation from which understanding can begin to form.

I realize this may all seem a bit too ethereal, but I believe it is possible—if only life itself and the society in which we live didn't get in the way. We are bombarded every day with forces that seek to shape our opinions, our degree of open mindedness, and our tolerance for people "who do not look like me." Our worldview is influenced on a daily basis by the media—in all its forms —and even by the ones we love.

That's a lot to overcome, and it can vary widely depending on where you live as you are reading this book. But I remain undaunted and humbly offer my story for you to contemplate, because we all have a story that deserves to be heard. This one happens to be mine.

CHAPTER ONE
HIDING IN PLAIN SIGHT

*"Growth is painful. Change is painful. But nothing is as painful
as staying stuck somewhere you don't belong."*
~ Mandy Hale

KEARNY, NEW JERSEY LIES EIGHT MILES DUE WEST OF
New York City. I had a clear view of the city's skyline, across the Mead-
owlands, from my high school. I like to say that I grew up in the shadow
of the city, and in many respects, I did—both literally and figuratively.
It was a place where I found out that feeling different from everybody
else meant hiding in the shadows at a very young age. For me, hiding
wasn't an option. I was a natural extrovert. On the playground, in school,
and at family gatherings, I was always the center of attention—and I
enjoyed the spotlight. So, instead of retreating to the shadows, I hid in
plain sight.

God, I wanted to get out of that town as fast as I could. By the
time I attended high school, I knew, beyond a shadow of a doubt, that
my future—whatever it was going to look like—was most definitely not
going to take place in Kearny. I feared that if I didn't go away to college,
I would be resigned to a life of pumping gas and on the weekends hang-

ing in some dive bar. But that only sounded good in conversation with friends. I was going for the laugh—and I usually got it. The *real* reason that I was running away was that I was running from myself. Wearing a mask every day was exhausting.

Leaving home meant that maybe I could finally leave behind the dirty little secret I held onto for so long. In my most private and intimate moments, when no one was around, and I could retreat from being the center of attention, I felt like a girl inside, not a boy. I realize now that it was the first of many attempts to eradicate this "sickness" inside me. It was a pseudo-sickness that I would battle in a series of epic failures both in the workplace and my personal life for the next twenty-seven years.

My socialization process as an overachieving male in the workplace and society was well on its way. My acquired machismo gave me a sense of competitiveness that fueled my successes and failures as a manager, executive, and a male in corporate life. My desire to compete and win has been a part of my personality my entire life, even after I transitioned. It is a trait that ultimately chaffed my male colleagues who were convinced that women should not act that way.

During that first part of my life, I had no one and nowhere to turn to with my feelings. There was no outlet for me to share my deepest feelings. No support group. No internet. So I just lowered my head and sojourned on, thinking that if I worked hard enough and did all the things that "manly men" did, I could destroy all traces of this horrible *sickness*.

GROWING UP DIFFERENT: WAS GOD JOKING?

I am the youngest of four children born to Jim and Rose Battaglino. I was born nearly twelve years after my middle brother and sister, fraternal twins, and almost fifteen years after my oldest brother. Despite the age difference—and what seemed like a generational difference—I got along just fine with my brothers and sister. But we only lived together in the same house, and in the case of my brothers and me, in the same attic room—for a few years. Both of my brothers were married and out of the house by the time I was thirteen.

I was raised in a very Catholic family. I was begrudgingly carted off to mass every Sunday at St. Stephen's Church. It was there that I first realized I was different from other boys my age, and more significantly, that it was a sin to feel that way. There was no way God could have ever created somebody like me on purpose.

I must have done something horribly wrong to have this happen to me. I couldn't determine if it was God's will that drew me toward my mother's closet that very first time. I was convinced that God was playing some sort of horrible joke on me. After all, he was watching me every single time that I would feel that overwhelming urge to slip into my mother's or my sister's undergarments and retreat into my fantasy world of being a girl—He knew I couldn't stop. God knew it was never going to go away. And, He was responsible for making me the way that I am.

Was this supposed to be my little version of hell on Earth that I was fated to endure for the rest of my life? I even thought it was all just some sort of supreme test that I had to pass to earn my place in heaven. I figured that I deserved it. After all, I couldn't stop myself. I had to be punished for feeling the way I felt. How could I ever be one of God's divine children? I was destined for the spiritual scrapheap. All I ever wanted was to wake up one morning and find that I was magically transformed into a girl. That was far too much to ask of God.

All of this served to instill a deep sense of guilt and shame in me that I was determined, at all costs, to keep hidden from everyone. How could I ever possibly tell one of the priests or the nuns about my feelings? That was just not going to happen. Ever. It was a pang of guilt and shame that

I carried like an ever-growing millstone around my neck for more than forty years.

I was very conflicted, and I wanted to do everything right. I made myself half-crazy trying to make everybody happy. Go to catechism classes and obey the nuns. Take all of my sacraments and be a good boy. Happy parents meant I could more easily get away with all the cross-dressing and all of the masturbatory fantasies of what it would be like to be a girl like my mom and my sister.

But this was all a sin, wasn't it? I was damned to the eternal flames of hell, wasn't I? Those thoughts would stop me, but only for a moment. They could not overcome the much stronger feelings of femininity I would experience when I went off to my secret world. Once there, I couldn't have cared less about all of the retribution. It was the furthest thing from my mind. But I would never get to heaven being this way. I even thought for a time that being a priest might be an excellent way to go. I could do the proverbial end around all of this. Thankfully, I decided that wasn't a good option for the Roman Catholic Church and me, after all.

THE TIMES THEY WERE A-CHANGING...

The world—as I mostly saw it through our furniture-sized RCA color television —was turning upside down in front of me. So many moments unfolded before my eyes: the war in Vietnam, Dr. King's and Bobby Kennedy's assassinations, and Woodstock. They all occupy, each in their way, an indelible place in my memory. But what rises above all of that are my memories of the women's liberation movement: Gloria Steinem and the ritualized, public bra-burning that feminists did in the early 1970s. These images were always on the news, and it hit much closer to home.

My sister Betty was a feminist in her own right. Well, as much as she could be a "feminist" in a very male-dominated household like mine—with parents like Archie and Edith Bunker of the hugely popular *All in the Family* television show of that same time. I can remember my sister and her girlfriends having the audacity to wear hot pants and go-go boots, which was the very trendy fashion choice of newly liberated women of the day, out to the bar they used to hang out at one particular Friday night—much to my father and mother's chagrin. But what stayed with me most was how women, including my sister and her friends, were celebrating their womanhood in the fashion choices they made, the cigarettes they smoked, and aligning themselves with the broader movement with the "Women's Lib" buttons they had on their purses.

In their way, these symbols of culture sent a message to the world around them that they were standing up to society and saying it was time we were treated fairly in the workplace and society as a whole—and it was time the men of the world realized that. It struck me as strangely empowering because it encouraged them to change how they carried themselves in the world. They seemed to have a newfound pride in being women and their solidarity with the other women in their social circle. And since I was so close to my sister at that time, my gender issues notwithstanding, I felt that connection too. It all made perfect sense to me. Times were changing, and it was all reflected back to me through the television and my sister's representation of what the movement looked like close to home. If it were me—and I so wished it was then—I think I would have been a part of the women's lib movement too. It was time for women to be treated fairly, I thought, on an equal footing to men in all aspects of society. Pretty big thoughts for a twelve-year-old kid. Little did I know that I would experience that lack of equal footing for myself later in my life.

But the reality of social change only went so far in my house. My mom and dad were very conservative in their views on the roles of men and women. Dad was the breadwinner, and mom was the homemaker. As the only girl among the siblings, my sister had it rough because my mom had her life all figured out. It was already pre-scripted: find a husband who will provide for you, have kids, and stay home and raise them. My mom—and my dad, too—certainly felt that my sister should be pursuing the whole "house with the white picket fence" thing. From my vantage point as someone who was trying to emulate, on some level, how my sister presented herself to the world, the script our parents had for her life created an uphill battle in her quest to be an independent woman.

Betty was trying to find her way as a working woman in the world, which in the early 1970s was still something of a new phenomenon. She tried to establish some independence measure from my parents, who had a more conventional idea of how things should be for her. I can remember it leading to more than one argument between my sister and my mother, especially when Betty presented them with the idea of moving out and finding an apartment. She made the mistake of asking their permission rather than just doing it, and it led to utter pandemonium. You would have thought my sister was declaring her allegiance to the Communist Party. Suffice it to say, it did not end well at all. At least she emerged from the confrontation still in possession of her bedroom in our house.

I believed my sister had the right as a woman to blaze her own trail. My parents held her back and forced her to conform to outdated social stereotypes. The social upheaval was running rampant in society, and my parents were simply not participating—and expecting my sister to do the same. It wasn't fair to her then, and it feels just as unfair today.

While the women's liberation movement of the 1970s undoubtedly created a tidal wave of change, it also marked the start of a debate about women's roles, and more broadly, gender roles in society that still rages to this day. While gains for women, particularly in the workplace, have certainly been realized since that time, it seems to me that so much more is still left to be done. The societal definitions of what women's and men's roles look like are shifting. The rigidity of gender roles seems to have softened. For example, men can choose to stay at home and raise the kids while their wife goes off to work each day. But in the workplace, this shift is less apparent. If it weren't, then perhaps we wouldn't still be talking about a phenomenon like the glass ceiling in the first place. The women's liberation movement may have started a revolution, but for many of the women I worked with, they were still waiting for that revolution to arrive.

I distinctly remember hanging out with my sister when she would be getting ready for work in the morning before heading off to school. In her room, the radio would be playing the hit songs of 1970, like The Carpenters' "Close to You" or "I'll Be There" by the Jackson Five, while she sat in front of her mirror and put on her makeup. I would sit mesmerized by how she would transform herself with each step of the process. First, she'd apply the foundation, then the blush, followed by her eye shadow, mascara, and lipstick. It was like she was taking on a different persona, ever so slowly, so precisely, one step at a time. I wanted to do that too. I wanted to be able to create a different "me" for the world to see, but I didn't dare. I couldn't—at least not when anyone was around to see. It was simply not in the cards for me then.

I wondered what it must have been like for my sister at her workplace. From the stories I heard, she was well-liked and had lots of work friends, but what was it like inside the walls of the now-defunct Mutual Benefit Life Insurance Company? I didn't think at all about it then, but I wonder if how she dressed, did her hair, and did her makeup had any sort of bearing on her status in her workplace.

I was captivated by my sister's daily transformation. She became *someone else* right before my eyes. And I found that strangely appealing. Her routine pulled me in. It was as if she had to create a mask of some sort every morning that separated the "around the house" person from the "working woman" person. Whatever it was, it was a daily ritual that I found myself doing in much the same way when I was preparing for my first day of work as my authentic self some thirty or so years later.

MY FATHER'S LESSONS

My dad was a Teamster—and a patriot. He was a veteran of World War II, where he served in the Pacific as a Seabee in the United States Navy. They were the ones who built the airstrips—among other things—after we had overtaken places like Guadalcanal, an island once held by the Japanese. He went off to war not long after my oldest brother was born. When he got back home, having no high school diploma, he found a job driving a truck. It was to become his life's work, and that's how he became a union man. "That was back when being in a union meant something," he used to tell me. The trouble is, when he finally retired from driving, his pension somehow became less than it was supposed to be. But his distinctly organized labor focus had an impact on me. It made me realize that as I grew up and began to think about what I wanted to do professionally, I most certainly did not want to be a tradesperson, or a truck driver like my dad was. I had loftier aspirations of nailing that executive position with all of the perks and the corner office. Fortunately, my dad was in full support of that vision. He often told me that he wanted a better life for me. That's one reason I knew that college was most definitely in the cards for me at a very young age. Despite never graduating high school, my dad knew that education was the most crucial prerequisite for my success in corporate America, and I ran with it. I don't think I've ever stopped.

Like many fathers of his generation, he wasn't exactly the nurturing sort; that just wasn't his way. I don't recall him ever saying the words, "I love you," to me. But he was always supportive of whatever I was doing in school and sports. I did whatever I could to make him proud of me. Not just in sports, in life as well. I couldn't ever tell him about who—or what—I really was. I doubt that he ever had a clue about the "real" me. I hardly knew myself. Was I overcompensating for not having the cojones, to be honest with him? Perhaps. I never really thought that much about it then.

When I was a kid, my father and I went to the Two Guys department store together, where he'd buy me a Matchbox car or truck. I loved playing with trucks and cars when I was little. I was always building some imaginary highway on the living room floor while my parents watched television. I never had any inclination to play with dolls or anything like that. I think the closest I ever got to that was my G.I. Joe collection that my uncle Augie started for me. He worked as a window dresser in New York and could bring them home for free after the display came down. My dad and my uncle also took me to my first baseball game (and many others) at the old Yankee Stadium.

I savor my memories of my time with my dad and uncle, even though they are a bit male-centric. My socialization process growing up was centered around being the alpha male in society. I went along willingly because it allowed me to hide my true feelings. I didn't embrace my feminine feelings. I ran from them until I couldn't any longer. That took over forty years! From around the age of ten right through my high school years, I was most vulnerable when I was all by myself. It was only then that I'd wander off into my fantasy world, thinking that, "If I did it just this one more time," that I wouldn't ever do it again. The only person I was deluding was myself.

I hid it from him, just like I did from everyone else around me. I didn't feel right about not being honest with him then, and even some eighteen years after his death, I still don't feel good about it. But my gender issues became such an immovable mountain in my mind that I felt like I had no other choice but to hide my true self from him and everyone else. I had fully compartmentalized the idea of being a girl into the deepest recesses of my brain. The mere notion that I would reveal the real "me" to the world brought nothing but abject fear. And not just any garden-variety anxiety. I'm talking about the kind of fear that permeates every fiber of your being and paralyzes you in a way that would make petrified wood seem like a wet sponge. Coming out to my father, or anyone else for that matter, was just not an option for me.

MY MOTHER'S PAIN

By all accounts, my mother had a pretty rough life. Like my dad, she was born in Jersey City, the third sibling of four. Both of her parents had passed away by the time she was fifteen. She dropped out of high school and went to work as a laborer in a cigarette factory in Jersey City by the name of P. Lorillard. That's where she learned to smoke for the first time.

But it wasn't the cigarettes that ultimately led to my mother's passing. She died of ovarian cancer in 1986, at just sixty-six years old. I was twenty-seven years old at the time. My mother was not present in my life very much in her last years because I had distanced myself both physically and emotionally. In the late '70s, I lived in Delaware and was floundering at life, working my way through two failed marriages and dealing poorly with my gender issues.

To this day, I never really quite understood what happened to her.

From right after my junior high year through college, my mom was physically present, but she had tuned us out. I can vaguely remember discussions among the adults in my house about the effects of menopause and low blood sugar, leading to "episodes" of bizarre behavior. Still, as I look back on it, I honestly think my mother had a nervous breakdown. She became a shell of her former self.

Before getting sick, she was a gregarious, warm-hearted woman who would welcome a first-time visitor to our home with open arms with a, "What can I get you?" After getting sick, she became vacant and swallowed up by all the pain she absorbed in her life.

I never saw my mother as any kind of role model of female behavior. She was too broken to be present in a nurturing way. Through no fault of her own, she surrendered her role as my mother during the most critical years of my life. She didn't share in any of my academic and athletic successes—or any other part of my life, for that matter. Everything I tried to accomplish in my early years was to make my mom and dad proud of me. It did not matter what I accomplished. My mother had checked out. I felt more isolated than ever before. Sure, I kept up appearances on the outside, but inside I was a mess.

CHAPTER TWO
SHACKLED IN AN EMOTIONAL STRAIGHTJACKET

"Very often, all the activity of the human mind is directed not in revealing the truth, but in hiding the truth."
~ Leo Tolstoy

THE FEAR OF BEING FOUND OUT PUT ME IN AN EMO-tional straightjacket that I doubted I could ever escape from. I had too much to lose; my entire life as I knew it up to that point. There was no doubt in my mind that if I came out to either of my parents I would be immediately rejected, thrown out of the house, and voted off the island. There was no room in my thinking for any other outcome.

And it stayed that way right through to each of their deaths. My mom died in 1986, when I was just twenty-seven years old and in the depths of my denial. She passed away never knowing about me. My dad didn't pass away until sixteen years later, in 2002. So I actually had many more years together with my dad. And while I am grateful for that, it also meant years of pretending to be someone I really never was to him. I loved and respected my father, but in the end it was not enough to overcome the fear of being as honest with him as I should have. In the end, he too died without ever knowing the truth about me.

When I was around twelve or thirteen years old I remember a conversation taking place in our house about something called "electroshock treatments," and that it should be something that my father should consider as a treatment option for whatever my mother's condition was. From my young kid's vantage point it seemed like my dad had already tried everything. He and my mom always seemed like they were going to a different doctor appointment with a different doctor all the time. According to the advice he received, these treatments could be the answer. But they weren't. In the '70s this was considered an acceptable and recommended treatment, but I didn't know that then. I had no idea how barbaric the procedure was for the patients either, lying there—fully awake and aware of what was happening to them. They would convulse as electricity coursed through their brain. The result was severe memory loss and numbness to emotional stimuli.

My mother must have been terrified. I just shudder at the mere thought of it. It stripped her of her personality and soul, but did little to alleviate her underlying conditions. It only made a bad situation worse.

The whole experience of my mother residing in a psych ward for extended periods of time, and seeing her life and dignity drain away, left me with a negative impression of the mental health profession. What's more, it only served to drive me deeper into my closeted world. If I was ever found out, I was convinced that I would have suffered the same fate as my mother- hooked up to a machine that would turn me into some sort of zombie with the flick of a switch.

"I'm not really like her anyway," I thought very dismissively. "I would never need *that*." In later years that self-talk would become rather stubborn, "I can overcome anything, without anyone's help." Turns out I was only fooling myself.

You see, there were no words back then to tell me what I was feeling. The term "transgender" wouldn't find its way into popular culture for another twenty or so years. There was no internet, no cable television, and no social media. Even if there were words for it, no one ever talked about this sort of thing. Certainly not in my house. Besides, I believed there couldn't possibly be anyone else on the planet as broken and damned to hell as me. That all changed when I heard for the first time in my life the word *transsexual*, which was what the media of the day used to describe Renee Richards when she made the headlines around 1972.

In the 1970s "transsexualism," as it was known then, was widely considered to be a perversion and was classified as a form of insanity. In fact, it was considered by the psychiatric community as a mental disorder until 2018.

RUNNING AWAY FROM MYSELF

As you might imagine, all of this had quite an effect on me in myriad ways. My first instinct was to just run away; get myself as far away as I could from all the madness. My mother's mental health struggles only served to amplify a situation that I already wanted to escape: my town, my gender issues, my overall unease with the conflict of my mind and my body. Leaving was the easiest route for me and the most cowardly too. As the old saying goes, "If you can't stand the heat, get out of the kitchen," and that is exactly what I did. My mother's situation taught me how to run away from life's problems. It didn't teach me to deal with them. I couldn't bear to see my mother convulsing wildly right in front of me time and time again. I already had experienced what it was like to restrain my mother and hold her down long enough to shove a tranquilizer down her throat without having it spit back in my face. It got so that I could sense when she was about to go off and I would just hop on my bike and ride away as fast and as far away as I could. One time I pedaled for miles nonstop and ended up three towns away from where I lived. I even knew about how long it took for one of my mom's episodes to last so that when I finally did pedal back home the episode would be over and she would be fast asleep.

Those experiences—and there were many—left an indelible mark on my psyche and how best to deal with a chaotic situation, whether it was created by someone else or by me and my issues. Just leave. Go far away. That way, I wouldn't have to address the situation or be a part of the solution. It became somebody else's mess to clean up. It was a lesson I learned well, resulting in a lot of pain and anguish for the people who came in and out of my life in the decade to come.

So I retreated, ever more deeply into my alternate fantasy world of cross dressing and masturbation. I picked my spots. In the beginning, grocery shopping night was popular. I was alone in the house and with mounting anticipation that made my entire body twitch with excitement as I carefully pulled out my mom's stockings, slip, and camisole and surrendered to the feeling of softness and femininity that washed over me in waves. I escaped into my fantasy. All I cared about was that I was as far away as I could be from my world. If for only a few minutes, it was my sanctuary. The only place where being *me* was okay.

I couldn't stop running my hands all over the silky material. The feeling left me breathless and beyond excited. I sought and found relief in masturbation. It just seemed like the appropriate thing to do while I was lost in this fantasy world, if only momentarily, away from my inner conflict and pain. I don't recall any specific fantasies, per se; it was more about being overcome by the sensations that were erupting all over my body that put me over the edge. And as soon as I caught my breath and my heart rate got back to normal levels the guilt and the shame would come. Damn, would it come. Stronger and harder than anything I had just experienced, wiping away the afterglow in the blink of an eye. But that was just the set up. They were merely the jabs to the uppercut of fear that coursed through my entire body. It was the fear of being caught, of being found out. The fear was so intense it propelled me right out of my bed and back downstairs where I made sure I put everything back precisely the way I found it. Making sure there were no new folds in any of the materials that could lead to a raised eyebrow, or worse yet, suspicion.

I was twelve years old and had the entire top floor of the house to myself to live out my fantasies of what it would be like to be the girl who I really felt like inside. It didn't hurt that one of my brothers left behind what seemed like his entire collection of *Playboy* magazines and other assorted "girlie magazines" and pornography. In the relative privacy of my attic room, I would gaze for hours and hours at the women in these magazines and wish that I could look just like they did. They had perfect bodies: long legs, flowing hair, and supple breasts. So soft and oh so utterly beautiful. I didn't just look at these pictures. I analyzed them. I scrutinized every square millimeter of their bodies, drinking in their beauty. I was supposed to look like them. To be very clear, crossdressing was the only way I knew how, at that time, to get in touch with the feminine feelings I had inside of me. It was my way of trying to find congruence in a sea of incongruity. It was my coping mechanism.

And that's pretty much how things went for me through my adolescent years and through college. Sure, circumstances were different, and what I would wear evolved, but the basic ebb and flow of feelings never changed. If anything, they grew stronger. Regardless of where I was living or what I was involved in at the time I always needed to retreat, to get away from whatever you would call my "life."

I learned, too, that there was a price to pay for all of the constant hiding and keeping my big secret from the world. It all took enormous amounts of energy to maintain. It was absolutely draining. Before I came out at work, I was hiding my true self from all of my colleagues for quite a while and it took its toll on me both physically and emotionally. I had to work so much harder when I only brought a portion of my true self to my job each and every day. Hiding took a lot of effort.

LIVING WITH NEVER KNOWING

When I was coming out to everyone in my life—except at work, which was still many months away—my friends and my fellow support group members would always tell me that I was "lucky" because both of my parents had passed away before I came out, so I was able to avoid all of the angst and potential rejection that came with revealing your true self to your parents. As much as I appreciated that unique brand of encouragement, it all seemed very hollow to me. The fact is I was haunted by the notion that I would never really know how my parents would have reacted to my coming out to them as transgender. I can picture various scenarios in my head about how those conversations would have gone, but in the final analysis, they are all just made up. I will never, ever really know how each of my parents would have reacted to their son telling them that he has felt from his earliest memories that he was born in the wrong body and was taking steps to live his truest life—as a woman.

That all came home to roost one cold, blustery, gray March day in 2005 when I found myself at my mom and dad's grave sobbing uncontrollably blurting out over and over again, "This is so hard!" I was crying out for consolation that they couldn't give me. At least that is what I thought the outcome would be. Like I've said before, I never have allowed myself the option of a positive parental response. Not for a moment. My sister claims that our mother would have gotten onboard pretty quickly. She may not have understood it, but her love for me would have won out over any inability she would have had to wrap her head around what it means to be transgender. My dad? "That's a whole 'nother story," my sister would say. And I tend to agree. I think it would have taken my dad some time to embrace the real me, if he ever did at all. By the time I decided to come out, I had new friends that celebrated the authentic me— Stephanie, but at that precise moment, inconsolable at their graves, I never felt so alone, or so vulnerable. I turned up my collar and with my scarf tight around my neck, I slowly made my way back to my car.

As I drove back home I thought about what would have happened if my estranged brother, who visited the gravesite somewhat regularly, had suddenly appeared. I wouldn't have run away. That wasn't an acceptable option anymore. It would have just been he and I, face-to-face. I wouldn't have had a bike to jump on and pedal away from the moment. And that would have been okay. I had finally learned to accept myself and to face the situations I found myself in directly and with honesty.

PARALLEL LINES NEVER CROSS OVER

I lived my life on parallel paths. One path was where I played the role of my former male persona, grasping at every nuance of maleness around me to perfect my portrayal. While the other path continued to be my fantasy world of crossdressing where I escaped in search of some sense of balance in my life.

I struggled with understanding what a man was all about. I didn't realize it then, but I wasn't wired like the rest of the guys. What came naturally to them was a painstaking and utterly painful experience for me because I simply didn't know what to do. A perfect example was dating. I was horrible at it! The truth is, for all of my outward, type A, big-man-on-campus persona I was beyond painfully shy when it came to asking a girl out on a date. I'd much rather have a conversation with them about clothing styles, hair, makeup, and shoes! If a girl was interested in dating me, I wasn't equipped with the male radar that detected such things. As a result, there was never any "high school sweetheart" in the cards for me, just quite a few girls who were my friends.

The fact is, I was playing the role of a male in society, the basic tenets of which never came to me naturally or innately. I was portraying a character that I hoped would position me in society so that I would be safe. Safe from being found out. Safe from being persecuted in some way. Safe from harm. I figured if I became involved in manly endeavors, such as sports, being able to fix things around the house (something I never really mastered to begin with), and do all the things that a male provider for their family does, I'd be okay. At least that is what I tried to convince myself.

I had to covertly watch and learn. But I was a quick study. No one ever knew, I mean *no one*.

I became very good at hiding from the real "me," whatever that was. I certainly didn't know. As I mentioned before, they hadn't yet come up with the word *transgender* to describe who I was. And because there was no internet, there was no accessible "community." I honestly thought, like so many trans individuals of my generation, that I was the only one. So seeing no obvious or viable solution to my problem—like coming out—I stayed in acting school and graduated magna cum laude. I was so lost and confused. I actually thought that living a lie like this was a wholly appropriate means to an end.

FLAILING—AND FAILING—AT LIFE

I took great pains to blend in as "one of the guys." Participation in a variety of sports was an easy way for me to accomplish this. God had blessed me with a modicum of athletic ability, and I could keep up my facade playing football (mostly the tackle variety without pads), basketball, and stickball, which were staples of my youth. Playing team sports was akin to a rite of passage on the playground and if you somehow didn't want to play you were just ignored. And I could never let myself be ignored. I was simply not going to let that happen. When I got to high school these were replaced with more organized sports: varsity football; wrestling (I was the captain and most valuable wrestler my senior year). I sucked at hitting a baseball, therefore, rowing, shot put, and discus occupied my time in the spring. I was most definitely a year-round athlete.

Football was my passion primarily because my middle brother, Tony, excelled at it. My parents and I went to all his games in high school and college, where he played offensive tackle. He was an all-star and if he didn't have knee problems when he was a senior in college, he may have been drafted by the Dallas Cowboys who were scouting him at the time. He was my instant role model! Just add water and follow the directions on the package. And that's precisely what I did.

I became obsessed with sports and became singularly focused, at a very young age, on being a success. It created a work ethic and an internal drive to be the best—at everything. I had to be number one in my classes and the best teammate and leader in whatever sport I found myself involved in. When I wasn't, I was devastated . While I will admit to actually enjoying school and the ego-stroking accolades I received from my athletic achievements, they were very much a means to an end for me. The equation was a simple one: Get good grades; excel on the football field; go to college and get as far from home as I could.

My drive to excel as an athlete landed me a football scholarship to the University of Delaware, where I quickly became a starter for their freshman football team (in those days freshmen were not allowed to play varsity sports) and to be a starter in the game that followed spring practice the following year. I burned out—all the hard work, sacrifice, the effort didn't seem worth it anymore. So I quit. I think I let a lot of people down when I did including my father, who remained mute on the subject. I still think about it to this day.

As I look back on my college days, which spanned the late '70s and all its excesses, I see that I was lost in a haze of drugs, low self-esteem, and utter confusion about who I really was. I merely drifted through my college years. While many of my friends were studying hard to get good grades and position themselves for a good job upon graduation, I clearly wasn't following that path anymore. Instead, after years of hard work, effort, and energy put into my plan to get away from home and hide the real me in the meantime, I was tired and now looking for the path of least resistance, not the path of greatest success.

I think my fascination with being stoned had a lot to do with that. It was in high school when I first discovered what smoking pot was all about. What an amazing way to leave my reality behind—if only for a few hours! It. Was. Life. Changing. My "real world" contained a lot of pain and confusion in those days. My mother's strange sickness, the pressure I put on myself to excel in the classroom and on the football field, the nagging sense that I was someone else and the guilt and denial it wrought were at times unbearable. When I got high all of that vanished, replaced by whatever trouble I was getting into with my friends. In the end, it served my ultimate objective—just to "fit in."

CHAPTER THREE
THE MISEDUCATION OF MICHAEL

"Don't let the noise of others' opinions drown out your own inner voice."
~ Steve Jobs

AS MY COLLEGE YEARS SLIPPED BY, THE REALITY THAT I would need to find a job and fend for myself leaped up at me from seemingly out of nowhere and grabbed me by the throat. I was not even close to prepared for it. So many of my fraternity brothers (yes, I even joined a fraternity in college as a means to blend in!) were frantically preparing for interviews with the big name firms that recruited on campus while I was looking for the next good time. Graduating and finding a job meant responsibility, and I was not at all ready for that.

You might think that something as startling as that would have shaken me from the funk I was in, but it really didn't. The fear of being found out, the fear of knowing I was different, the fear that I could not shake this disease inside of me was pervasive. So I did the only thing I knew to do: I ran from it. But this time I reached for something completely different from my bag of tricks. Sometime late in my junior year I met and became involved with a woman who would become my first wife. We dated steadily for the next year or so and I actually moved into her off-campus apartment for the majority of my senior year. We became engaged toward the end of that year and were married less than a year after I graduated. What was I thinking?

All my efforts at leading my life as a man seem now like desperate attempts at achieving some sense of harmony or dare I say it, normalcy, in my life. I was fighting a battle raging inside of me but I did not know who the enemy was. It didn't have a name. But through the sports, the drugs, even the girlfriends that I actually had in college, it was ever-present. I didn't have a name for it, it was just there all the time. Never far from my thoughts, it was another place to go. A place to get away and detach from everything around me. It became the place to go. It was the other track I spoke of earlier. For me, this is what the closet was called.

For every LGBTQ person, especially those of my generation, the closet is a wholly personal experience. While I'm sure there are common characteristics, the closet is a decidedly individual reality. For me it was the darkest of places. It was a prison. Solitary confinement for the soul.

But it was also a place of contradiction too. I would find relief in my closet. It was the only place where I could explore those intrinsic feelings of femininity that were very much a part of me. But the door of my closet quickly slammed shut on those fleeting feelings leaving just the empty shell of shame, guilt, and denial behind. That was always my reality. That was what my closet looked like—for four-plus decades of my life.

The fear and the pressure to conform to a lifestyle that everyone around me was thrusting upon me was insufferable. I was patently ill-equipped to manage my life at all, let alone as a married, straight, male in the world. I knew I had made the absolute wrong turn at this most critical juncture in my life, but I couldn't help myself. The voice inside me was screaming at the top of its lungs, "don't do this!" but off I went. I wasn't sure I wanted to get married. I was barely twenty-one years old! Deep down inside I knew that I had not addressed my gender issues at all. And I wasn't about to start. I somehow convinced myself that I would be able to manage through it, despite the voice inside of me screaming to the contrary.

My decision tore at my soul, but I knew I had no choice. I was trapped inside of myself. There was no way out. The only real choice I had was how I handled it, and I was about to screw that up in grandly tragic fashion. I was determined to fight off this thing inside of me but in a way that was destined for failure from the start. I was going to disregard my own feelings and live the rest of my life based on what everyone else in my life thought I should be doing. It was never about what I wanted. I had no time for that. I had to get on with becoming a responsible human being in the world of the 1980s. And the best way to do that was to make everyone else happy. And why not? I had perfected that strategy since I was a child. I couldn't care about what I was feeling—this was all about survival, pure and simple. If I stood still for too long the fear would envelop me. It was the fear of finding out—once and for all—who I really was, and of being found out by everyone in my orbit.

I was on a collision course with a life that would bring me to these same crossroads twice more over the next twenty years or so. You would think I would have learned, but I sorely lacked the wisdom to do so. I could not summon the courage needed to look in the mirror and see the real person staring back at me. I just dove headlong into the lie and the unknown world before me. I had no safety net to catch me. I landed in the workplace as a broken, tangled, and conflicted person in a constant battle with my inner true self. I didn't realize it at the time, but it was a battle that was only just beginning.

FROM THE INSIDE OUT

I was running out of time. My college years were coming to an end and I needed to find gainful employment. I was soon to be married to my first wife, Lynn, who I had met the year before while working at a dining hall on campus, and I needed a job. After all, it was what I was supposed to do at this point in my life.

For a time I thought I would embark upon a career in radio as a DJ. I had been a regular on the campus radio station for all four years I was at school and I was pretty good at it. I did all of the research. I read each issue of *Rolling Stone* cover to cover so I could be well-versed on all that was happening with the music scene and bring it to my show. I studied the styles of the top jocks at the Philadelphia and New York stations that I listened to and tried to emulate them in my banter and the music sets I curated. Back in the late '70s progressive FM radio was still a thing and I thought I could make a career of it. But I knew I'd have to start out at some small market station in the middle of nowhere if I was really serious about it.

But I wasn't.

If I was, I would have busted my butt and created a killer audition tape cut from my on-air checks, made multiple copies, and sent them out to every single FM radio station across the country. But I didn't do that. I thought that was not what everyone was expecting of me. What would my parents think? They paid for four years of college for me to become a *DJ*? That's just not a *responsible* thing to do. And I was engaged, for crying out loud. I couldn't drag my new wife to some remote corner of the United States so I could pursue my dream. I didn't believe in it enough for it to really be a dream in the first place.

In the end, I talked myself completely out of pursuing a career in radio. No exciting relocation to a new part of the country as a single male to pursue my dream as a big time radio personality in New York. Or LA. Or San Francisco. I can't honestly say I had a dream when I gave up on it before it ever got off the ground.

The irony of it all is that I did send out some half-assed inquiries to a handful of stations. And after I had made my mind up to go off and do God-knows-what for a job I received a response from one of them. A station in Worcester, Massachusetts was interested in bringing me on to cover weekends and fill in during the week to start. They asked for an audition tape. I stared at the letter for hours, my mind churning the entire time as I read it over and over. It was paralyzing. It was as if this letter was a divine message sent to tell me what to do. But I shrugged that notion off, paying it no mind whatsoever. All I could think about was that I would have to undo an awful lot of things I had already committed to—including my commitment to my fiancée—if I was to make this leap. So I did the easiest thing I thought I could do. Nothing. I threw the letter in the trash and never told anyone about it. As the saying goes, "I had made my bed, and now it was time to *lie* in it."

I didn't realize it until many years later, but I learned a very valuable lesson about what it feels like when you compromise on your hopes and dreams.

A CASUALTY OF RETAIL

As the days toward my college graduation dwindled down to a precious few I still did not have anything lined up for work. I was starting to get frantic. All of my friends and fraternity brothers who had what I thought to be as more *substantive* majors in finance, computer science, or accounting were all interviewing with recruiters from the Fortune 100 that had made their way to my campus. They were most definitely not looking for communication majors like me. I spent a lot of time in the latter stages of my senior year at the "Career Planning and Placement Office" scouring the listings of recruiters that were visiting to see if I qualified for an interview.

Most of the notices were for business majors only, precious few if any listed liberal arts majors like me as people they were interested in. While I thought I should have majored in business administration or engineering, I wouldn't have lasted five minutes in either of those majors. But the thing is, I had always wanted to major in communications. I had made that decision in high school when I was formulating my plans for a career in the radio industry. And, the availability of that major was one of the first things I asked about when I was being recruited to play football. It was somewhat of a fledgling department back then, but the classes in my major were the only ones that I was interested enough to do well in.

Seemingly out of nowhere a notice popped up out of the mix that I could interview for. A retail company that was completely foreign to me called Jefferson-Ward was launching a regional chain of stores in New Jersey, Pennsylvania, and Delaware and they were hiring college graduates for their management training program. I immediately applied, and in a matter of just a couple of weeks I had my interview and received a job offer.

I wasn't interested in a career in retail at all, but it was a *job*. I was beyond relieved that I found something that paid me money to be a trainee for nearly a year before being assigned to a store in the region as an assistant manager. That worked for me because it allowed me to defer, or more precisely *avoid*, making any real decisions about my work life for a while. Another big positive was that all of the locations were within a ninety-minute drive from where my first wife and I lived in northern Delaware.

But the most important positive was that it checked the biggest box of all: It fulfilled the expectations of what others had about me. It enabled me to keep up appearances which ensured my safety, at least for a little while longer. I was really just kicking the can a little farther down the road. And that helped me keep the truth about me from being revealed: I was a slacker with serious unresolved gender issues.

To be clear, I absolutely hated working in retail. It was simply a horrible match from the beginning. Once the excitement and the newness of the grand openings faded away and I was assigned to a store, my job quickly became a grind. All in all, it was too much like *work*.

To escape I almost immediately began crossdressing in my wife's clothes whenever I got the chance—which was quite often. I even picked up some things to add to my wardrobe at the store. I was like a kid in a candy store when I learned I could take things out of there and not get caught.

I was ashamed of what I'd become, but I was powerless to stop it. Part of me knew I was better than this, but a much larger part of me lacked the wherewithal to change it. I was unchallenged at work, unhappy with my life, and I simply didn't care anymore. I was feeling very unfulfilled professionally, but what I failed to realize was that it was all of my own doing. I never took responsibility for my actions because if I did it would somehow lead to me revealing the truth about who I really was. And I could never let that happen.

As almost a natural consequence of all of this, I got myself fired. And for the stupidest, most easy to uncover act: I started taking a little off the top of my cash register till every night. I somehow convinced myself that if I didn't steal "too much" that they'd never find out about in the counting room at the end of the night. Who was I kidding? Certainly not my colleagues in the counting room. All it took was a few weeks for the pattern to establish itself and there I was in the store manager's office being told that I was being fired and that - as a favor to me! - they wouldn't press charges. In the final analysis it wasn't a lot of money, but that's not really the point. The mature thing to do would have been to simply find another job. But no, I had to go out in much grander style.

And of course I lied to everyone about it. I crafted a ridiculous story about how I was somehow wronged by store management, and that it was just as well because it all amounted to a complete waste of my considerable talents. But my family and friends bought it, because when you hold the lie as the truth inside you it's easy to actually believe it yourself. Then delivering it to those around you is a piece of cake.

This foray into retail is what served as my maiden voyage in the world of work and it set me on a professional course that, in hindsight, stunted my career growth.

THROW ME A LIFE PRESERVER

I had not stopped the drifting that had set in during my college years. I was still caught up in a maze of hiding and confusion about who I *really* was. My work ethic had been seriously eroded by my continued fondness for smoking pot, partying, and my nonstop preoccupation with crossdressing. I still had my fantasy world to hold on to. I found clothes to crossdress in. I'd get stoned and dress up while Lynn was at work. Because of my coverage schedule at the store our work schedules were very different. This presented me with increased opportunities to get away from my reality for blocks of time. I hated my life and this was my coping mechanism. It always had been since I was young. I found myself surrounded by conflict and confusion about who I really was at every turn. This was my safe haven. It was the only way I knew how to bring balance to a world that seemed so *unbalanced*.

Time and time again I would beat myself up mentally because I still didn't know how to commit to my life as a male. I so desperately wanted to. Life would be so easy if I could somehow flip a switch and feel like a man inside. I had yet to realize that I was never born with the internal wiring or the ability to do so in the first place.

I was divorced from Lynn some time in 1982 after a whopping fourteen months of marriage. The official cause of the dissolution of our marriage on my part should have been "disinterest." I was unable to commit to the lifetime ideal of marriage like she had. I was guilt-ridden that I had kept a secret from her the entire time we were in each other's lives. That was so unfair of me and more than just a little selfish. She deserved so much more.

Just like everything else in my life up to that point I just drifted away from it, never once showing any ounce of genuine devotedness. And caught up in that drift were all of my college friends, any friends that my ex and I had, and most of my fraternity brothers. I just brushed them all aside, figuring that my destiny was to trudge through life pretty much on my own, just using people as props in my game of hide-and-*don't*-seek.

To that end, I put up the appearance of devotion and commitment, because that's what I was supposed to do as a young married man. And for a time it fooled everybody: friends, family, and yes, it fooled her too. She was devastated by our divorce and I sank into a deep funk of remorse and regret.

I hurt her so much. I was so uncaring of her feelings. In my drive to run away from my true self I had become a cold and detached person devoid of empathy, who did not possess the ability to truly love someone. I felt like I was being slowly separated from my soul and I didn't know how to stop.

The 1980s had only just begun and I was off to a rousing start. In the span of two years I had been essentially fired from my first job and had my marriage go up in flames. One would think that I might have used it all to turn my life around and learn from my mistakes, to perhaps chart a new course for my life's direction. If you are a fan of fairytale endings you can think that if you'd like, but you'd be profoundly mistaken.

Instead I went in search for whoever and whatever I could *use* to keep the charade in place.

PICKING UP THE PIECES

For the first and only time in my life I found myself unemployed and with no place to live. But thanks to some savings I managed to put aside and the good graces of one of my fraternity brothers who was looking for a roommate, I was able to start over.

As I began to pore over the classified ads in the local paper each day, I applied for any job that I thought I could do. I was sending out resumes and making phone calls every waking hour of every day. My family back in New Jersey beckoned for me to come home, but I just couldn't. In the early months of 1983 I equated all of that with failure.

I was determined to make it on my own. I interviewed to be an insurance agent, to work as a manager in a paint store, to sell trucks (because, hey, my dad *drove* a truck), and to even work as a purveyor of bananas and other assorted fruits at a large food company. Each one resulted in polite thank yous—and no offers of employment.

Just as I was beginning to wonder if I would ever find another job, a law was passed that gave large banks incentives to move their credit card operations to Delaware. It created jobs—and one for me—almost over-night. My new career as a "banker" began in the collections department of Maryland National Bank in downtown Baltimore. Not exactly the most glamorous job in the financial services industry, but I was energized by the notion that if I did well I could move into management. At least that was the enticement at the time I was interviewed and I took the bait wholeheartedly.

While *reminding* hundreds of people a week to pay their credit card bill wasn't exactly what I had gotten a college degree for, I did my best to make the most of it. And I was good at it.

My personal life was still a hot mess; I had compounded the prob-lems I already had with my gender by starting to date someone who would go on to become my second wife. Her name was Hannah and she had no idea what she was in for. But the idea, the *optics*, of having a steady relationship that I could show the world led me right into another one, right on the heels of my previous one. It would turn out to be a recipe for another marital disaster.

It was shortly after we made the move to our permanent home in Delaware that my boss called me into his office to tell me that I was being promoted to supervisor. I was ecstatic. Finally something positive was happening in my professional life. At last I had a real honest-to-goodness accomplishment that I could hold on to.

It was a watershed moment in my fledgling career in the sense that I would never return to the rank and file ever again. I was a manager again, but this time I felt like a *real* manager.

And a white, male one at that.

That is to say that for the first time in my life in any setting, I felt very *empowered*. And given my gender and my skin color it was much easier for me to be *seen* by those around me—regardless of gender or race—as having power and authority than if I were a female and/or of a different race. It was the nature of the culture at the bank, and perhaps many others, in the mid-1980s. Management was very white and very male, so I fit right in. Because of this I, perhaps, didn't have to work at it as hard as my female and non-white colleagues did in order to achieve the recognition that had just been bestowed upon me.

The truth is the only power and authority I ever had was over the collectors in my unit. I had some measure of *privilege* as well but that didn't really manifest itself in anything tangible. Sure, I got to go to management meetings that the rank and file weren't privy to and openly discuss individual members of the staff, but that was about it. Privilege didn't mean a whole lot to me then, mostly because I couldn't recognize it. I couldn't feel it—yet. Perhaps if I had I might have been better at recognizing and then working the culture I was in for my own personal gain. But I wasn't that organizationally savvy yet. I wouldn't develop that skill for a while.

I came to appreciate the spoils of male privilege even though I was not thoroughly cognizant of it every waking hour of every day. It would just have a knack for showing up at critical times in my career. This male privilege would make its presence known in the way I was treated: how the opportunities came to me, how I seemed to always be at or near the front of the line. Or, how it would reach out and save me from harm while those around me were being laid off. I used to trick myself into thinking that it was my shining performance that kept me safe, and that may have been true—to a point.

But there was another safety net that was in play. My privilege would accompany me wherever I went in my career. Like a guardian angel, it rode silently next to me embedded in my maleness and my whiteness. And at this early stage of my managerial career I saw a fleeting glimpse of it for the first time. But I was too preoccupied with my ongoing battle with my true self to ever pay any real attention to it. In my short stint in retail I had developed some pretty bad habits—like laziness and not giving a damn about anything. There was no place for those habits now. And that I was cognizant enough to actually realize that was an accomplishment all by itself. That's not to say that I wasn't struggling every day with who I really was—and how to hide it. Let me be clear: that never went away. I wore my gender struggles like a thorny crown every single waking moment of my life.

If there was a glimmer of hope for the "professional Michael," it was purely accidental. I still was completely unversed in the ways of managerial tactics or politics. I had absolutely no freaking idea what to do or where to begin with the supervisory gig that had just been handed to me. I hadn't learned anything from my retail experience that I could apply.

I was green. I was working with other managers and superiors who were older than me and much more hip to the office vibe and how to maneuver within it than I was. They sent me to training, or "finishing school" as I liked to call it, and that helped somewhat, but there was a lot I had to figure out on my own.

But the bigger thing that was happening was that the seed had been planted about becoming an officer of the bank. To my way of thinking that was a big deal and the ultimate badge of honor in my new world. What I didn't yet grasp was the fact that the banking industry was very hierarchical, which meant lots of levels and lots of titles that didn't mean a whole lot. They certainly didn't mean much more money.

But I was blinded by the prestige of being an officer, the cache that it had. I glamorized it so much that I romanticized it in my mind as somehow being the pinnacle of my profession. It became the one thing that got me out of bed every day. I obsessed over it for the entire time I worked at banks in Delaware. Getting promoted to officer might even get me out of the collection department.

This goal refueled my desire to perform, to excel. But not in a good way. What now passed for "drive" was more like a jaundiced obsession to succeed. I needed to succeed to survive, at any cost, whether or not I possessed the skills to do so in the first place. I was overcompensating for all of the perceived shortcomings and insecurities I had as a failed retail manager, and as a human being. I created a mental diversion to take my mind off of the daily drudgery of keeping my gender issues at bay. I was attempting to press the restart button on my career, but all it did was ramp up my levels of anxiety and paranoia. Instead of holding my desperation at bay, I was being swallowed up by it.

I made mistakes. Lots of them. I must have made every mistake a rookie manager can think of. Instead of being the *manager* I was, I instead tried to be a *friend* to all of my people. I was trying to be the *cheerleader.* In the world of collections, where it is all about money and lowering delinquency percentages, being your collector's friend or bringing pom-poms to the office just won't cut it.

It was right around this time that I began to think that perhaps I didn't have the proper internal makeup to be the stern, all-business, all-about-the-numbers boss. To put it another way, I didn't have it in me to be an asshole. And that would be what ultimately held me back from achieving the officership I so desperately desired. What I wouldn't admit to myself then was that innately I did not possess the internal wiring required to be a badass, testosterone-filled collections manager on the fast track. That was simply not in the script for me.

I was trying to apply the same "fake it until I make it" strategy that I was failing at in my personal life to my professional life as a manager. And I thought that somehow the outcome was going to be different. The only person I was fooling was myself.

I started thinking that there have to be other jobs in other areas that were more suited to my *personality* than the one I had.

It was right around this time when I first encountered what many a manager has heard ever since there have been managers: I was "too nice." It would become an ongoing problem for me that became a hallmark of my time working in banks in the 80s. That label never served me well.

My frustrations began to mount. The pressure to "get the numbers" was never-ending. The stress associated with trying to overcome my niceness was mounting as well. I beat my head up against a lot of brick walls in those days. But nothing helped. I was beginning to feel trapped in a world that I was getting less and less fond of.

This was compounded by the intensifying strain to progress up the ranks at work. I sensed I was being passed over. Again. And again. And again. Each time someone else got promoted and it wasn't me, my frustrations mounted to even higher heights. Most were other white guys that I came into the bank with. And there were some women too, both white and Black. People were moving up and moving out of collections and I was jealous. They had gotten what I wanted and I was angry because I was being left behind. I was beginning to think my bosses had it out for me. I convinced myself that I was being punished somehow, that I was being screwed. Paranoia can be a very insidious thing.

And none of this changed my outside-of-work behavior. I was getting high and crossdressing almost every day. When I couldn't crossdress because my roommate was around, I made sure that we both got stoned. I was caught in a vise with no way out.

My paranoia heightened with the arrival of my new boss. In my mind I thought this guy had it out for me from day one and was looking for ways to let me go. For all I knew, when they hired him they told him one of his first duties was to get rid of me. Turns out my greatest fears were realized that way.

He wrote me up for things that I thought were totally unwarranted, but I must admit were true: my lack of monitoring my collectors' calls and the poor results of my unit. For a short time he made my life a living hell. I hated him. The reality was I had one foot out the door and he was pushing the other one. My days there were numbered. It took about three years, but I was doing the same thing I did at the end of my retail debacle. Not giving a damn about a job I had learned to hate. And instead of doing something proactive about it, I just watched as things crashed and burned right in front of my eyes.

It all came to a head one night in the office parking lot. An all-employee anniversary celebration had just wrapped up and I had a few too many cocktails. I sat in my car with Hannah, who I was engaged to by then, and as we were getting ready to pull away we were having a conversation about the people at work, when the subject of my boss came up. The mixture of the alcohol and the subject matter was all that was needed to light my candle.

I completely snapped. "I should be an officer, I should be an officer" I screamed. I was seething with anger from every pore of my body. I was crying and slobbering all over the entire front seat. I started banging on the dashboard with clenched fists. Each thrust was harder than the last. The surface started to crack and break into pieces. I was destroying it right before my eyes. I didn't even notice that my fists were starting to bleed. Everything—all of the anger, frustration, and pressure of not just work, but every other aspect of my life, came out of me in a torrent of rage.

Hannah finally got me to stop by screaming at the top of her lungs at me. It startled me and brought me back to the reality of the moment. In an instant, I became very ashamed of myself for what I had just done. I got very quiet, like a child who just got caught playing with matches, and just bent over and started rocking myself back and forth. I scared the daylights out of her but I could not find any words to tell her I was sorry.

I had already ensnared her in my selfish charade of "marriage will fix me" right on the heels of my first marriage and I couldn't bring myself to apologize. She had a front row seat to all of the self-imposed crap I put myself through and never once wavered in her devotion and love for me. She deserved so much more than what I was able to offer, which wasn't very much at all. My sense of guilt over what I just did, and what I was in the process of doing to her, was so overwhelming that all I could do was quietly mutter totally indiscernible gibberish.

I was having a nervous breakdown.

CHAPTER FOUR
FROM THE FRYING PAN INTO THE FIRE

"Knowing what you should do and doing it are two different things."
~ Kyle Idleman

I KNEW IT WASN'T RIGHT FROM THE BEGINNING.

But yet again, I ignored my inner voice and just went along with my relationship with Hannah. Why would I subject myself to all of this emotional turmoil so soon after my first failed marriage? For one thing, I *had* to be married. In my twisted mind I somehow saw being married as my mark of normalcy. I mistakenly thought that this marriage would be the one that put me over the top and freed me from my secret world. I just had to pursue it, even if every single person who cared even an iota about me was telling me, "don't do it!"

My family definitely knew something was wrong. They tried to talk me out of it—in their own way. They implored me to rethink what I was doing. I will never forget my sister telling me that I was just going "from the frying pan straight into the fire." And she was right. But I still thought that this was what I was supposed to be doing at this stage of my life, primarily because it allowed me to hide from the world who I really was. Even if it meant going *against* my family, who were the group of people I was trying to impress in the first place.

I insisted on tearing myself in two.

There was one part of me that was still very much into getting high. And my roommate was the perfect partner. My getting high served as a counterweight to everything else that was going on in my life: the never-ending slog of my gender issues, my less-than-stellar work performance, and this wrong-from-the-start relationship that I kept trying to convince myself was right for me.

Even though I was sharing an apartment with someone who had no idea about the real me and how I lived another life deep in the closet, I could not resist the temptation to acquire new clothes, shoes, and a wig to change into. I had to be extra careful not to get caught, but that only added to the thrill. So whenever I found myself alone in the apartment, I went back to my bedroom, closed the door, and got away from my life for a while. It was a temporary salve for my soul and kept the reality of my fractured world at bay, at least for a little while. Just as it always had.

And, just as it always had, life came roaring right back at me. I could never escape from it. The guilt and shame I felt only got worse. It snapped me out of my secret world and back into the false reality of the successful white professional male that I was once again attempting to construct. Armed with a renewed determination to "get myself right," I threw myself into another ill-advised relationship that was headed inevitably toward another failed marriage.

"Getting myself right" never meant subjecting myself to some sort of "conversion therapy"—a movement that had gained considerable momentum at the time. There existed a school of thought, espoused primarily by the Christian Right, that being gay or trans was a curable *disease*. There were plenty of licensed therapists around that were willing to perform this course of treatment, also known as "reparative therapy," that was specifically designed to change a person's sexual orientation or, in my case, gender identity. At the time, I didn't even know it existed, but even if I had, I would not have entertained the idea of undergoing such a program. To do that would mean that I would have to *admit* that I had an issue with my gender identity. I would have to come out to get treated, and revealing my true self to the world was not something that I was even remotely focused on. I thought that if I pushed it away and compacted it deeper and deeper in my emotional closet that it would somehow magically disappear. I didn't need to pay someone money that I really didn't have to do that.

So I told myself, it would be different. I would *sacrifice*. In my increasingly twisted logic I thought that the only way to succeed would be to deny major parts of my life experience—partying and crossdressing. I would, once and for all, leave my closet behind and get on with a more serious approach to life. It meant making a deliberate decision to leave that all behind and move forward with what I thought I *should* be doing, and that always meant getting married. I decided I was going to go "cold turkey," and just walk away from all of the crossdressing and the partying.

Getting married was my only way out. It ensured the lie would remain intact and sent a signal to those around me that I was "normal." It was the perfect cover. There was absolutely no way I was going to come out at work or in any other aspect of my life. I was running, always running, from my authentic self. To stop would mean I had succumbed to the "gender demon" that was chasing me. To get caught was to lose. To get caught would mean the end of everything. I would be found out once and for all and shunned by everyone around me. I would be abandoned by my family and set adrift—alone and unloved. That was what I thought the end game looked like for me. That outcome was bereft of hope.

So I got married—again. But the weight of being in another marriage and trying to conform to a life that was not my own just sat on my shoulders like a thousand pounds of bricks. I thought I could "tough it out" and perhaps one day I would just wake up and I would be a *normal* male and I could finally stop running from myself. But that day never came. Out of sheer perseverance, my second marriage and second banking job lasted around four years. They were four years of being in the wrong place, at the wrong time, with the wrong job, and in the wrong marriage.

As for the new job, it was better, but not ideal. It was still in collections and I still wasn't an officer, but I got away from a bad situation that would have only led to more pain and anguish. It felt like a "win" just to be wanted again by an employer. It was at this stop in my career that I began to pick up a few rules of the road. It was here that I first learned to be more politically astute about how to work within and around the company culture.

For example, I learned the basics about knowing who to impress and when to impress them. I saw others doing it, and I knew that I could do that too—and probably better. After all, I was good at putting up appearances. This was no different. While it never actually bore the fruit of promotion that I hoped for, I also watched and learned from my colleagues who were better at it than I. It became a trait that would ultimately serve me well as I moved on with my career.

But the problem was that I was trying to impress my bosses in spite of my continued uneven performance as a manager. I never escaped the dislike I had for working in collections and always having to "chase the numbers" each and every month. Those facts didn't help me at all with my aspirations for promotion.

In the final analysis, I was still overlooked. Again and again. But rather than punch my way through a car dashboard in utter rage, I decided that perhaps it was time for a complete change of scenery.

As much as I might have been marginally successful at somehow muddling through at my next job, I was most definitely not a success at my next marriage. Hannah and I grew distant from the start. Whatever sexual attraction we once had for each other before we were married was gone. I found my release myself, picking up where I had left off a few years back with crossdressing in her clothes and masturbating. I once again found refuge in my alone time, my private fantasy world.

Throughout this entire marriage I was really trying to be someone I wasn't. But I tried. I really tried. I doubled down on shutting off the past, but that only seemed to drive me further and further away from my roots. Try as I might, I would always be on the "visiting team" if I stayed in Delaware. I could not suddenly morph into someone I was not. But that's where I was. That's how far off the rails I had gotten. I thought that by denying my own *lineage* that I could somehow make it on my own in my professional and personal life—and be seen as a "normal" male in society.

I could not have been more wrong. I was more miserable than ever, and I was getting homesick. It was around this time that my mother died and I felt the pull of family starting to draw me back. Inevitably, the second divorce came. The indifference we had toward one another was like a concrete wall between us. There was never any talk of raising a family or anything remotely related to that. I did not have children during my first two marriages, and it's just as well. I do not think that becoming a father would have been a good thing for me then. I would have felt even more trapped. I can vaguely remember my first wife Lynn and I talking about starting a family, but it was further down the road, not for a few years. That marriage ended before it began with no chance of that ever happening.

With my marriage to Hannah it was different in that it stretched on for nearly four years. Four years of trying to be somebody I never was to begin with. But even with that longer period of time, the subject of kids never materialized. We weren't mature enough to have kids anyway. Hannah was younger than I by some four years or so and was still very closely tied to her mother. We all got along, but starting a family never really was anything we seriously considered.

Through it all, I couldn't escape the fact that I was a failure at life. I was so unhappy. I felt like life was just passing me by like a parade on the Fourth of July. While I sat on the curb in my lawn chair I watched, remorseful and dejected, as everyone went by having a great time, singing and dancing and really *living* their lives. That was *their* reality, I thought, not *mine*. I saw my life slipping away from me and I felt helpless to stop it.

Another mistaken attempt at normalcy ended in pain and anguish for her and for me. Another marriage that I drifted away from. The guilt enveloped me. I had hurt someone as a result of my own selfishness— again.

After my divorce I lived alone, which only served to reignite my fantasy world. I bought all kinds of clothes and crossdressed and got high every day, with few exceptions. I was like an alcoholic on a bender and mine lasted for nearly two years. I guess I figured if I was ultimately going to leave the state that had caused such hopelessness, I was going to go out in a blaze of glory.

Through some miracle of divine intervention, I survived all of that, but in its wake I realized that I was absolutely done with Delaware and all of the frustration, pain, and heartache that I will forever associate with it. It was time to say hello to New Jersey—again—and begin a brand new chapter of my life.

And it worked—for a while.

YOU *CAN* GO HOME AGAIN

When I left Delaware I tried as hard as I could to make a clean break from my past. I cleaned up my act. I stopped smoking pot and I discarded any lingerie and any other clothes that I had re-accumulated during the two years I lived by myself. I even started to run and began to lose a lot of weight as a result. I was determined to start anew in all aspects of my life. Having a job that I could really embrace and completely throw myself into helped.

But I also met my third wife, Mallory, a month or so before I left. So perhaps my break wasn't as clean as I originally hoped. But this felt different than the other two relationships. I didn't jump right into it. I took my time. I didn't meet her until nearly two years had passed since my last divorce.

It might sound strange coming from someone who had already been married twice, but I felt what I thought was love for the first time in my life. As we did the long-distance dating thing throughout 1989 and all the way to when we were married in late 1990, I increasingly felt like this love would be the one that would be the answer to completely eradicating my gender issues. It's actually a common theme among trans people of my generation. But, alas, that hope eventually turns to despair. As the new year began I knew that I had to concentrate on resurrecting my career from the ashes.

A former connection set me up with a job at First Fidelity Bank in New Jersey. I only worked there for about a year and half before a huge layoff came that signaled the end of my time in the banking industry. But during those eighteen months I learned more and achieved more than I ever did during my "lost years" in Delaware. The frustration and anger were soon replaced by multiple successes and an ever-increasing confidence and self-esteem in my work and about myself as a person.

I saw it as sweet vindication for all those times I was passed over. I always knew that I could succeed. I just needed to find the right situation that was a better match for my skill set.

I worked for a great guy who gave me the opportunity to develop my skills and business acumen. I owe a lot to Louis. He took this totally green kid and somehow, over the course of a little more than a year, turned him into a business professional. Louis and I were responsible for the marketing of the bank's small business products (think loans and checking and savings accounts) via the bank's extensive branch network. My connection may have gotten me in, but I still had to prove myself. Sure I was back home, but I had a lot to learn about the bank and its culture. And Louis was my guide. We just hit it off. We meshed really well from the start and accomplished a lot in our relatively short time together.

He also told me who to stay away from and who to align myself with. Louis seemed very comfortable with where he was in his career. He was a vice president at the largest commercial bank in New Jersey and he gave me credit for my ideas and he was my advocate to management. So much so that I was promoted to a higher level office—assistant vice president—within my first year. I even received a bonus for all of the work I had done, and it happened at a time when no one else got one.

Would it have been different if I was a woman? I believe it would have, and here's why. Women at my level were clearly in the minority. Even though there were a lot of women in that area of the bank at that time, only a handful had progressed to assistant vice president and beyond. It was a direct reflection on the culture at the bank then.

In the C-suite the group consisted of four men and one woman. Only two of Louis' vice president peers were women. The rest—about a dozen or so—were all men. We had some diversity, with a few Latinos among us, but not a lot. There were no Black officers, but there were plenty of Black administrative assistants. When you think banking in the late '80s you think "old boys' network" and honestly, First Fidelity was no exception to that.

What *was* different for me was that I was a white male with a good amount of privilege and a good reputation. It allowed me to progress steadily and quickly through the ranks of the department. I do not believe I would have that same freedom of movement if I were a woman in that culture. And it's not like I was aware of it every single day I came to the office. But it was there nonetheless, and I rode the crest of its wave, most unconsciously.

Then it all came crashing down almost overnight.

The bank had made quite a few bad loans that had severely impacted the bottom line. A new chairman was brought in and he immediately started slashing staff across the entire bank—and my department wasn't spared. This all happened shortly after the holiday season in early 1990. The day HR came in, set up shop in a conference room, and started calling people in to tell them they were being let go, is a day that is seared into my memory. I had never experienced anything like it before. It was excruciating—for those that were let go after years and years of service, and for those like me who were saved.

I was one of the "lucky" ones. Louis pulled me into his office the day before to tell me I had been spared and swore me to silence. He told me he was going to be okay too. But there was a catch. In the aftermath I would no longer be working for him, or in that department. I was being reassigned to—wait for it—a collections position in the bank's leasing department!

It was the irony of ironies! The good news was I still had a job. The bad news was it was collections—again. Apparently, somebody noticed my past experience when they were deciding who should stay and who should go. So, the job I hated the most from my past, actually saved me.

I immediately began looking for another job. While it was a very different type of collections work—these were large equipment leases like aircraft and commercial printing equipment—at its heart it was still collections and I knew I was not about to start a new career in the equipment leasing business. Besides, the bank was on shaky ground and my new supervisor felt I had been forced into her department, which meant we did not get along. It was time to move on to much greener pastures.

HITTING THE BIG TIME

Some of the best days of my professional life were the days I worked at AT&T. In the decade that I worked there I made huge strides in my career, improved my management style, and learned how to navigate the corporate landscape to my advantage. My career had jumped to another plateau. I actually thought that I would retire from AT&T, that's how much I loved working there.

I had come onboard in the middle of what would become known as "the long distance wars," when every other commercial on television was about switching your long distance carrier. The early to mid '90s were the days before cellular service was launched, so if you had a phone in America, you had a landline. I found myself in the middle of it all as a manager in a marketing group that was responsible for creating and sending out the millions of direct mail pieces that implored you to sign up with AT&T and drop our hated competitors, MCI or Sprint.

It was a fast-paced, work hard, play hard culture and it all spelled one thing for me: opportunity.

I jumped on this train and rode it for as long as I could. Because I truly loved what I was doing it showed in every aspect of my performance. I was quickly identified as a "high-potential manager," which in AT&T-speak meant that I was seen as a future leader of the company.

I had a very solid reputation for doing what I said I would and doing it well. I had a group of internal clients, mostly product managers, who trusted me implicitly. I know this because they told me so. My first manager and the person who hired me, Abby, told me at the very beginning to "make sure that every one of your clients feels like they are the only client you have." And I took that to heart.

Someone once told me that moving up the ranks at AT&T was the most political game that anyone could ever engage in. It was a huge organization. The organizational structure was extremely hierarchical. The only way to progress with one's career was to work your way up through the organizational labyrinth. It was a big company with many divisions and units—consumer, business, domestic, international—just to name a few. To get noticed and advance you had to make sure that you align yourself with people at higher levels than yours that were seen in the same light. It all became a bit of a game. And the culture facilitated that in every way by rewarding those who played the game well.

To do that effectively meant you had to proactively manage your career. No one was about to do it for you. If you were interested in a particular area or assignment it was up to you to position yourself for it. That meant making sure the individuals who worked in those areas knew about you and your reputation. If they happened to be one of your clients, so much the better. It was all about selling yourself.

I came to regard my reputation as unassailable. The few times that colleagues tried to take shots at it for their own gain, I defended it instinctively and stridently. And I became very good at it.

So much so that in those ten years I was promoted three times and sent to a program that was reserved for the "future leaders of the company with a passion for winning" and nominated by their bosses to attend. I got to meet two of our chairmen in person, Robert Allen and Michael Armstrong. I traveled internationally to places like Singapore, London,

Brussels, and Amsterdam. I managed large-scale global projects that saved the company millions of dollars in the process. Because of my status I was able to steer clear of no fewer than four mass layoffs that befell the company throughout the '90s. I was on quite a roll.

I do think that it would have been possible to achieve this if I were a woman, too. I worked with some really sharp women who survived the layoffs like I did. I witnessed my female colleagues being promoted as well. There were quite a number of women at the "future leaders" program as well. It just seemed like a more equitable workplace for women—at least in comparison to all of the banks that I had worked at. But then again, that's arguably a pretty low bar.

By all appearances, women seemed to be treated more fairly at AT&T than at any of the banks I worked at. There were women at the highest levels of management—think senior vice presidents and above—who oversaw vast organizations. One of my mentors was just such a woman. Interestingly, all of my bosses at AT&T were women. The majority of my internal clients were women. I received my last promotion at the company because my Black, female boss advocated for me.

And it was there where I first experienced working alongside out, LGBTQ colleagues. AT&T was the first company that I ever worked for that actually had an employee resource group (ERG) for its LGBTQ employees. It is called LEAGUE, and it is one of the oldest LGBTQ ERGs in corporate America. It was established three years before I arrived, in 1987, and is still going strong today. But before you get any ideas about whether or not I contemplated joining—even as an ally—I did not. The thought of associating with LGBTQ people was something I avoided like the plague, because I thought that somehow people would think I was gay if I mingled with my LGBTQ colleagues. So there was the image piece of it. I thought that my grand plan for advancement up the corporate ladder would be stifled by my mere association with these people. I was so afraid that if I spent any time with them my secret would be revealed—and I could not take that chance.

I worked side by side with one particular gay man for a number of years in one of my assignments. We got to know each other very well over dinners on the road. Roger was well-liked and respected by all of our colleagues and I thought he was so incredibly brave. Braver than I could ever be, still mired in the closet for so long. He had a partner who had recently died of AIDS. I really empathized with him when he spoke to me about it. I didn't want to admit it to myself, but we shared a "community connection" of sorts and I could feel it when we were in conversation.

IT NEVER REALLY GOES AWAY

I had attempted time and time again to contain and compartmentalize my other life for a significant portion of the '90s. This time I thought I might actually have a chance at eradicating my true feminine self. I had fallen madly in love with the person who I thought would make it all go away; I went years without touching a stitch of women's clothing; I was super successful at work; I got married yet again, bought a house in the suburbs, and witnessed the birth of my son.

That event, more than any other, was life-changing for me. When Mallory and I decided to start a family I did so with a clear mind and honest intent. There were no little voices inside my head telling me this was a mistake. When Andrew was born I can remember holding him in my arms—he was barely an hour old—and I didn't know what to do. The nurse who gave him to me sensed what was happening and she said, "go ahead, you can talk to him. He can hear you." It was at that moment that I told him that I loved him with my entire being and that I would always be there for him. I would forever be a father and for years after, that's all I really saw myself as. Maybe, just maybe, I had this gender thing licked.

As the turn of the century drew near, things began to change and I realized I hadn't really conquered anything, partly because of work and partly because my feminine self was beginning to re-emerge. What served as a huge catalyst for this re-emergence was my newfound love of the internet. Through my dial-up connection I started surfing the web and realized very quickly that there were thousands of people out there just like me. I was most definitely not alone. And in the chat rooms and websites I visited most of these transwomen wanted to get together. I got very excited. I could share my most intimate feminine feelings with like-minded people. It felt like I hit the jackpot.

I started accumulating a wardrobe again and became very conscious of how I looked. I lost weight, got rid of my facial hair and began contacting people in my area. I started meeting other trans women like me—in secret. While the run up to every meeting was met with a mixture of exhilaration and nervousness, the aftermath of every meeting left me in a guilt-ridden heap. I was playing my own version of Russian roulette and I was endangering everything I had achieved. Or, to be honest, my reckless behavior was threatening to bring the grand facade crashing down. To put it mildly, this was not the most shining time of my life.

In addition to everything else I was, I now could add being a sneak and a cheat to my personal resume.

Meanwhile, it was becoming very apparent to me that I had reached my ceiling at AT&T. After "graduating" from the future leaders school, I landed in a network consulting division that catered to our largest business customers and it was good—for a short while. The woman who hired me into this unit turned out to be someone that I did not mesh with. I quickly began to feel unwanted and unappreciated. And my personal life was getting complicated: my marriage was showing signs of strain, I was out cavorting whenever I had the opportunity, and I was beginning to unravel. I even fell back on some old habits of not caring much at all for what I was doing.

As I realized that this may not have been my best career choice, I also knew that the internal movement across the company was being severely curtailed. There were rumors of yet another downsizing. That meant that there weren't a lot of other opportunities available to me. I even tried going back to the department I had started in. But they weren't bringing anybody in—and I was now three levels higher than when I left. There's an old saying that goes something like this, "as you move up the ladder you realize it's really a pyramid, and the higher you climb the fewer opportunities there are."

It became apparent to me that my train was slowing down and reaching the end of the line. Before things got out of hand I decided that perhaps my best next move was to leave. I took a long look at where the business world was at the dawn of the new millennium. The telecommunications industry was changing before my very eyes. The emergence of cellular service was a truly transformative event that changed AT&T forever. It was also the time of the "dot-com boom" and there were job opportunities everywhere. I had just won an industry award for a website redesign project I had overseen, so I thought of myself as a hot commodity.

I realized that if I got out now I could go out on top and earn substantially more someplace else. It was time to test the market, I thought, and make the most of this moment.

And that's when New York Life came calling.

A NEW BEGINNING . . .

I was recruited to join New York Life as their first-ever (as far I could tell) internet marketing manager. I had never in a million years thought that I would end up working at a life insurance company. I'm not exactly sure why. I think it had something to do with what the times were like then. Tech companies of all stripes were very much in vogue and I had interviewed with a few start-ups, so I somehow envisioned myself at a more "tech-oriented" company.

A life insurance company seemed so conservative, so . . . brick-and-mortar. I never would have imagined they were looking for someone to do internet marketing of all things. But as I discussed the job with the recruiter it seemed like a solid opportunity with a solid company. The more I thought about it, the more I thought I could leverage my new-found skills and make the jump to a higher level of management.

I found myself as a corporate vice president in the small but mighty corporate internet department of New York Life. It was a relatively new area within the company and was responsible for both the company's employee intranet and its external website. The vice president who hired me was a long-time employee of the company and had worked in a number of different areas before he was tasked with starting up this area. Apparently he had been working with a group of consultants to bring the company's internal and external internet presence to fruition and the plan called for the hiring of someone to do "internet marketing." If it sounds a little vague, that's because it was. I don't even think my new boss totally understood it either.

. . . 9/11—THE BEGINNING OF THE END

I was in Manhattan, in the New York Life building some two miles north and east of Ground Zero on that fateful day. It all unfolded right in front of me. I saw the second tower get hit on our conference room television. I heard the never ending wail of the fire engine and ambulance sirens. And the F-18s as they flew overhead. And I saw the survivors, covered in soot from head to toe as they haltingly walked up Fifth Avenue.

I felt something inside of me tear apart when I saw the towers collapse. Even though I didn't lose anyone, I was shaken to the core. And when I saw that they had hit the Pentagon I was frightened at the thought of what was going to happen next. I was in pain.

The final months of 2001 quickly became one of the worst times of my life. I was still reeling from the aftermath of 9/11. I was confronted with the terrible reminder of the tragedy every day on my daily commute. At stations along my train line cars were parked with flags draped over them to honor the owner who never returned from work that day. On my eight-block walk across Manhattan all I saw on every pole and every fence were handmade signs of the missing. The daily news was equally horrifying. Letters laced with the deadly chemical anthrax started showing up in the U.S. Mail. A plane crashed just after takeoff from Kennedy Airport killing everyone on board—over 250 souls were lost.

My heart broke every single day. I became numb all over. A malaise came over me that I could not shake.

And then, just when I thought it couldn't get any worse, my boss pulled me in to tell me my job was being eliminated. I wasn't even there for two years and they were already showing me the door. My malaise turned into defeat.

The towers' fall was a powerful metaphor for what was happening in my life. I felt caught in a confluence of forces. My job had vanished right in front of my eyes. My career was on the brink. My gender issues had re-emerged and all of my clandestine trysts had caught up with me. My marriage was on very shaky ground. Once again, I was playing a game of whack-a-mole with the real person inside of me to somehow salvage my life as I thought I knew it, and I was uncertain of the outcome.

Relief, at least from an employment perspective, came from a very unexpected source. I was scheduled to have lunch with Paula, a colleague who I had met some months before and hit it off with. She was being promoted to chief marketing officer of a newly formed marketing unit. I wanted to talk to her about how I could support her new unit from an internet marketing standpoint. Between scheduling the lunch and actually having it, I was informed about the elimination of my job so my lunch was transformed into a plea for employment. I tried not to sound too desperate, but I am certain that I did. She assured me she would try, and after enduring one of the most agonizing holiday seasons ever, I was told that they had created a position for me.

I was saved—from the unemployment line. But not from myself.

I was on a collision course with my true self and my life would soon be turned upside down. I had reached an inflection point in my journey that required me to face the reality of who I was in its entirety and in every facet of my life.

And I wasn't ready for it.

Like the juggler who keeps spinning plates from falling to the ground, I would soon find myself under a sea of wobbling plates that I had to keep from crashing to the floor.

No less than my life depended on it.

CHAPTER FIVE
PLATE SPINNING

"It's no use going back to yesterday, because I was a different person then."
~ Lewis Carroll

EVERY TRANSGENDER PERSON'S TRANSITION STORY IS different. Depending on several factors, such as where they live and what their specific living situation is, one story can be vastly different from another. Please keep in mind that as I tell you my story it is my story. While it is uniquely mine, it is by no means meant to stand as the example of what transition is like for every transgender person who makes the heroic decision to live their truth.

What I can tell you is that for me, coming out was a truly multidimensional experience. It's like being a plate spinner. I remember back when I was little my family would gather round the television on Sunday nights to watch the *Ed Sullivan Show*. It was a variety show, much like the late night talk shows of today, that those of us of a certain age will remember.

Ed often had on jugglers to balance out the bill with the big-name stars that appeared on his show each week. One such juggler was the plate spinner. These performers balanced plates on long sticks and would spin them and keep them from falling. The trick is, the more plates you have spinning the greater the challenge, because you risk a plate slowing down, falling, and breaking if you don't pay attention to it. The plate spinner must remain vigilant to assure a disaster does not happen—and keep calm, cool, and collected—all at the same time. The second challenge is that if one plate falls, it will likely hit another plate in the process and create a domino effect of knocking all the plates to the ground.

Keep that visual clearly in your mind because I can think of no other metaphor that so aptly represents what my life was like when I came out. Because you just don't proclaim to the world you're coming out and suddenly get to live happily ever after. Oh, if it were only that easy! The reality of the matter is that when you come out you do not do so in a vacuum. You, quite literally, come out to everyone in your life. It's essentially unavoidable. Everyone, like it or not, comes along for the ride.

Each plate represented a person or a venue in my life. One plate was my son. Another, my siblings. Yet another represented my workplace. Still another was all my friends. My mail carrier. The guy at the 7-11 I bought my coffee and lottery tickets from. Hell, if we still had milk men (yes, once upon a time before Amazon.com milk was delivered directly to your door from your local dairy) I would've had to come out to him too! As I came out to a person, I mentally put their plate atop a stick and began spinning it. Meanwhile, I had to pay attention to all the other plates that were already in the air.

When a transgender person comes out, there is a physical transformation that happens. If you choose to be on estrogen and testosterone blockers like I was at the time it's unavoidable. You are changing your body's chemistry. This biological 180-degree change in direction creates variations in one's physical appearance. It is a much different experience than that of my gay and lesbian brothers and sisters. When they come out there isn't much of a change to their physical appearance. Society doesn't see anything different and that's the biggest distinction.

When I started my transition, society most definitely saw something very visually different. It casts light on society's perceived notions of what male and female are supposed to look like. For a while, I was looking like a little bit of both, and that can be very disconcerting for people. Despite increased visibility in popular culture and the media about the concepts of the gender continuum and gender fluidity, we still live in a very gender binary world—in and out of the workplace. By that I mean, for many, it is simply a matter of what sex you are designated at birth. Depending on your external physical sex characteristics, you were either deemed a boy or a girl by the doctor. They cannot conceive of the notion that someone's internal sense of self is somehow misaligned with their birth sex. It isn't something much of the population ever thinks about. There is no in-between. But for me, and the rest of the trans community we live our life in the in-between.

Some people, obviously perplexed by the notion of my being transgender, would attempt to wrap their brains around this foreign concept by saying something like, ". . . so you're gay, right?" Well, not exactly. It's important to understand that because one chooses to transition that they do not automatically become gay. It doesn't work that way. Permit me to explain via a little "Transgender 101."

Everyone—not just trans folks—possesses both a *gender identity* and a *sexual orientation*. There are many definitions of each, but for our purposes here, let's go with these:

◊ *Gender identity* refers to a person's internal sense of being male, female, some combination of male and female, or neither male nor female.

◊ *Sexual orientation* describes patterns of sexual, romantic, and

emotional attraction to members of the opposite sex (het-
erosexual); attraction to members of the same sex (homosexual); and attraction to members of both sexes (bisexual).

Even more important, perhaps, than the definitions themselves is
the fact that these two variables are independent of each other. In my
case, I possess a gender identity of female, and I am attracted to other
members of the same sex: homosexual.

If these definitions still flummox you, I'll make it very easy to remember: Gender identity is *who I am*, sexual orientation is *who I love*.
How's that?

So yes, I am gay, *but* I also identify as trans. More specifically, I am a
transwoman who happens to be happily married to another transwoman.
That is my distinct reality. Your head just exploded, right? Gosh, I hope
not. I happen to be in a lesbian relationship with another transwoman,
so I guess that makes us . . . *transbians*? I actually think it has a nice ring
to it—transbian. Consider the term officially coined.

I should point out that my coworkers, themselves one of those spinning plates, were noticing my physical changes and modifications to my
outward presentation. I found out, some time after I came out at work,
that the running commentary around the office was "What is Mike going to show up looking like today?" Around that time I was already divorced and living on my own and with the exceptions of when I had my
son (I had joint custody) and when I was at work, I was presenting to the
world as my true self, as Stephanie. Trouble was, it was beginning to spill
over and I wasn't about to stop it. The boundaries of those spheres of my
life were by no means solid lines.

I had convinced myself that it was okay to start wearing women's
slacks, blouses, and flats to work and no one would really notice. After
all, I had been wearing women's undergarments for awhile anyway. I

even went so far as to put a little eye makeup on—nothing too overt, or so I thought—and show up at the office that way. I no longer wanted to wear male clothing. In my bedroom closet at the time were two distinct sections: on the left side was a rather large—and growing—collection of women's clothes and shoes. On the right side stood an ever-shrinking section of men's clothes, or "Michael clothes" as I called them. Some trans women call them "drab clothes," for obvious reasons. As time went on, I had very little use for the clothes on the right side of my closet.

Clearly, I was only kidding myself. The parallel from the popular media that comes to mind is when Bruce (now Caitlyn) Jenner began her transition. I had the pleasure of serving as a consultant on the television program she ultimately came out to the entire country on—Diane Sawyer's *Primetime Live*. By that time the world was beginning to see a very different Bruce. There were distinct physical changes that had all of the tabloid magazines buzzing. Her hair was growing out, she had some facial plastic surgery. I'm sure you remember all of the coverage she was getting at that time. To me and my friends it was very apparent: Bruce Jenner was transgender and she was beginning her own transition.

I think she may have been kidding herself, too. For a variety of reasons that were only known to her, she wasn't quite ready to come out to the world—and for her, unlike me, it was the entire world. But she had passed the point of being able to conceal it. The physical changes had become too apparent for the public to ignore. Perhaps she had her own plates spinning, too.

I actually think there are a number of parallels between my transition and Caitlyn's. We are of the same generation. We transitioned later in life. We ran from our gender issues through our participation in sports. We spun the same plates. Okay, so maybe I don't have an Olympic gold medal hanging in my den and I'm not a multimillionaire, but you get the idea.

Because of these parallels, I consulted on the *Primetime Live* episode in which Caitlyn came out, and had the surreal experience of watching a different version of my story being told. I can remember feeling that way as I sat with Diane and her production team as we watched the pre-recorded footage of the program just days before the live show was to air. I could immediately feel Caitlyn's anguish, her pain and her struggle. I really could. In a strange way, it is precisely these emotions that bind all of us together as a community. It's the struggle.

We all go through it in one way or another. But we are driven forward by that inescapable light inside of us that draws us ever closer to our authentic selves. The problem is, unlike Caitlyn—and to a lesser degree—me, the vast majority of transgender people are taking their journey under much more trying socioeconomic and racial circumstances. To put it another way, they do not enjoy the same privilege that society affords those of higher economic standing and white skin.

It's not that we don't want to admit it to ourselves—I was way past that point in my transition. I had finally embraced my true self, but not all of the planets were aligned just yet. I still had to keep all of the spinning plates from falling to the ground. Practically speaking, I couldn't come out at work because I was not yet out to my son. So I compromised. I pushed the envelope with my appearance when I could, but I was only fooling myself if I thought my colleagues didn't notice. I did what I could to strengthen the grip on my feminine self and make it through those portions of my life where I was not yet able to introduce the real me. And it's for those reasons that I was the last to grasp what had become patently obvious to those around me.

As I look back on this period in my life, from 2003 to late 2005, it all strikes me as being such a very exhausting experience—both mentally and physically. And that's because it was. But I couldn't stop to think about that for too long, or it would paralyze me in the journey I was finally taking. Up to this point I had wandered aimlessly through what passed for my adult life and I wasn't about to turn back. Once the genie is out of the bottle it is hard to put her back in. But by that time, I was on a mission—a mission to finally embrace my true self—and I was not going to stop for anything. Or so I thought.

THE ROAD RISES UP TO MEET YOU

I can specifically trace the real beginning of my journey back to a conversation I had with my soon to be ex-wife in the fall of 2003. I was firmly ensconced in my house-of-cards suburban life at the time, hanging on by my fingernails to what had become a very unstable and disintegrating marriage.

We were still living with the after effects of something that had happened a few years prior. Mallory had found pictures of me crossdressed and absolutely flipped out. It was New Year's Eve and I had just returned from a trip to the store to stock up for the evening's festivities when I was confronted on the front lawn by my ex. I knew immediately by the look of horror and anger in her eyes what had happened. She literally threw the briefcase, full of pictures, at me. In that moment time stood still, my head started buzzing and the only words I could hear were my own muffled cries of "I'm sick, I'm sick" for indeed that is what I thought I was. It was at this precise moment that I felt my two worlds collide as the lifelong facade that I had so stridently kept in place come crashing to the ground. I quickly gathered everything off the lawn and rushed inside fearful the neighbors saw everything that had just transpired. A few panicked phone calls later Mallory and I found ourselves in our pastor's living room where I was made to recite an act of contrition and agree to see a therapist so this would never happen again. Oh if it was only *that* simple. Happy New Year!

Looking back on the whole debacle I wonder if I somehow wanted to get caught. Why else would I bring home pictures of me crossdressed inside my briefcase when they would have been perfectly safe - and unseen - in my office drawer under lock and key? So I could somehow admire them during a private moment over the holiday weekend? The reality is that after literally decades of hiding and denying my truest feelings from myself, keeping the lie in place was getting harder and harder for me to do and, in a very major way, I screwed up.

But there's more to the story. The origin of these fateful photographs involves revealing more about a checkered part of my past that I'm not very proud of.

For me, back to the '80s, the only place where I could find another image of a transgender person was at my local adult book store, where a certain section had pornographic magazines featuring "transvestites." The interesting thing about these magazines is that they all had a "Personal Ads" section where other transwomen would post ads—many with provocative pictures—where one could send in a written response with the hope of connecting in person. The main problem was that you never knew how up-to-date these magazines were. As a result, any written overtures I made resulted in returned mail marked "addressee not found," or "moved—no forwarding address." Scanning personal ads was all too often an exercise in futility.

By the time the mid-90s rolled around, the internet was more than coming into its own as a meeting place for transgender individuals of all stripes. Chat rooms and websites abounded that offered an opportunity for connection and community that had never existed before. That was certainly the case for folks of my generation.

As a result, it was relatively easy to connect with someone of like mind for meetings—typically in a hotel or motel—where we were free to express our femininity within the confines of the room. Taking pictures to memorialize how feminine we looked and felt—these moments of being our authentic selves—was a necessary component of the experience. Sometimes sex was involved, but not all the time. It all seems so clandestine, so in the shadows. Because it was. Trading one closet for another, I guess. The search for connectedness can take one to very interesting and dangerous places. That's where the pictures came from.

But this is where my two worlds existed at the time. In one sphere was my normal life. In the other, my secret life that I found myself holding on tighter and tighter to. I was caught in the middle of a clash of emotions that was tearing me in half, but try as I might I could not break free. In a very weird way I became comfortable living in the vortex of these two worlds. Had my search for some sort of balance in my life become so jaundiced that it led me to this crossroads? Apparently it had, and I crashed and burned the moment she saw them.

Can't say that I blame her. It amazes me that we didn't split up then, but I can remember vowing to change and get help so I could "cure the sickness" that I had.

Yes, that's what I called being transgender back then—a "sickness." I couldn't be "cured," because there was nothing to cure. I was light years away from embracing my authentic self. And though I did try for a while, I couldn't change who I am, and eventually we did divorce. I was scared—yet another failed marriage! This can't be happening again! But in fact it was. I had spent the better part of two decades running from something that would never go away and I was about to burn through a third marriage doing so. I was a complete failure at life, certainly at living as a male in the world.

After each of my prior divorces, I can recall going off to some place where I could be alone with my thoughts. I would quickly find myself sobbing uncontrollably over the pain that I knew I had caused to those who extended their love to me. A love which I did not have the capacity to reciprocate because I was not bringing my truest self to the relation-ship. Through no fault of their own they were caught under the grand facade that was my life back then.

But here's the thing: my first two exes never knew about all of the crossdressing and my true inner feelings. I had hidden it all from both of them. It's not like I'm proud of that by any means, it's just what hap-pened. The failed marriages were all on me and my inability to face my own reality.

I cried, too, because I felt altogether helpless to stop it. I simply could not resolve the push and pull of wanting to express my true self, the intense guilt and fear it created, and the pressure to conform to life as a male in the world the way my family had envisioned it for me. The intensity of the spotlight I put myself under withered my soul. I was incapable of reconciling it all.

I should have run to some place far away so I couldn't hurt anyone anymore. I was toxic, a hazardous substance to myself and anyone that got close enough to me. But instead I would selfishly draw them in, ig-noring everything that happened before, hoping beyond hope that "this woman will change everything." Off I'd go with another relationship that, despite all the hoping, I knew would eventually end in disaster. I couldn't help myself.

In some awful, insidious way, all of my hiding from who I really was rendered me emotionally unavailable to these women on a deeper level. The totally ironic thing about all of this is that I had this twisted notion that if I somehow fell madly in love and got married I would rid myself once and for all of the feelings I harbored since my childhood. That was a losing proposition from the start. But when one is helplessly grasping at the straws of life these thoughts can seem quite plausible.

Yet there I was facing divorce number three squarely in the face, so what did I do? I sucked it up, got rid of the wigs, the makeup, the shoes, and the clothes I had accumulated and vowed to never go back again. But of course I eventually did. My "beginning of the end" actually lasted for nearly five years!

I soldiered on. I actually had this delusional thought that I could somehow manage to live a double life, make it all work and keep everyone happy. I had yet to shed the paradigm of living my life for the fulfillment of others' expectations. I had lived so much of my life up to that point trying to do the "right thing," not ever really knowing what that meant. I was living my life on other people's terms, on what I thought I was supposed to be doing as a now forty-year-old married father. I didn't want to disappoint those closest to me—all the people that loved me and supported me throughout my life—but I was failing miserably. As I remember it, it was all just so excruciatingly painful.

So there I sat, in the fall of 2003, at one end of the dinner table with wife number three at the other. Andrew was off playing or watching television in another room in the house. I can recall a rather uneasy silence hanging in the air. She suddenly said, "I know this isn't going away." It was immediately clear to me that she had been doing some research on the internet.

I responded, "You're right, it's not." "And," I added, "if I do this, I'm going all the way." I knew that transitioning was my ultimate destination. Reflecting back on it, I have to say that it was the most authentic moment I had experienced in my life up to that point. I had recently started seeing my therapist so I was slowly beginning to not be so ashamed of who I was. Or, to put it another way, I was finally starting to own who I was. It was as if at that moment, I was standing on the edge of a great abyss and as I looked down all I could see was blackness. There was just nothingness. Try as I might I could not see the bottom.

I knew that if I stepped off the edge I risked losing everything. The life I had created for myself would come crashing down. On some level,

I actually thought I had it all: the white picket fence, the house in the 'burbs, an established social circle of friends and neighbors. Who was I kidding? I was in complete denial.

But step off I did. And you know what happened? Instead of tumbling down into the darkness all alone, a road rose up out of the gloom to meet my step. What exactly was on that road? It was a new path for me to travel on, a path to embracing my true self that over the years has been populated by friends who have become my new chosen family. People who would understand and celebrate me for who I am. They have been there for all of the good times and the not-so-good times, too.

As it turned out, many of these people were my coworkers. They embraced me for who I was as a person—and as a colleague. Keeping that plate firmly in the air would require a lot of perseverance, mental toughness, and a whole lot of logistics.

My good friend, Scotty, an engineer at Raytheon Technologies, who also happens to be a trans man, characterized his moment of truth in a decidedly different way:

"I was at the center of a hurricane. A storm built inside me. I was dealing with conflict, perceptions, gender rigidity and gender baggage of others around me all the time. As I began the transition process, and it bloomed into a hurricane, but I was standing in the eye. I was feeling good about myself, and things were progressing, but the storm had spread out to everyone around me. They now had to deal with what was going on."

As for me and what happened next? I really do not have any specific recollection. I kept seeing my therapist. Kept going to work every day. Kept up appearances to our neighbors and friends.

That all changed just a few months later in January of the next year, 2004, when Mallory told me she wanted a divorce. We agreed very quickly that we'd have joint custody of our son and that I would move out of the house as soon as I could find an apartment, which I moved into in March of 2004. Our divorce was final on Tax Day, April 15, 2004. I think it was the fastest divorce on record in the state of New Jersey. It was ninety days of me giving up a lot (as my attorney told me on several occasions) just so I could put it all behind me and move on once and for all.

What I do remember is when we told Andrew we were getting divorced. He was nine years old. To this day I say it was the hardest thing I ever had to do. The anguished look on his face, the tears, as he said, "no, no." It hurts deeply just to recall it all. I can recall my therapist unpacking that reaction for me in one of the sessions we had after we told him. She told me that, among other things, a child mourns the loss of the family unit more than a lot of the other things commonly associated with a divorce. That is why my soon to be ex and I did everything we could to assure him that he would always have both of us in his life. That's a promise I am proud to say we have kept in all of the years since.

MY SON, MY HERO

Without question, one of the most important plates I had spinning was the one that represented my son. I wasn't very concerned about what was going on in the courts relative to our divorce. There was no trial. I didn't have to appear before a judge. It was all handled by the lawyers, just one big paper chase. I was more concerned with establishing my new life and what that was going to look and feel like.

I found a new apartment not that far away from where we had lived as a family. I got new furniture, which Andrew helped me pick out. One piece of which was the convertible sofa that would become his bed on the nights and every-other weekends he stayed with me.

I was trying to work through all of the logistics of moving, of telling my siblings and friends that we were divorcing—and somehow avoiding the real truth in the story I told each of them. I told my boss, but honestly, work was the least of my concerns. No one in my life at the time, with the exception of my girlfriends, therapist, and my fellow support group attendees, knew the actual reason for the split.

Not even Andrew. I couldn't lay that on him then. Besides, I didn't have the ability to. That would be well over a year later. The fact is, I was scared to death. I was afraid I was going to screw it all up somehow and lose him. As I slowly, haltingly began my new reality it felt like I was balancing all of these spinning plates on the head of a pin.

One realization broke through all of the self-imposed fear: regardless of whatever happened to me, he was the most important person in my life. Out of all of the marriages, divorces, angst, shame, guilt, and denial I was given the greatest gift in the world—my son. He is my hero because he taught me what unconditional love truly means.

As I looked out at the road ahead of me, before I could preoccupy my mind with thoughts of what my new tomorrows would look like, I had to ask myself these simple yet hugely important questions:

◊   Who do you want in your life after you transition?
◊   Who do you want to be there next to you when you live into your truest self?

For me those answers were instantaneous: my son. Total slam dunk. I would not and could not exist without him in my life. No way. I was going to do whatever I needed to do to ensure I was in his life and he was in mine.

But I was lucky in that Andrew was young enough that the opportunity existed to bring him along slowly and not lose him completely, if at all. A close friend of mine at that time, who really served as my role model in coming out to one's employer, had older kids when she came out—and she lost contact with every one of them. It seems they were highly influenced by her ex-wife's completely negative and hateful reactions to her transition. Over the years she made repeated attempts at re-establishing contact, but they all ultimately failed. I suspect her ex had completely poisoned their minds by that point leaving no hope for a reconciliation.

It pains me to think of how some people, in this case ex-wives, weaponize their morality and/or their religious beliefs on their exes. What is the root of that behavior? Do they feel so wronged, so deceived, so betrayed that they believe that the only course of action available to them is to ruin their ex's life? It was, unfortunately, a very common theme at the support groups I went to. One tale after another of transwomen being voted off the island and quite literally thrown out on to the street to fend for themselves. The phrase "hell hath no fury like a woman scorned" comes clearly to mind.

Look, I will never feel those emotions or have those reactions because it has never been done to me. But it would be very insensitive for me to say that these women shouldn't feel this way. Who am I to say that? I will never know their pain and their anguish. It was just so hard to see it unfold right in front of me like it did.

We would talk for hours about it at her apartment and I just felt so helpless. I could console her and of course I did, that's what friends do, but I was powerless to change her reality. It saddened me then and it saddens me now. The upshot of this story is that it is not an uncommon occurrence for a majority of transgender people. You come out. You lose people. Some come back, as my brothers eventually did, for example, but many never do. It's unfortunate and unfair, but it comes with the territory.

Remember how I said I was afraid of screwing things up with my son? Well I dodged a bullet in that regard about a year or so later.

As the months passed, I was getting my feet under me in my new digs and in my new life. I had established a social life as Stephanie and I was getting out in public a good amount of the time—outside of work hours and the times I had Andrew. I guess I was beginning to get a little full of myself and I decided that a great way to bring my son along was to put out pictures of me with one or more of my girlfriends. I thought that maybe they might help him put two and two together and realize that one of those women in the photograph was his dad.

It was, to put it bluntly, a very bad idea. While I did not get any reaction from my son in the few weeks they were scattered around my apartment, I found out much later from him that all it did was muddy the waters in his mind. It just really confused him.

When I told my therapist about it she completely flipped. "How can you do that? Why would you do that?" she shouted at me. I felt like such an idiot. She continued, "How can you put all of that on your son? He doesn't understand any of that." She was not at all happy with me—and she was right. I was absolutely out of line. While this may seem rather harsh, it was indicative of the professional relationship she and I had and, more than anything else, it was the wakeup call that I needed.

I distinctly remember leaving her office shaken to my core. What had I done? How self-absorbed with my transition had I become? My mind was racing. How selfish was I getting? Had my desire to be completely out overtaken my concerns for my son's well-being? Apparently, it had. As soon as I got home I got rid of all the pictures—that was the easy part. The much harder part was reassessing my transition. How fast was I really going? Sometimes you have to get off the moving train and view it from the side of the tracks to really get a sense of how fast it is travelling. Had I lost control? Were the plates teetering on their sticks about to fall to the floor? The short answer is—yes.

There was only one answer—I had to slow down. For me, and for many transgender folks of my generation—after decades in the closet—it was one of the most difficult things I had to do. Up to that point I had fully embraced the mindset of "Let's go! Let's get this party started! Look out world, here I come." I realized I had to walk that back—a lot. I realized that I just could not go at that pace anymore. Andrew wasn't ready, and as hard it was for me to admit it to myself—I wasn't ready either.

So in the weeks and months that followed, I did slow down. It actually wasn't nearly as hard as I thought it would be. Like so many of us, my approach to life closely mirrors my work ethic—I put a lot of pressure on myself. I always have throughout my career, before and after my transition. So taking my foot off the gas, even just a little bit, had a surprisingly calming effect on my psyche. I think I finally realized that transitioning is not a competitive sport, it has no World Series or Super Bowl attached to it. Although I think I approached it that way and that's what got me into trouble in the first place.

FREAK SHOW DAD

Regardless of how serene I had suddenly become, the fact that I had a long road ahead with my son was not lost on me. There would be hurdles to jump over and mountains to climb on his journey to acceptance of me for what I was becoming. We had our moments together along the way. We had our ups and our downs. What else could I expect? To think for one moment that this was all going to progress without any significant bumps in the road would have been very unrealistic of me.

We had some knockdown, drag out shouting matches when he was in his early high school years. I'm talking about nose-to-nose screaming matches. Each of our positions usually came from the same place every time. He was very upset about all of the excess baggage I was putting on him because I wasn't at all like his friends' fathers and I think it just all got to be such a burden for him from time to time. I'm sure there was more to it, but he never shared all of the reasons. Just the anger.

It would build and build, he'd then get very quiet, I'd prod a bit too much for an answer to what was going on and—*boom*—off he'd go. I would immediately go on the defensive and shout back some nonsense about how this is what I am and I can't change who I am and blah, blah, blah. It was just such a hot mess.

After things settled down and he went off to his room, we'd invariably wind up hugging each other and exchanging "I love yous." I can remember him saying on more than one occasion after these eruptions, "I love you, Steph, but it's all the other stuff that is hard." I totally got what he meant.

After I received that rather thorough dressing down from my therapist, the one thing that I always tried to ground myself in was the actual reality of where I was at the moment I was currently in. I couldn't allow any overly idealistic images of what the future was going to look like post-transition to creep into my daily mindset. I had to anchor myself in the reality of now—each and every day.

This "living in the moment" mentality was very hard for me at first, but when I strayed too far away from my focus I always had those essential questions I spoke of earlier to re-center me. I honestly think that mentality has helped me in my professional life. Having a plan is one thing, but having the tactics of that plan tied to a specific goal or outcome keeps you on track and can serve as your true north when all of the noise that swirls around you seems designed specifically to pull you away from it.

One of the major hurdles I encountered with my son was a direct result of the physical changes I was going through at the time. I became a "Freak Show Dad" for a while. He actually called me that. "Freak Show

Dad." I vividly remember the first time it happened.

I was picking him after work on one of the evenings I had him, and I remember he didn't come to the door right away. His mom and I were both just kind of waiting for him in awkward silence. It hit me pretty quickly that there was quite a bit of reluctance on his part to come with me that night. His mom yelled out for him to "hurry up, your father is waiting." He finally emerged and said something like "gotta go with Freak Show Dad," and into the car we went. The drive from the house to my apartment was no more than ten, maybe fifteen minutes, tops. There was complete silence. I had no words. No snappy retort. I may have apologized at some point that evening, but I honestly don't remember. I just felt like the wind had been taken out of my sails. He had a right to feel that way, I thought to myself, and that was that.

Why did he feel that way? Well, for one thing I certainly was not looking like most of the other dads out there in suburban northern New Jersey at the time. I was getting my eyebrows waxed. My ears were pierced. My hair was growing out. I was going through the various stages of laser hair removal of my facial hair, so I was looking rather splotchy. I had been on hormone treatments for the better part of a year. When you put it all together I was looking pretty funky, and my son did not know how to deal with it.

I remember taking him aside one day and having what has turned out to be a very pivotal conversation with him. I knew I had to do something. I knew I needed to help him get past the physical manifestations of my transition and connect with him heart-to-heart. So I said to him:

"Andrew, there is something I would like you to try to understand. I will always be your dad.

"You can always call me Dad. It doesn't matter to me. You can call me anything you want, but I'll always be your dad.

"Now I get it, I'm going to look different than other dads, but will I somehow forget how to throw a baseball? Or a football? Nope.

"Will I still yell at the television on Sunday afternoons when the New York Giants make yet another bonehead play on the football field? Absolutely I will.

"Just remember one thing," I said as I leaned in closer to his face, "I'm not your mom. Your mom gave birth to you. I'm your dad—and no matter what I will always be there for you. Okay?"

"Okay" was all he said in return. But what I remember most about that conversation is that he was really listening to every word I was saying. We never lost eye contact. I hoped that it had the intended impact—and I think it did.

He needed to hear that. And you know something, I needed to hear myself say it. It steeled my resolve to make my transition as manageable for him as I could at that time. I knew that as he reached puberty and his high school years that if I didn't have some foundation of love and trust already established, things could become very difficult for the two of us. And if you think about it for a minute, isn't that true of all relationships between parents and their children?

The part that might be difficult for you to understand is that my being transgender is not a choice. It is who I am. But where I do have a choice is deciding how and when to come out, and dare I say it, if I ever do. I must point out that just because these are decisions that I felt I was faced with does not mean that transgender folks of younger generations feel that they have to face them at all. Their lived experience is very different from mine. You don't have to *come* out when you've always *been* out.

These decisions were driven by my age—I was forty-six years old in 2004, and in the closet—a very real place that existed in my world for nearly as long. But like I mentioned before, when you make that decision, everyone in your life, like it or not, comes out with you. In as much as I had a choice, Andrew did not. Faced with that reality, it was my responsibility as his parent to prepare him, but on his terms, not mine.

So we devised our own ways of navigating public spaces together. It wasn't about me at all, really. It was all about making sure he was comfortable. I can recall a conversation about it that went something like this:

"So when we are out shopping together somewhere we could come into contact with some people that might refer to me as your mom. But you and I both know that I'm not, but they don't know that. So as long as we are in on it together we're cool, okay? We get it, but they won't know—and that's okay. Just remember when we are in Home Depot or the supermarket and you're on the other side of the store from me you might not want to yell 'Hey Dad!' at the top of your lungs to get my attention because it might just confuse a few people that are waiting in line with me, all right?"

He nodded his head in reply, "It's cool. I got it. I got it."

This came full circle a few years ago when I went to my son's university graduation. We had decided to go out for lunch to one of his favorite downtown restaurants and celebrate. Turns out there was a guy at the bar who my son knew. He saw us and approached the table to say hello. The guy introduces himself then turns to my son and says, "This must be your . . ." and before he could finish the sentence my son and I answered in unison "mom!" It was the perfect moment for both of us.

But it is important to understand that we didn't just arrive there by accident.

Both of us, each in our own way, had to do the "inside work"—all of the little things that nobody sees, the individual moments that bond a father and a son—to reach a place of common understanding, acceptance, and love.

I have learned that progress toward one's goals, or progress in one's life for that matter, doesn't happen solely in bold sweeping strokes seen by many—quite the contrary. It has been my experience that it's more about a collection of little moments, unseen by everyone except yourself, that when strung together move you forward, or in this case, move *us* forward. Sometimes that can bring you to place that you never thought was achievable, never thought was remotely possible. But then, somewhat suddenly, there you are. You realize in that moment that you have attained the dream you have held onto so tightly for so long.

One such moment was during my son's sessions with his therapist. I should first explain that, despite my ex's misgivings, through my therapist we found someone who worked with kids who my son could talk to about his feelings toward me. These went on for quite a while until one evening all the pieces came together and made sense for him. I remember it well. His therapist stepped out of his office, turned to me and said, "Stephanie, Andrew has something to tell you."

My heart skipped a beat. I wasn't sure what was going to come next. Did he hate me? Was all of this just a colossal waste of time and money? My mind began to race. So I sat down on the couch next to him, took a deep breath, and braced myself for what came next.

Andrew furrowed his brow and said to me, "So a crossdresser is a boy who likes to dress up in girl's clothes." I nodded yes in reply. He continued, "but a transgender person is a boy that feels like a girl inside—and that's you, Dad."

Well you could have knocked me over with a feather! He got it! Tears began to stream down my cheeks as I acknowledged his newfound revelation with a big hug. That was the moment the switch flipped. He got it. He understood, in terms that worked for an eleven year-old brain, what so many adults still do not understand about gender identity and about being born incongruent with one's internal sense of self.

In the years since that day he has never missed a pronoun and he has never gotten my name wrong. Ever. He mostly calls me Steph now, but throughout high school and even college he has called me Dad too— and I love it. After all, I *am* his father. And just because he calls me that doesn't somehow invalidate my lived experience as a transgender woman. Not for a second.

With that hurdle successfully cleared the next obstacle on our journey together was the socialization piece: how to explain to his friends that his dad is transgender. I decided the best course of action was to give my son a wide berth. Stay out of the way and for heaven's sake, don't try to push my own agenda on him. In short, I let him lead. I had to let go of the reins and trust that he would find his way.

Middle school was tough, but not so much because of me, because I tried to keep myself at a safe distance from that part of his world. I didn't want to complicate things for him. I made sure I was closely involved in his academic life. On the days during the week I had him I would always drop him off at school on my way to work. I made most of his parent-teacher conferences except when a work obligation that I couldn't get out of got in the way.

The tough part for Andrew was the fact that he was adjusting to a new school, new friends, a new town, and a new living arrangement, as his mother sold the house we used to live in and moved in with the man who a few years later would become her husband. In short, he had a whole new life that he didn't have any control over.

I remember telling him high school was going to get better: more kids from other middle schools meant there was a greater chance that he would make friends with kids who had similar interests. And that's precisely what happened.

What I learned is that kids are extremely resilient and a lot brighter than we adults give them credit for. They are amazing points of light. They can navigate their spaces better than we can because those spaces are theirs, not ours. Children and adults have different mental guardrails. In my humble opinion, as parents we instill in our kids a set of values that we believe and hope will serve them well as they grow up and make life decisions for themselves. Sure, we can serve as a sounding board for them—I certainly have throughout my son's life thus far. But in the end, it's his decision. He has to own it. Just like I had to own my decision to transition and live my truth.

So one day, he says to me totally out of blue, in a completely matter-of-fact tone, "By the way, all my friends know about you." I nearly fell off the couch.

"What? Are you kidding me?"

I steadied myself. "Wait a minute. Say that again."

"All of my friends know about you, Steph," my son replied.

"That I'm transgender, right?" I asked.

At this point he was becoming a little irritated with my disbelief. "Well, yeah, of course."

I was in shock I guess, and caught more than a little off guard.

I replied, "What do you mean, 'yeah, of course'? This is huge. Do you know how big this is?"

"No, why?" he asked.

"Do you know how courageous it was for you to do that? The risk that you took? That could have all gone downhill in a hurry! You are my hero!"

To this day I'm not really sure if he fully appreciated the enormity of his achievement. That has everything to do with the fact that I am recounting this from my perspective. From his point of view, as I found out later from him, is that it may not have been as momentous an accomplishment. It was clear he had surrounded himself with a solid group of friends. He simply told them what the situation was. Turns out, every one of his friends was cool with it.

And you know what was even cooler? So were their parents. I got to meet all of them at his high school graduation. The parents had all gotten together to create an after-graduation party which we all chaperoned. Like most high schools, the last thing anybody wants is for newly graduated students to be out drinking and driving on graduation night.

The kids went on a boat cruise around Manhattan and then were bused back to the high school gym—transformed into a nightclub of sorts with music, couches, games. It was all very lounge-y. All of them were very welcoming and each one had so many wonderful things to say to me about raising such a wonderful son. It was beyond gratifying.

"I'm so glad to finally meet you," they said to me. I had no idea. My son, the hero, blazing a trail—for me! I could not have been prouder.

Frankly, there are a million lessons you can glean from the journey I have taken with my son. From all those lessons, the one I believe in the most is that you create your own reality. How people treat you, how they initially react to you, is all a direct byproduct of the energy that you put out into the world. To put it another way, how brightly do you allow your light to shine wherever you go? How steadfast are you in the conviction that what you say matters to people, that you have a right to be in whatever physical space you find yourself and that you have a right to be heard?

It has become a universal principle that I carry with me to this day. It has guided all aspects of my daily life, and it has caused me some amount of consternation, especially in the workplace.

I suppose some people call that courage, but for me it's really a survival mechanism. When I came out, with all of those plates spinning in the air, anything less than approaching my new life with the steadfast conviction that I would succeed in all aspects of it was totally unacceptable. As I like to say, "I can only do *me* one way." I soon found out that a straight-on, full-speed-ahead approach could have its drawbacks with some people.

FACING MY FEARS

As I was bringing my son along with me on my journey of transition, there was still one very, very important plate that I had yet to spin. And that was coming out to my siblings. To be honest, I was holding off on this one for as long as I could because I was quite terrified of how things would turn out. It was very difficult for me to view the outcome as being anything but a total disaster. Fear can do that. My fear always manifests as fear of rejection and isolation, and this instance was a prime example. I never knew how insidious it could be, how it could seep into every pore of my skin until my entire being was taken over by it. But the prospect of coming out as transgender to my two brothers and my sister was utterly horrifying. To put it mildly, I got myself very worked up over it.

My siblings were over a decade older than I was and their lived experience up to that point, as far as I could tell, never included a transgender person. I can recall having many conversations with my therapist about how I just loathed the thought of sitting down with each of them—to have three separate and distinct conversations, I might add—and telling them that their "kid brother" was not really their *brother* at all.

As much as I dreaded the idea, there was a part of me that also felt like I owed them an explanation for all of the divorces, especially the most recent one. For each one I would just brush off the questions of "What?," "Why?," and "How come?" with some utterly vague explanation about how "we just grew apart" or, "it was a mistake from the very beginning." It was all just made up nonsense. I could not bring myself to tell them the real reason. Among other things, I was just too embarrassed. I had failed. And failed again. And failed again.

So after much cajoling from my therapist I finally arranged a time to meet with each of my siblings separately and have "the talk." Much to my surprise, there was no screaming and yelling, I was not thrown out of anybody's house, or physically accosted. It was very apparent in each case that as I spoke the word "transgender" and attempted to explain what it meant *and* that it was me they were quickly bewildered. But I continued to try to explain. I had come this far in overcoming my fears so I wasn't going to get shortchanged on talking now.

I came out to my sister Betty first. That was an easy decision. She and I had spent the most time together when I was growing up. She was the one who made time to play with me when I was little. She was the one who functioned as my surrogate mom when my real mother was simply unavailable. All of the shining moments in my life I had always shared with her; and the ones that weren't all that great too. She was my biggest fan.

I recall her listening very intently to me. She knew I was having a very hard time getting all of the words out. I remember her trying to take it all in and saying something like, "If that's what you need to do, fine, but I don't want to see it." So what did that mean exactly? I didn't stop to ponder the consequences of that statement. I just finished up and then said my goodbyes just knowing I had created more problems than I was trying to solve.

That's the way it basically happened. I could see them attempting to process the information, but it was very difficult. This was probably—no, make that *definitely*—the last thing they were thinking I was going to talk about. In fact, my middle brother had already made up his mind that I was going to come out to him as gay, so the curve ball I threw him was most definitely unexpected.

When I finished with each, there was an immediate weight lifted off my shoulders, but it was fleeting. I realized very quickly that I was not finished coming out to them. Quite the contrary. This initial conver-sation only served to open up the proverbial can of worms. This wasn't going to happen in one tidy little chat. This was not a "one and done" scenario. How could it be?

I had miscalculated something very important. And that was the history that each of my siblings had with Michael. I was forty-six years old when I did this. Forty-six years is a long time. They had seen, from whatever distance, me grow up and make a life for myself, regardless of how fractured it was, and all they knew was Michael.

I needed to cut them some serious slack, but just like with my early mistakes with my son, I was trying to rush this along so I could get on with my new life. The main reason for the added velocity of this spinning plate was my intense desire to just get it over with. This was all so very torturous.

But I learned some things from all of it. Instead of just plowing through it as I had always lived my life up to that point, I realized that having tough conversations with people, whether they are your family or your colleagues, is an inevitable thing. What makes the difference is how you show up to each of them. This taught me that one cannot cower and hide from their beliefs or the truth. Quite the contrary. You have to meet people where they are, with an open heart and an open mind.

What were the results? Well, the good news is I have my brothers and sister in my life. In fact, my amazing sister became a real advocate for me among our family, our relatives, and close family friends. It didn't happen overnight, but we always stayed in touch. I knew we had reached a point of acceptance—and a major milestone in my new life—when my sister said to me, "You are the little sister I always wished I had."

With my brothers, though, the road was a bit more winding. They were slow to come around, despite repeated coaxing by my sister and sisters-in-law. We didn't speak for about two years. I wrote letters that were never read. It was tough. But they did eventually come around. It was awkward at first. Lots of missed pronouns and the use of my former name. But they were trying. They corrected themselves. Perhaps another person would have been more militant about it. I was just glad to have them back in my life and rolled with it, knowing their mistakes were not coming from a hurtful place.

Sadly, I lost my brother Jimy, as I used to call him, in April of 2020. He died of brain cancer at the height of the COVID-19 pandemic. I was on lockdown and couldn't go to the funeral. Nobody really could. It was heartbreaking.

A lifelong diabetic, he was an Army veteran and someone who before I ever transitioned, was always in my corner. We shared a lot of laughs, closed a lot of bars, and shared many a late night/very early morning breakfast at the local greasy spoon—the Arlington Diner—afterward. He taught me how to work on my car, how to restore a car—the 1970 Mustang we worked on together will be forever etched in my memory— and how to fix things around the house. He was simply great at all of those things. He had the cleanest garage and most well-organized tool box that ever existed. It seemed to come so natural to him. I was envious. What seemed so easy for him was a monumental undertaking for me.

Thankfully, we had our time together after I came out.

The most memorable occurred at the annual family Christmas Eve gathering in 2006. I had been estranged from both of my brothers since I came out nearly two years prior. Everyone else in my family, thanks to my sister's advocacy, were on board with me, including my brother's wives. So the stage was set for the grand unveiling of Stephanie. I was, to put it bluntly, a nervous wreck. I lingered for what seemed like hours over what to wear, finally settling on a very appropriate knee length wool skirt, turtleneck sweater and boots. This was New Jersey in late December after all. I arrived at my sister's house early and plied myself with a couple of scotches while waiting for everyone to arrive. My sister, who had already been in my company several times before, gave me the once over and a thumbs up on my makeup, hair and outfit.

I just sat at the kitchen table twirling the cubes in drink waiting, and waiting, and waiting. A half-hour seemed like an eternity. But in that time I just kept telling myself that everything was going to be fine, and that at the end of the day we really all loved each other. Finally the door opened and the first to arrive was my brother Jimy and my sister-in-law Ceil. I made a beeline for the door where he and I made eye contact. And upon seeing me for the first time, the next words out of his mouth after we exchanged Christmas greetings was "nice boobs." We hugged and kissed, and he explained to me—although he didn't really have to, about why he thought that would be a good ice-breaker. He didn't have to say another word. That just told me volumes about how much he cared.

And what did I learn from all of that you may ask? Simply put, my brothers needed to come to what acceptance looked like to them in their own time. There was no way I could ever dictate what that timeframe was going to be. It was out of my control.

And therein lies the other learning: you can only control what's in your control, nothing more, nothing less. I suppose it's my short version of the Serenity Prayer written by the American theologian Reinhold Niebuhr:

God, grant me the serenity to accept the things I cannot change, courage to change the things I can, and wisdom to know the difference.

The last, but by no means the least, plate I had yet to spin was the one that represented coming out at work. I guess I was saving the best for last.

CHAPTER SIX
OUT WITH THE OLD . . .

The life you have led doesn't need to be the only life you have.
~ Anna Quindlen

FROM THE MOMENT I TOOK THAT INITIAL LEAP OF faith, I knew that I was pushing the restart button on my life. My existence as a white male living a relatively affluent upper-middle–class lifestyle in the suburbs of Morris County, New Jersey, was about to come to an abrupt end. Caught up in all of this were the relationships that I had forged with the circle of friends my ex and I had developed over the past nine or so years. But these relationships were built on shifting sand. I was not being true to who I really was when I established these relationships. They were just another level of my cover. That's not to say that I didn't have good times with these people and that we didn't share some personal moments along the way; we did, but I always kept the secret of who I really was out of their view. I knew these relationships would never withstand my transition.

So I knew how it was going to end before it even began. I wasn't just turning a page, or beginning a new chapter of my life. I was closing the entire book and starting a brand new one. I suspected that the whole concept of being transgender was about as foreign to them as anything they had ever experienced before. It turned out I was correct on all counts.

But it wasn't like I didn't try. I did engage with a handful of male friends I was closest to and while they did their best to process what I was telling them, it was painfully obvious that the concept was too alien for them to really understand. As each one of these friendships disappeared, they became a part of the blackness of the abyss I had stepped into. But the good news is that as I set out on my new life a road rose up to meet my step and that road led me to new friends that were to become my new family and contribute greatly to the new sense of self I was embracing. I no longer had to pretend to be someone else, or worse yet, hide who I really was, from these people. I would soon learn that we shared a much deeper connection.

FINDING MY KINDRED SPIRITS

Over the years I have received many emails and calls from trans people seeking guidance on what to do as they prepare to take their first steps in the world as their authentic selves. Almost always the first thing I say to them is "find community." I would remind them that you don't get any bonus points for taking this journey by yourself and that the road to your true self is best traveled with people who celebrate who you are.

I know that because I have experienced it for myself.

I found my kindred spirits at my first support group. That is where I experienced the diversity of the transgender community firsthand and learned about the issues it faces through the eyes of my fellow "groupies." It is where I cried an ocean of tears and laughed so hard that I thought I was going to hurt myself. It is where I celebrated the triumphs of all my plate spinning and felt the love and empathy of others when things didn't quite work out the way I had planned. I became a part of each of them, and they became a part of me—my past *and* my future.

It is where I found myself.

I remember coming to the group for the very first time - sometime during the fall of 2003 and I was really late having totally miscalculated the time it would take to drive there from a friend's place where I had changed, as I was still a few months away from moving into my own apartment. I was a nervous wreck. I was perspiring so much that I thought all of my makeup was just going to run down my face. This was the first time that I was going to reveal myself to total strangers and I was having serious second thoughts. As I raced down the highway I kept thinking of excuse after excuse to get out of it. Flat tire? That could work. Engine trouble? That was another good one. But I pushed each one of those thoughts aside because I didn't want to let my therapist down. After all, this support group was sponsored by her practice and I had already called to tell the group facilitator I was going to be late. She was expecting me.

So I finally got there and the place was packed! Leave it to me to make a grand entrance. There must have been close to twenty people there, maybe more. I looked around and said to myself, "I have just been teleported to the Land of Misfit Toys." But a nanosecond later I followed that with "and I fit right in!"

Someone pulled in a folding chair and I sat down and gathered myself as the person who was speaking when I arrived picked up with her story. While it may have looked like I was paying attention to what she was saying, I was really just trying to get my heart to stop beating so fast. A couple of deep breaths later, I scanned the room to see what my fellow group members looked like. There was quite a variety of people. Mostly transwomen, each one with their own unique presentation. There were transmen there too. It was the first time I had ever seen a transman—and there were three there that day. I took it all in and began to relax a bit.

I listened intently as each person told their story of what had happened in their life over the course of the month since the last meeting. There were many stories that were very different from mine. Some were difficult to hear. People had been disowned by their families and thrown out of the house. Others were dealing with significant mental health issues and addictions of varying types while at the same time trying to manage their gender issues. And I thought I had multiple plates to juggle? By comparison, I had it easy.

Still others were experiencing issues with finding a place to live and finding meaningful employment. Back then, most companies had no idea how to handle a situation like that, nor did their hiring policies protect transgender applicants from discrimination. Rather than attempting to accommodate the trans applicant they would simply move on to the next candidate—one who they would be more *comfortable* dealing with. Unfortunately, that was a very common story in our group over the years. I wish I could say that it doesn't happen anymore, but unfortunately there are "less enlightened" companies that still do this to trans people.

And then there were others whose stories paralleled what I was going through. I realized very quickly that while my own story may have been unique *to me*, there were common elements like issues with family acceptance, divorce, and child custody that others were dealing with too. That's where I felt the first sparks of connection with the others. I could empathize with what they were going through and they, in turn, did the same for me.

When it came time for me to talk, I introduced myself and told everyone where I lived. That was significant for everyone to know because there weren't very many transgender support groups around at that time and some people travelled hours just to get there. For me the drive was about an hour down the New Jersey Turnpike, which was significantly less crowded on the Sunday afternoons that the group met. I found out later that others in the group travelled twice as long as that, and in some cases more, because that was their only option to find support and community at that time. With introductory remarks behind me, I just started to tell my story. And I put everything out on the table.

I explained that after four plus decades of shame, guilt, and denial I had finally arrived at a place where I could no longer deny who I really was. As a result, my marriage was crumbling before my eyes. At that point I wasn't sure it could survive, and I didn't want to lose my son. After that admission I just kind of lost it and broke down under the weight of the entire day. As I started sobbing everyone was really wonderful about consoling me. They had all been there in one way or another.

That day marked a turning point in my journey. Looking back on it now it signaled the beginning of the end of how I was living my life up to that point. I had been living what amounted to a double life for a while. I would go off and meet other transwomen and then come back to my other life as a church-going husband and father who dutifully got on the train every morning for the commute into the office in New York. It all seemed so unseemly, so false. I didn't feel all that great about the person I had become. I wasn't being true to anybody, let alone myself. I was a fraud.

For years I carried around in a large duffle bag the entire existence of my feminine self. I kept it hidden from the rest of the world under lock and key, only to be brought out when I thought it was safe to do so. I used to joke that this was my "Stephanie in a Bag" phase. And it had its share of gut-wrenching moments.

Every time I would change back into male mode before going home after one of my get-togethers I would be overcome by a rush of guilt and dread as I scrubbed off all of my makeup—and probably a few layers of skin along with it. It became very difficult to look at myself in the mirror as I turned back into the person that I knew in my heart I was not. I felt like Cinderella as the clock was striking midnight. I was being transport-ed back to the drab, colorless, and hopeless reality that was my life. Back to someone and someplace that, apart from my son, was feeling more distant and less like home with each passing day.

But as time passed, and I began to sort out other aspects of my tran-sition and my life with the help of those in the group who knew me the longest, I could sense a growing confidence in myself. I was starting to move on with my life. Sure, I had obstacles to overcome, but I somehow knew that I would make it to the other side of each of them. Having people to share the journey with made it seem less arduous, less trying. It was through connecting with people who experienced that same need for kinship that I gained strength for the road that was unfolding before me.

THE TRANSKETEERS

I met my first real girlfriends Terri and Jill at our group. We bonded together through our own shared experiences of struggle and loss. We were all close in age and had come out later in life facing similar obsta-cles. Terri and I were going through divorces and dealing with estrange-ment from family. For her, it was her adult children. For me, it was my brothers. Jill was not married, but faced quite a bit of resistance from her parents, who insisted on calling her by her former male name and using male pronouns every time they saw her. She also was dealing with a fair amount of difficulties at her job.

We realized very quickly that we lived within a very short distance of one another, so it didn't take long for us to get together at one anoth-er's places and carpool to the monthly group meetings. Over time, we became inseparable. If you saw one of us somewhere, the other two were always close by. One day, as we arrived at the support group meeting, one of the group's co-facilitators, Terry, somewhat off-handedly proclaimed, "Here comes the Transketeers!" Everyone had a hearty laugh at our collective expense, but from that point on that's what we were called. The label stuck.

A year or so later we added a fourth person to our little group. Sherrie, who had recently moved into the area through a job transfer, found our support group. It was there where we all met with her and very quickly added her to the fold. She was a Black transwoman who was out to her employer, but seemed to be facing continuous hostility from some of her colleagues. We would talk for hours about what she should do to report these people and rectify the situation.

We all had our own particular plates to spin, and through it all we were there for each other. We were just trying to live our lives the only way we knew how and get from one day to the next. Having one another to lean on made it all a little bit more bearable.

And isn't that really what true friendship is all about? Of course we hung out together, but it wasn't just about that. There was something going on at a much deeper level that had connected us as sisters. Our individual journeys may have been different, but we shared a common core, an inner flame that was constantly moving us forward toward our truest selves. We may not have reached our destinations quite yet, but we knew where we were headed and shared each and every step.

It saddens me to say that while the Transketeers will always be vibrant and alive in my memory we have drifted apart over the years for various reasons. Terri passed away a couple of years ago. Sherrie retired and moved back to her home state of Ohio. Jill moved a couple of times and now lives in Pennsylvania. If it weren't for Facebook, we wouldn't be connected.

But they each taught me, in their own unique ways, what true friendship looked and felt like. And for that I am eternally grateful to each of them.

PUTTING MYSELF OUT THERE

One of things I talked a lot about with my fellow Transketeers was the need to get out into the world and experience it firsthand as our authentic selves. These conversations took place right around the time that I had moved into my apartment and my divorce was final, in the spring of 2004. For the first time in my life, I was free to explore the world as my true self but I was a little unsure of how best to do it. Partly, it was a matter of logistics. I only had so much latitude in my weekly schedule given that I had my son two evenings a week and every other weekend, so any time that I could devote to having social time as myself in public would need to be arranged around that schedule.

The other part was that I was a little scared. I would be doing this all by myself, so I would be subjected to all the little voices in my head telling me that the entire world would be watching my every move. I was fearful of being seen—and judged—by others as something that I knew in my heart I wasn't: a guy in a dress.

So I leaned on one of my friends, Sherrie, for support. I decided to go to the mall for the first time as "me." The mall. Really? How Jersey could I get, right? But, back then, and perhaps still to this day for some, the mall was very much seen as a rite of passage for a trans person like me.

It's hard to say why exactly, other than it was a place with a lot of people in it. And you got to parade around as your true self in front of all of them. How liberating. Or terrifying. Specifically, I was very hung up on being "clocked," which is the euphemism for being "seen" as trans by straight people. The accepted notion at the time was that as soon as you were "found out" the straight person(s) would, presumably, make a big scene about discovering you, which would inevitably lead to you cowering in shame and running for the nearest exit. I could care less about that now, but back then, it was very much on my mind. Regardless, passing the mall test was seen as a coveted stamp to put in one's mythical trans passport. Sherrie was totally down for coming along with me and talking me through the entire experience. It was sort of "been there, done that" for her and she was happy to do it.

The first thing I needed to realize was that this was a mall, not a ballroom dancing competition, so the high heels and the dress would remain in the closet. Who goes to the mall dressed like that anyway? A sweater, jeans and a pair of flats would more than suffice, I thought. I wanted to *blend*, not stick out like a sore thumb. This was very much about *harmonizing* with the flow of the people there, not bringing attention to myself. My therapist was very supportive of this endeavor and she pointed out, very correctly, that most people there wouldn't really pick up on anything anyway. They are far too wrapped up in their own world to notice in the first place. This was my first taste of the realization that this was not all about me, and I took great comfort in that.

When Sherrie and I arrived, I was pretty nervous. When I am nervous I tend to talk a lot, and on this particular day I must have talked her ears off! But Sherrie was very patient with me and very reassuring. We walked through the mall and into and out of a number of stores without much issue at all. I think I may have bought something, just so I could be carrying a shopping bag with me and thereby achieving the aforementioned "blending."

We had been there for a while and I was feeling much more comfortable when out of the corner of my eye I saw a gaggle of teenage girls looking our way. "Oh crap, here we go," I thought. They were kind of snickering among themselves and looking over at us. But they just continued walking along. They were some distance from Sherrie and I. I suspect we were the subject of some conversation on their way home, but that was the last thing I was thinking about at that moment. I'm not sure Sherrie even noticed until I exclaimed in a not-so-hushed tone, "they are looking at us!" She shrugged. There were no further issues at all and it was getting around the time for us to leave anyway. I had passed the whole mall ordeal without any real issues. It was time to celebrate and go to dinner. It was the least I could to thank Sherrie and it was a situation that I was much more comfortable with given that it was a restaurant we had been to before as a group, so it was considered "trans proofed." Or is that "Transketeers proofed?" It didn't matter, we still toasted to my triumph.

But it always amazed me how the teenage girls seemed to just have the "radar." By that I mean they could pick out a transwoman without hesitating. I heard a number of theories as to why this was the case. The most plausible, and completely unscientific, explanation made to me was that young girls of that age are very conscious, perhaps even more than a little insecure, of their own image so they are already attuned to what another woman's style is and are apt to judge them—on their clothes, their hair, their makeup, and so forth.

The funny thing is, I have the same radar. I guess I always did. It actually became more accentuated once I found myself on the other side of the glass ceiling. After I came out at work I found myself thinking about all of the elements of my *presentation* through a very different lens—the lens of the workplace. This was a new setting for me. A new "backdrop" against which I had to "perform." There were different rules that I had to conform to. It wasn't just that it was "me" either. Make no mistake, I was beyond ecstatic that I could finally bring my whole self to work. But I also had to function as an officer of the company—a female officer to be more precise—and I felt a pressure to be *seen* as such by all of my col-leagues. I had to *look* as well as *act* the part. Being very observant of how the other women I worked for and with comported themselves would be valuable input for me.

There was another element at play in all of this that was best ex-plained to me by my friend, Kate. Kate, who always considered herself to be a crossdresser, was someone who I met online and became very good friends with. She explained to me that as a crossdresser it gave her a dif-ferent perspective than me about femininity. While she deeply *admired* the female form, I wanted to *become* it. She had a very insightful take on the whole notion of "radar." She said as transpersons we don't just look at other women in some casual or fleeting fashion. She believed that we observe them on almost a microscopic level, paying the closest attention to every nuance of their behavior. Every gesture, every inflection in their voice, did not go unnoticed so that we could incorporate it into our own presentation. I don't disagree.

What my friend Kate was really getting at was how we develop our *gender expression*. While I was born with a feminine *gender identity*—an internal sense of self that is female—my *gender expression*—the outward manifestation of my gender—can be a very societally-driven concept. Why? Because it is society at-large that processes the cues that I trans-mit to the world—such as my name, the pronouns I choose to use, my clothing, my hairstyle, my mannerisms and my voice, just to name a few—as either masculine or feminine.

In the beginning of my journey the cues I chose to use were, admit-tedly, very well thought out. It was extremely important to me that I was transmitting signals that society interpreted as *feminine.* Nowadays, as I have grown into who I am as a person, I don't really give it that much thought. As the song goes, "I am what I am," and that feels more than right and comfortable for me.

I have explained all of this to cisgender women friends of mine and they are amazed to hear it, because these are things that they don't even think twice about. It's just a part of who they are and they don't even notice it.

So, can gender expression be seen as a matter of *nature* or a matter of *nurture?* The answer: Yes.

YEAH, YOU BLEND . . .

From the very beginning, I have always wanted to be seen as a woman in the world. This was of paramount importance to me when I was heading to my first support group meeting and it was no less important on my first day at work as myself. It has and always will be my guiding principle. My view of being a "woman in the world" is driven completely by what my own mental image is of what a woman—me—should look like. It is wholly my own.

For example, when I was first getting out in public I was very conscious of my hair. My hair was much too short—or so I thought—for me to ever *pass* as a woman. So while I waited for what seemed like forever for my hair to grow out, I wore a wig. And not just any wig, it had to be a dark auburn, almost brunette in color and it had to be shoulder length. It couldn't be shorter and it couldn't be any other color. My therapist solved the riddle when she told me that for whatever the reason—perhaps because my mother's hair color was similar and from whatever I was exposed to in popular culture over the years—that my internalized image of a woman was one that included shoulder-length dark auburn hair.

Equipped with this notion of what I should look like to the world, I made a conscious effort to get out in public by myself as often as I could. I was determined to experience my life as it was always intended to be.

To be clear, I was never trying to deceive anyone. I didn't have any agenda of any kind. I just wanted to get out as much as I could and experience the world as me. I was simply expressing my sense of self the only way I knew how at that time. Frankly, I was still learning so I couldn't focus on anything other than being myself. And I wanted to look as good as I could—but for me, not for society at-large.

But this is not to say that I was haphazard with my behavior when I was alone in public. I had a healthy concern for my own safety, and I was always very mindful of placing myself in situations where I felt safe—like my local coffee shop. I wasn't looking to attract any attention. I just wanted to be *present* with the world around me. To be seen as a part of the milieu. There is a difference between being obvious and being indiscernible.

In the beginning, before I was out at work, I would get changed after dinner and head over to my local Starbucks. Since my apartment was just a stone's throw from downtown Morristown it was easy for me to just hop over in my car, grab a latte of some sort, find a seat, and write in my journal. People would come and go, the staff was very friendly, and I could just "be" for an hour or so. It was very chill and very good for me. Sometimes, especially around the holidays when all of the downtown area was decorated, I would go for a walk. It was a pretty lively place in the evening, with restaurants and a few bars, so there were always plenty of people around. In those days, I had to nourish the emerging person inside of me and during the week this worked perfectly.

ON BEING ALICE

As time went on I found myself graduating to the big time: going into New York City by myself. I was always exposing myself to larger, more public, spaces and you couldn't get more public than the City.

Many of these trips were actually out of necessity. My endocrinologist's office and my hair salon were in midtown Manhattan, just a few blocks away from each other. My doctor appointments for my hormone shots were every two weeks and I made it a point to make it a full day out in the City.

A big part of the experience was the trip itself, as *how* I got to the City was just as important as *what* I did when I got there. On my very first trip I took the New Jersey Transit train to Penn Station. I carefully checked the schedule in advance so I knew exactly what train to catch from my local station so I'd make it to my appointment with time to spare. I was like a little girl at Christmas going to see The Rockettes at Radio City.

For a change, I was not nervous at all. It was familiar territory for me. I had been commuting to my office every day for the past four years on the exact same train line, and I was on it just the day before in male mode. But now I was riding the train as my true self for the very first time. That was a huge deal to me. Breaking new barriers is how I remember thinking about it. I even used my monthly pass for the ride. I remember the conductor making his way slowing through the train car, checking tickets. When he finally got to me he shot me a warm smile, kind of tipped his cap and said "thank you, miss" as I showed him my pass.

I was floating over my seat on the inside while trying to remain cool, calm, and collected on the outside. It wasn't the first time I was referred to that way, but it was just where I was mentally at that moment, on that spring morning. I was feeling very within myself, that made it all the more sweet.

By the time we arrived at Penn Station I just floated off the train and over to the subway for my trip uptown. While still busy, Penn Station on a Saturday is nothing at all like the mob scene it is during a weekday rush hour. As I glided through the passageways to the subway platform, I felt a sort of lightness come over me. It would happen a lot when I ventured out on my own. I think it had much to do with the growing confidence I had in myself. But on this first trip in, it felt like I was tapping into a source of divine energy for the very first time in my life. It sharpened my focus and put a spring in my step. I'd like to think that it was always there just waiting for me to draw upon its magical powers one day.

Sometimes I would combine my appointments. I'd get my shots and then head over to the hair salon where my dear friend Michael Todd would work his magic on, at first, my wig, and then once it grew out, my real hair. After that all of Manhattan was mine, or so I thought. I was free to go anywhere I wanted. Take the subway and head to Greenwich Village. Grab lunch at one of the zillion diners that were around and take a stroll through Central Park. Maybe go to Macy's at Herald Square and do some shopping. Sometimes I had a plan. Most times I didn't. It was exhilarating. And life-changing on so many levels.

As my confidence grew with each trip I too, I really felt like I was experiencing life for the very first time. I was surrounded by people, places, and things that made me feel so *alive*. I loved every moment of it. I was relating to my world for the first time as the person I always knew myself to be and it was nothing short of a profound experience. It's as if an electrical connection came on line the moment my soul interacted with the external stimuli that only New York City can deliver.

I found it all so very *empowering*.

I was surrounded by colors that were more vivid. The sounds, and even the smells, of the City were all somehow sharper and filled my senses like never before. There was something new to explore and experience at every turn.

I felt a little like Alice in Wonderland, but without all the angst.

I had embarked on a quest to find my true identity and I could feel it beginning to take shape with each interaction I had with the world around me. I was growing up all over again, but in a profoundly different way. There would be no turning back.

A LITTLE HELP, PLEASE . . .

As if by some divine intervention, the timing of all this could not have been better. I was bruised and battered emotionally from my divorce, the logistics of finding and moving into a new place, and starting all over again at the tender age of forty-five.

It wasn't like I was wanting to go back to my old life. There was no room for going back, that simply was not part of the equation. My mind had been made up quite a while ago. I had set a course for the rest of my life on that day the previous fall when I told my ex- that, "if I do this, I can only do this one way and that is all the way." My fate was sealed the moment I stared down the abyss and said to myself, "I'm jumping!" And I was comfortable with that We all make choices in our lives and I own mine in every way. I wouldn't change a thing.

But instead of feeling hopeful, I was feeling very uneasy, like a sailor trying to get her "sea legs" in turbulent waters. And my emotional waters were particularly turbulent around this time. I was carrying a lot of guilt with me. Guilt over the dissolution of my marriage, and guilt over what the loss of the family unit was doing to my son's world. I certainly had moments where I sat alone in my new apartment just thinking "what have I done?"

While I may have been feeling remorseful, I was certainly not regretful.

When I looked up all I could see was plate after plate spinning—or wobbling—in the air. Coming out at work was still a hoped for outcome that seemed so very far away. It would be well over a year before I would even begin to seriously consider it. I was only just starting my journey with my son, Andrew. All I saw were mountains in front of me. I waged a constant battle with the sickening feeling of being overwhelmed by all of it. There was just so much that I had to handle. There was absolutely no way I could do this by *myself.*

I needed help—my friends and my sisters and brothers in arms. I needed to have my spirit nourished, and I was beginning to find it through all the people that I could now count among my friends. I was very lucky. God blessed me with friends that became my chosen family.

Although I may not have been thinking about it at the time, all of these people and all of these experiences came along for the ride on my first day at work as my authentic self, and each and every day thereafter. In so many ways, I carry a piece of each of these people and adventures with me. Their stories and our shared experiences, gave me the strength and the courage to move forward with my life's journey and helped shape me into the person that I am today.

CHAPTER SEVEN
I HAVE A PLAN

All you need is the plan, the road map, and the courage to press on to your
destination.

~ Earl Nightingale

TRUTH BE TOLD, AT THE START I HAD NO PLAN ON how to transition at work. I wasn't quite sure at all how I was going to pull it off. I do remember it being a frequent topic of conversation during the support groups I attended. During this time, which spans all of 2004 and 2005, I was a regular participant in groups hosted by my therapist's practice in New Jersey and at the LGBT Community Center of New York in Manhattan. It was in these group sessions where I found community and connection with my transgender brothers and sisters. Many of the transwomen who attended these groups were in the same boat as me: they were coming out later in life and they were attempting to jump the same hurdles and scale the same mountains as I was regarding how to handle the embrace of their true selves with their significant others, kids, and coworkers. But it was through that exchange of successes, failures, horror stories, and triumphs that I began to convince myself that I could actually come out to my employer and still have a job on the other side.

The initial feelings I had about coming out at work were much the same as they had been with preparing to come out to my siblings. Fear dominated my resolve. But this was a different flavor of fear all together: I could lose my job. That was beyond frightening to me. Losing my job could really stop me dead in my tracks. No amount of planning could ever overcome the fact that if I lost my job I could risk losing the roof over my head and the ability to pay my bills, and pay child support and alimony too. I would have to start all over again and I was terrified that I would not be able to get anyone to hire me. I had very little faith that there were companies enlightened enough to hire an out transwoman.

Making matters worse was the fact that back in the early 2000s there weren't many places in the United States that had policies or laws that protected transgender workers from workplace discrimination. I was working in New York, and the state didn't have protections for transgender people until January of 2019.

I began working for New York Life Insurance as a corporate vice president in the spring of 2000. It is in the company's DNA to be conservative. When you buy life insurance you are buying it as protection for the long term. As a result, a prudent company like New York Life invests conservatively, ensuring that the company is going to be around decades down the road to pay on the death claims for the policies they issue.

Why does any of that matter? The company's culture was also on the conservative side. They wanted things to be stable, and did not like when people challenged the status quo. It wasn't some hip, west coast, tech start-up, where employees were encouraged to bring their skateboards to the office. Quite the opposite. It is the third-largest life insurance company in the United States, the largest mutual life insurance company in the United States, and is ranked within the Fortune 100. None of these wonderful and well-deserved statistics made me feel any better about transitioning on the job there.

Someone once told me that the company had an old advertising campaign based on the words "large, conservative, and dull . . ." Again, not helping with my anxiety level! I had resigned myself to the fact that the moment I came out they were going to run me right out of town, never to be seen or heard from again, my existence permanently expunged from the human resources database.

Thankfully, my good friend Terri was about to come out at her place of employment. It was much smaller than New York Life, but it also had a pretty conservative culture. It was through what seemed like hundreds of conversations over dinner or glasses of wine where she shared with me how she was approaching things. It all seemed very thoughtful, logical, and straightforward. Terri was a good six to nine months ahead of me in her planning, so it gave me the time to figure out if I could apply the same tactics in my workplace. It was how my grand plan was hatched.

It's important to point out that Terri and I were by no means the first transgender women to ever come out on the job. There were many others of our generation who had done so before us. It was through the magic of the internet that we were able to read other workplace coming out stories, so that we could compare notes.

Many of these stories gave me hope that mine would ultimately go well. But there were many more that were stories of heartache, humiliation, and loss that weighed heavily on my plans. Fifteen years later, navigating a workplace transition can still be a very perilous exercise for a transgender person, often resulting in the loss of their job. Some things never change.

By the summer of 2005, I had crafted a plan. Part of the plan was based directly on the steps Terri had taken in her workplace transition. Another part came from the internet research I had done. The final part was more of a gut feeling on what I thought the right thing to do was. I always felt that I worked with a group of kind and sincere people. That's not to say that they didn't have their stressed-out moments, we all did. But I just felt that they all were centered in that most human of virtues, decency.

I resolved to come out individually to those colleagues I was the closest to. They were the ones in my department who I had worked the most with on a daily basis and on various projects. They were the ones who I had worked with the longest and had gotten to know on a personal level. I thought the best way to do that was to schedule lunches outside of the office so we could have the chance to talk privately. I figured that by doing so, my base of support would slowly yet methodically grow before I came out to the head of my department, our chief marketing officer. Coming out to the most senior person in your area or department was a common approach taken in those days. Terri had used it with much success earlier that year, too.

I honestly don't remember how many people I came out to individually that summer. I do remember there were a lot of lunches, though. I kept a scorecard of sorts in my office. To keep track of each person I talked with, I took a hard copy of our departmental phone list and would check off each name in red ink and date the entry after each lunch.

While most of the specifics of each lunch are a bit hazy now, I do remember approaching each in a very deliberate way. The fact is I had an agenda for each and every one of them: to reveal something about myself that I had kept hidden from the world for my entire life. I might have thought that I had an idea of how they would react, but the reality is anything could have happened. I was taking a risk. A calculated one, but a risk nonetheless.

But what I remember the most was the empathy each and every person had. They may have been hearing the word *transgender* for the first time in their lives, but they cared enough about me and what I was going through to just listen and hear me out. I also asked each of them to please hold the conversation in their confidence. I explained that it had much to do with the fact that it wasn't public knowledge and that I was going to let our department head know in a few weeks' time.

I didn't realize it then, but I was asking an awful lot of each of them to keep my secret.

As I look back I don't think I was being terribly fair. But as far as I know, each one of them did keep our talk just between us. The truth is, I have no way of really knowing. If my lunches stoked the gossip fires I was totally unaware of it. I do remember worrying about it, but I was so relieved that I had come out to them in the first place that I didn't give it much more thought. I had no Plan B if any of them had violated my trust.

I appreciate that much more today than I ever did then because it just speaks volumes about the integrity of the people I had the privilege of working with then—and for years afterward. Their grace and empathy nourished me and gave me the strength I needed to continue moving forward.

I remember one colleague, when I was having a lot of trouble getting the words out, just grabbing my hand and telling me "it's okay, whatever you have to tell me, it's okay." Another colleague responded after I stammered through my story, "If that's what God wants you to do, then that's what you do." I couldn't have been more blessed with the outcome of each one of these moments. I am eternally grateful for their individual acts of kindness.

THERE'S SOMETHING I HAVE TO TELL YOU

As the fall of 2005 approached, the stars were beginning to align. All of the plates were somehow miraculously still simultaneously spinning. At that point, my son Andrew had been in therapy for nearly a year, and earlier that summer had come to his own level of understanding with who I was. I had come out to my siblings in the spring of 2005 and while that was still very much a work in progress, it wasn't keeping me from coming out at work.

On top of that, I was getting my feet under me with respect to just being out as *me* in public, which began in earnest when I moved into my own apartment in the spring of the previous year. Simple things that most people don't even think twice about doing took on greater significance because I was going about my daily life, for the first time in my life, as the person I had always known myself to be. Going to the grocery store, the mall, or going out to New York City whether it was alone or with my friends all played a part in *living into myself* as I like to call it.

My checklist of coworkers who I came out to had been completed. I was feeling more confident about my chances with my chief marketing officer. It was time to schedule the most important lunch of my life. I can recall being concerned about how long I might have to wait to get on her calendar. She was a pretty busy person. Surprisingly, I didn't have to wait forever to set up the lunch that would change my life.

Paula is a Black woman, and a lawyer by trade. I had known and worked with her since my earliest days at the company. I liked her a lot. I respected her as a woman—and a leader—in the workplace. As such, I felt that I needed to properly prepare for our lunch with a clear idea of what I was going to say and how best to say it.

The day of our lunch finally arrived. Surprisingly, I slept quite well the night before. I think that's because I tired myself out running through all the different conversation scenarios in my head. Unlike any of the meetings I had with my colleagues, Paula didn't have enough time available for us to go out to lunch, so the company cafeteria would have to do.

Unfortunately, that meant that I would have to wait until we got back to her office to share my "big secret." I wasn't about to do that surrounded by tables full of my coworkers and many of the people who reported to me at that time. Besides that, any time *anyone* had lunch with the department head eyes tended to wander over to that table to see who it was.

I came by her office to pick her up and off we went. Inside, I was vibrating with anxiety, but I tried to keep a calm and cool exterior the entire time. It's a little weird to say, but I was just marking time until we had the "real" conversation when we'd get back to her office. But here's the thing: how did I know that she wouldn't shoo me out of her office as soon as we got back because she had a meeting or a conference call? The fact is I really didn't. My plan could have gone up in smoke right then. For all of my planning I certainly did a lousy job of coming up with contingencies, or at the very least, checking with her administrative assistant to make sure she didn't have anything on her calendar immediately after our lunch.

Despite this, I had reached the point where my mind was made up. I was going to do this and the chips were going to fall where the chips were going to fall. I was well past the point of no return.

As we made our way back to her office she mentioned to me how collegial she found the culture of the company to be. She shared a story about a person who returned to the company after an eight-year absence and was warmly welcomed back with hugs and well wishes all around. Did she have a sense of what I was going to be telling her in a few short minutes, and that was her way of easing my anxiety?

Once we got to her office doorway, sensing that this was the moment, with my heart beating like a drum inside of me and straining to stay outwardly collected, I asked her if she had a couple of minutes. She said yes she did, and as she sat down at her desk I slowly moved over to her door and closed it. I sat back down in front of her desk and said—again, with as much calm as I could muster—these words:

"Paula, I'm transgender and I . . . "

Unexpectedly, she completely cut me off and finished my sentence, "and you're transitioning!"

All I could say was, "Yes, I am." She kind of stole my thunder. But in the absolute best way possible!

In the moments that followed, Paula told me how courageous she thought I was and that, most important, I had her "one thousand percent support" and that she would call Human Resources and let them know what was happening and get the ball rolling on my transition. She even told me that her mother was a lesbian! Evidently, Paula's mom had come out later in life to her family.

"Wow," I thought, "and I got all anxiety ridden over this moment and it turns out my boss's mother is a lesbian!" I just kind of shook my head.

Last, she told me about a conversation she had with my boss, who's name was Ben, a couple weeks prior. I had been pushing the envelope with respect to my outward appearance since at least the spring of that year, by slowly incorporating women's clothes into my work wardrobe. I started with blouses, then over time added slacks, shoes, and finally a touch of eye makeup to my "new look." I suspect that it may have sparked a meeting. She said, "You know, I told Ben you were transitioning and he said to me 'transitioning to *what*?'" We both shared a chuckle over that one.

As I left her office I remember having this immense weight lifted off of my shoulders. The feeling of utter relief was beyond palpable. I had done it! I had come out at work! That spinning plate most definitely did not crash to the floor! An immense sense of accomplishment washed over me.

But the truth is, I really hadn't come out to *everyone* just yet. Turns out, there was an entire company I had yet to reveal my true self to. Well, maybe not exactly. My department had roughly fifty-five people in it. They would all be coming along for the ride with me for sure, as they were all people I interacted with nearly every day. The building where I worked at the time was home to nearly a thousand employees in total, and a portion of those people—maybe another fifty or so, were either internal clients of my unit or supported my team in some capacity. I figured I would need to reach out to each of them as well. As for everyone else? The office grapevine would most definitely take care of notifying them.

So, just like when I had those initial conversations with each of my siblings and their spouses, this was just the first step. Albeit a hugely important first step, but there was much *inside work* still to be done. It's the detailed work that I knew I needed to do to make sure my work transition would progress as smoothly as possible. It's the work that nobody would see.

The reality was that this was merely the beginning of what would become a process that I would need to lead to some extent because this was all new territory for the company. I didn't anticipate any issues, but I needed to foster a spirit of collaboration to make sure there weren't any. The only way I knew how to do that was to be my own champion and blaze my own trail.

THE LEAD UP

Now that the cat was partially out of the bag, things began to move fairly quickly. Paula, true to her word, had contacted Human Resources and made them aware of the situation. I met with two HR vice presidents to discuss my transition plan in the company's headquarters, located on Madison Avenue in the heart of Manhattan.

I had a few days before I had to go into the City so that gave me plenty of time to think—and plan—for the meeting. So I took stock of the situation. There was a good chance I was the first trans person to transition on the job at New York Life. It would be important for me to take a proactive position in this meeting. This was the most important meeting I would ever take part in in my career. There was no way I was just going to sit back and let the meeting come to me. I had to take charge and guide the discussion, but within the boundaries set by my rank in the organizational hierarchy of the company. I was a corporate vice president. My HR collaborators were vice presidents. Even though it may seem contradictory, I was—organizationally speaking—outranked.

My friend Terri had transitioned at her company only a few months before me, so I leaned on her experience a lot in planning for this meeting. I learned, over dinner and several glasses of wine, her plan had a lot to do with *logistics*. Many things within the company would need to change, such as my male name to my female name. I accepted that it was my responsibility to bring these items to the table. I could not assume those in charge would have thought through everything that needed to happen.

The day before the meeting I finished my agenda and made copies to hand out. It wasn't anything elaborate, just a series of bullet points wherein I tried to capture everything I could think of that would need to change from Michael P. Battaglino to Stephanie C. Battaglino.

I should point out that by this time I had already had my name changed legally. The court order was signed just a few months prior in July, 2005. It was something that I always knew I was going to do, as it is for the majority of trans people. The process of changing one's name, however, can vary widely depending on the state one lives in. There were, and still are, a lot of online resources that walk you through how to do it in each state. Some states require an appearance before a judge. Others, like New Jersey, do not. Still others have rather interesting little quirks to their name change laws.

In New Jersey, name changes are administered on a county level which isn't all that extraordinary. But there was a requirement at the time, now rescinded, that a legal ad be run in the newspaper for thirty days before the order is granted to, in theory, give the public the opportunity to comment or contest the name change. My attorney, who took care of all of this for me, although I was prepared to do it all myself, explained that it has more to do with ensuring that nothing fraudulent is going on than anything else.

For agenda purposes, I listed the following items that needed to have my name changed on them:

◊ all of my existing employee records
  • payroll
  • health benefits
  • employee savings plan (401k)
◊ ID badge
◊ email
◊ caller ID on my office phone
◊ nameplate outside my office
◊ business cards
◊ fitness center registration

In addition, we needed to discuss the following accommodations

◊ which bathroom I should use
◊ which fitness center locker room to use

Armed with this document I was ready to face the HR VPs. I had never thought for an instant that I should come to this meeting at our headquarters location as anyone other than my authentic self, as Stephanie. I didn't stop to think that I might run into someone I had worked with that might recognize me. I never asked for permission or anything like that. I just felt that I should and that I could.

Much of it had to do with the fact that by this time I had been coming to the City as Stephanie for several months. For support groups, doctor visits, shopping trips, or just to stroll through Central Park. I was becoming increasingly more confident with my comportment and I saw it as yet another opportunity to continue that progression. It was kind of an automatic thing for me; any time I came to the City I did so as Stephanie. All a part of what I like to call "living into my authentic self." It's an expression that helps me describe what it feels like to embrace the person you have always known yourself to be each and every day. This would be no different.

So as it turned out, this meeting actually was the first time I ever showed up at New York Life as Stephanie. I wore the same business suit that I would wear in a few weeks' time for my first day. Same blouse, same shoes, same wig. It was important to me that I made a good first impression. I'm nothing if not consistent.

It didn't "officially" count as *my first day* because it didn't happen where my office actually was. That was in Sleepy Hollow, New York, where I commuted to every day from New Jersey. But it didn't count for a much more important reason: When I went back to my office the next day I was back in Michael mode. That was the biggest difference. I had still had a month to go before I didn't have to concern myself with switching back and forth anymore.

But despite that notion, it just felt like making this visit as "me" was the right thing to do at the time. I may have been nervous about the meeting, but I was never nervous about bringing my whole self to it.

Walking into the lobby of 51 Madison Avenue can be an awe-inspiring thing. All you have to do is look up and you'll quickly see you've entered one of New York City's treasured landmarks. The ornately painted coffer ceiling and travertine walls are quite impressive. As I walked in through the revolving doors, having realized that I was standing inside this amazing building as my true self for the first time, I just stopped for a moment, looked up, took a deep breath, said a quick prayer, and off I went. I actually think I felt a chill go down my spine—in a good way. It didn't matter that I still had an ID card with my soon to be "old" picture on it. I simply waved it at the security guards, who only really needed to see the distinctive blue square logo in its corner and into the elevator I went.

As I walked in, the VPs were already seated and were ready for business. But I'm not so sure they were prepared to meet Stephanie. There had been no advance discussions at all about how I was to show up. In retrospect, perhaps they thought I would come to the meeting as my former self. That might explain why they had such deer-in-the-headlights looks on their faces. Regardless, that was my cue to distribute my agenda as I said, "I've prepared something that will help guide our discussion today." You could immediately see the look of relief take over their expressions. I thought to myself, "this is going to go well," and it did.

One of the VPs commented, "We want to make this transition as comfortable as we can for you." There was such a feeling of sincerity in her voice as she said it that I felt reassured that everything was going to go well. Even though the process had already begun after my lunch with Paula, I still had lingering concerns about how things would go once HR got involved. Since the VPs were Human Resources officers I knew that I didn't have anything to worry about.

I remember they both asked me what my name was, and when I said Stephanie, I remember one of them commenting that one of his twin daughters was named Stephanie. After the meeting they sent out a number of emails and made phone calls to ensure all the changes were made to the various internal systems that housed my information.

When we talked about the timing of my first day, I wanted it to be as soon as it was possible. I was excited and ready to go. It turns out my first day would be gated by how long it took for the system changes to take effect. None of us knew how long that was going to take, but it most certainly wasn't going to be in a few days. We all agreed that there was no need for something as grandiose as a company-wide communication because my job function did not touch every area of the company.

We did agree, however, that I could write and send an email to a list to all of the individuals I knew personally and that I had worked with at various times as it related to the discharge of my role. Since I led a group of nearly twenty-five people who created marketing and product materials, that list was pretty long. As it turned out, there was going to need to be a sequence of communications to my department that would have to take place within seventy-two hours of my first day. The VPs promised to get back to me on the specific details of what that was going to be.

It wasn't until years after my transition, when I was working with other companies on their transition plans, that I realized all of the behind-the-scenes work that had to have been undertaken to facilitate my transition. Since I was the first officer-level employee to ever transition in the company's history, there was no specific roadmap in place. Although no one ever communicated directly to me, I am sure there were several conversations with our lawyers about how best to navigate these uncharted waters. While I would like to believe that the actions of the VPs were totally altruistic, I am not naive to the fact that concerns over the company's liability, if anything were to go awry, were of much more paramount concern.

I began wondering how far up the ladder the news of my transition had traveled. At New York Life as well as just about every other company, news (that is, office gossip) can travel very fast, and my transition was most definitely of the front-page variety. Would it ever make it to our chairman's office? In the years since, I have heard anecdotally that it did, but in the final analysis, I'll never really know—and you know what? It doesn't really matter.

What I do know is I was fully cognizant of the bigger picture and what it all meant as all of this was unfolding. Once I found out that I was the first officer to do this *in the entire existence of the company,* it became very apparent to me that there was a much larger message that needed to be conveyed to the rest of the world outside the hallowed halls of New York Life. I was focused on the specific details of my workplace transition because I had to be. I knew, even with all of the outward expressions of support and assurances that the company would "make this transition as smooth" as they could, I still needed to act as my own advocate, and soon thereafter as an advocate for others just like me who were attempting to do the same thing at their companies.

This was when I first knew that there was a larger mission for me to pursue. As I have often said since, I get that when people exclaim that they have a *passion* for transgender workplace inclusion they truly do mean it. Their actions more than affirm their feelings. And that is a good thing.

For me, it is something much different, much deeper. It is my *calling.* Trust me, that is not a word I choose to use lightly. I believe I was put on this Earth to tell my story and do the work I am doing.

There is plenty of room in the movement for everyone. The greater the number of voices that the collective has, the greater the array of stories are told, and the stronger the collective becomes as a force for change.

Trailblazer? I've been called that more times than I can count and I am beyond grateful for the recognition. I'll own that, because in truth, that is what I was at that moment in October of 2005 and I cannot escape the fact that I *knew* it then. I guess I took my first step down that path when I looked up at the VPs as we parted company and said, "I may be the first, but I am certainly not the last."

IT'S ALL ABOUT THE BATHROOM

There weren't any issues with any of the areas I had on my list *except* one: What bathroom should I be using? I can remember one of the VPs saying, "Ninety-nine percent of the employees won't have any problems with you using the ladies' room, but I have to concern myself with the 1 percent who might." I can recall being taken slightly aback by his comment, but I did not want to press him on it. Up to this point in the conversation things were going pretty smoothly, so I instead opted for a problem-solving approach. I put out the possibility of using a single-use bathroom—as long as one existed in my building back in Sleepy Hollow. I had no idea if one actually did, nor was I prepared with any encyclopedic knowledge of the blueprints of my building.

Nowadays, a key component of any workplace transition plan is bathroom use. It ensures that facilities be made available to the transitioning employee that are, among other things, conveniently located and easily accessible. Back then (and to this day unfortunately), that wasn't always the case. I can recall reading horror stories of trans women having to walk great distances just to access the bathroom designated for them. Often, many of these facilities were not in the most desirable locations, well off the factory floor, or in other buildings, for example.

One such story is courtesy of my friend Scotty, whose bathroom situation turned into something decidedly different:

"Everyone was worried about the bathrooms. At one point I was only allowed to use the bathroom in the medical department which was in another building fifteen minutes away. Someone had seen me coming out of the men's restroom and so I was referred to the medical department.

It had become a security question. The original report came from someone who knew what gender was written down on my paperwork. They reported it to the security office as adverse information, because of my security clearance. They called the medical office to refer me to them.

I had a lengthy interview with the head of the medical department about my transition. After a couple hours of questioning, the doctor's prejudices began showing, and he was asking me very personal questions he had no business asking. He wanted to know how long I really planned to continue to work there.

The best part of the interview was when he asked me how long I had been on testosterone, and I told him six weeks, at which point his jaw dropped. He was shocked about how masculine I already was even after such a short period of time.

I was upset with the questions and how invasive they were. The medical office director wanted to keep tabs on me. I took the situation to the company's ethics office. I explained what happened. I did not want to cause any problems, but I told them I would not do it again.

They allowed me to use a single stall bathroom in the lobby. I could get to those easier. This became a policy change for others who came after me. The bathroom had plagued me since middle school. I would either hold it all day, or wait until class started and get a pass. I could not go between classes with everyone else."

So, what did we agree to? Up until such time as I had my gender reassignment surgery, which I had scheduled for the following summer, and had made known to the VPs during our meeting, I was to use a single-use bathroom in my building one floor down from my office. It was actually near a couple of rarely used executive dining rooms adjacent to our cafeteria. They gave me a key and everything, so I would not be disturbed. It turned out I only used it for a short time, opting for a bathroom in our medical department—with our nurse's consent—that had much better lighting. Once I had my surgery, I was free to pee wherever I wanted to.

As far as I can tell, and in all the years since, the only thing that women want to do in the bathroom is, well, go to the bathroom. You do your business, you wash your hands, and off you go. To think that I would want to do anything other than that is just silly. Unfortunately, society isn't nearly as enlightened as we like to think and the notion that trans people are going to do something inappropriate within the confines of the ladies' bathroom still persists.

The most ironic thing happened to me immediately after the meeting had concluded and I parted company with the VPs. I really had to go to the bathroom. It seems as though the multiple cups of coffee I had that morning had caught up with me. Now I realize that going to the bathroom isn't necessarily an ironic act, but where was I going to go? I had absolutely no idea where a single-use bathroom might be on any of the forty-one floors of the building!

So I immediately looked for the nearest women's bathroom on the floor I was on, found one just down the hall from where I had come out from the meeting, took a deep breath, and pushed the door open. No one was there but me, not that it would have mattered all that much anyway. I did my business, washed my hands, and as I was getting ready to leave, another woman came through the door. We made eye contact, exchanged smiles, said hello, and out the door I went. As I was waiting for the elevator I just started chuckling to myself and then I burst out laughing to no one but me. So much for not using the women's room!

THE LAST DAYS OF MICHAEL

It turned out that all of the system changes that needed to happen were going to take around four weeks. My first thought was, "Four weeks?! Really?! That's an eternity!!" But there wasn't much I could do. Updating the computer systems was akin to an ocean liner at sea that takes miles just to make a right turn. I had no choice but to wait—and ruminate over what needed to be done. Like, what do I wear? What do I do with my hair? This was like my first day at school and I had to look right. It's a self-confidence thing. To turn the old saying around just a bit, I was a firm believer that "the clothes make the *woman*."

I decided that your standard business pants suit would work just fine. Taupe color, nicely tailored. A collared blouse. Slingbacks with a sensible heel. It was essentially the same outfit that I wore when I met the VPs in the City. I thought about changing it up with a skirt, but only briefly. I figured I'd save my coworkers from seeing my legs for a while. Besides, it was getting cold out anyway.

As for the hair? Well, that was a different story. I had been wearing a wig ever since I first started going out in public because I was very self-conscious about the length of my real hair. It hadn't yet grown out to a length that I was comfortable with. But for some unknown reason I was actually contemplating ditching the wig for my first day. What was I thinking?

My hair stylist and dear friend Michael Todd and I had a rather brief conversation about it on my trip to the salon a week or two before the big day. I said to him, "So what do you think—stick with the wig or maybe go with my real hair?" He just looked at me incredulously and said flatly, "the wig." Well then, the wig it is!

I discussed the actual date with Ann, one of the HR VPs who became my point person on the logistics. We arrived at a date of Friday,

November fourth. It gave the systems people enough time and personally I just liked the idea of it being a Friday. I knew that I would need the weekend to decompress and we both thought it was a good idea to give my colleagues the weekend to process it all. In the years since I suspect that I became the subject of more than a few dinnertime conversations that weekend.

The last piece of the puzzle was figuring out how people were going to be notified that Stephanie was going to be making her debut on November fourth.

It was decided that everyone would attend a departmental meeting on Thursday while I was at home. There, the HR folks and my unit head, Frank, were going to let everyone in on what was going to happen the following day. Frank was to follow that up with an email that evening that was to serve as the lead-in to my very own email, which is something I saw as the most critical piece.

I wanted the opportunity to share my innermost feelings with the employees most impacted by my transition and to others that I had previously worked with who I hadn't seen for some time. It was my way of reaching out and sharing a small piece of my journey with each one of them.

THE EMAIL

Most times when I have to write something, I tend to put it off. I procrastinate in grand fashion. I do everything else *but* write. Rearrange the sock drawer? Of course. Clean my apartment? Every nook and cranny. Whatever keeps me from being alone with my feelings and putting pen to paper.

But what I did know about this communication is that it was my one shot to share with the over 100 people on the list what my life had been like, to connect on a human level, and ask for their support. I decided it wasn't a time to try to educate them on every aspect of what it means to be transgender. I didn't have nearly enough space for that. And besides, it would have been a pretty foreign topic to the vast majority of them anyway. This was no time for "Transgender 101."

I figured that everyone on the list had already worked with me as Michael in some capacity for well over five years, so why try to deny that they ever did? I thought about all the interactions I had with each of them. Most were good. A few were not. I didn't really know for sure, but I hoped that each one of them saw me as a competent, intelligent, fair, and at times, pretty funny, guy. Even though I thought I had always gone out of my way to establish a relationship with the people I worked for and with, I had no way of knowing if people saw it that way. I hoped that they saw me as an upstanding person, because it would make my transition easier.

Once I sat down to write the email all of my thoughts coalesced rather quickly and I wrote it all within twenty minutes. The words were always in my head, I just had to stop doing everything else and let them rise up to the top of my consciousness so I could write them down.

To My Colleagues and Friends,

Many of you may have noticed changes in my physical appearance that have taken place recently. The simplest explanation I can provide is that I am transgender. I have been struggling with my gender issues all of my life. After decades of shame, guilt, and denial I have made the decision to fully embrace my authentic self.

On Friday, November fourth, I will begin reporting to work as my true self, as Stephanie.

While I may be changing on the outside, please know that I am still the same person, only happier and more fulfilled, on the inside.

I sincerely hope that I can continue to count on each and every one of you for your support and friendship in the weeks and months ahead.

Sincerely,

Stephanie (Michael) Battaglino

I sent it over to Ann as she had requested, thinking that it was going to come back to me with multiple deletions and corrections. There were none. Nor did she ever ask to see my rather lengthy list of recipients. I really appreciated her expression of trust.

The only thing that she asked me to do was that when I sent it, to check one of the preference boxes that restricted the forwarding of the email by the recipient. It was a way, electronically at least, to confine the spread of the buzz that it would create. If it were only that simple.

This happened no more than the week before my coming out day. As eager as I was to have it go out, I knew it was in my best interests to just wait and forget about it.

Finally Wednesday evening came. Most people had gone home for the night by the time six o'clock came around. I had finished up my work for the day and was—very carefully—creating my note and re-checking the list of addressees.

I specifically remember clicking on the "prevent recipient forward-ing" box, triple checking my spelling and flow, and then just waiting. Frank's office was not within my line of sight, but he assured me that at 6:00 pm sharp he would hit the send button on his email. Sure enough, at no later than 6:01 pm, his note went out. I briefly scanned it, not really paying much attention to its contents and then clicked the send button on mine, sending it off into the ether.

I did not wait for any responses. That would have to wait until tomorrow. I shutdown my laptop, threw it in my backpack, and headed straight out of the building to my car without stopping.

Friday, my coming out day, would come soon enough.

CHAPTER EIGHT
THE DAY BEFORE

It always seems impossible until it's done.
~ Nelson Mandela

THURSDAY WAS NOT MY USUAL DAY OFF. I WAS NEVER off during the week unless I took the day for some reason. On this day, however, I was told to stay home. The HR meeting to discuss my transition with the entire department was taking place that day and it was decided—and I agreed—that to avoid any issues it would be best that I not be present.

Technically it would be noted as a "personal day" in my attendance record, which in retrospect was pretty prophetic. It became a day for me to collect my thoughts, and more than anything, reflect on all that had happened in the weeks and months that led to that day. I would characterize my emotions as more contemplative and expectant.

After all, I had been successful in keeping all of the spinning plates from falling up to that point. I had talked one-on-one to colleagues, come out to my department head, and charted a logistical course for my workplace transition with Human Resources. All while managing to keep my son's evolution of understanding of who I am on track.

I got up after a pretty restful night's sleep, went for a run, made coffee, and had breakfast before ever getting around to opening my laptop.

Okay, so I may have procrastinated just a little. I gingerly opened up my laptop and sat down at the dining room table which served as my home office. The anticipation was definitely building as I waited for what seemed like forever for my computer to boot up.

I clicked on the icon to my email program and I held my breath. As I watched my inbox load up I was floored by what I saw. My inbox was overflowing with responses to my note! I just froze as I stood over the table and waited for it to finish. I'm sure it only took a handful of seconds, but it felt like an eternity.

I grabbed my coffee mug and took a seat and began to slowly open each of the emails. Some were no more than a few words. Some were much longer. Many contained words like *brave* and *courage*. Others wished me happiness. A few sent me heartfelt prayers for God's blessing. One even complimented me on how beautifully written my note was.

As magnificently different each response was, they all shared one common characteristic. Each one, in its own unique way, was a personal expression of support. As I read each one I became more and more emotional. Tears began to run down my checks and on to my keyboard. By the time I had reached the last one—and a few actually came in while I was reading—I was sobbing uncontrollably and my computer was getting pretty wet!

I didn't want to respond to the emails, because given the emotional state I was in I doubt I would have made much sense. I was content just to leave everything as it was. I was beyond grateful and feeling very, very blessed.

After I had a chance to compose myself, I created a new folder and made sure I put all of the responses there for safe keeping. I'd be lying if I told you that I didn't go back and re-read them several times in the days, weeks, and months that followed. I held on to them for quite some time. To me, they were the tangible outcome of perseverance, tenaciousness, and accomplishment. They gave me a sense of confidence that would serve me well as I navigated the twists and turns of corporate life as an out transwoman.

MY FIRST DAY

I awoke on the morning of Friday, November 4, 2005 full of nervous energy but with a definite sense of enthusiasm for the day ahead. I had made arrangements with my ex to switch coverage days with my son that week so that I would not have to concern myself with dropping him off at school before heading to the office. Also, I made the conscious decision in my planning the date to do so before a weekend that I did not have Andrew, so I didn't have to worry about picking him up that evening. I just wanted to "clear the deck" logistically so that I could focus completely on the task at hand.

Like it was my first day at a new school, I gave myself extra time to make sure my hair and makeup looked just right. I took great pains to lay out all of my clothes the night before. I chose the same very professional business pants suit that I wore to meet with the VPs in the Home Office. It had quickly become my "go-to" outfit. Well, it was really my *first* outfit. And, more than anything, I felt very confident when I wore it.

As I was putting the finishing touches on my appearance—what earrings should I wear?—I could sense that confidence building inside of me. As I got into my car and headed off on my forty-five-minute or so commute to the office I could feel that confidence—and the nervous energy—building inside of me.

As I made my way to the office, I had plenty of time to reflect on the road that I had traveled to get to this moment. I kept reminding myself that I had done so much of the groundwork already.

Now all I had to do now was show up—and make sure that I didn't look like a train wreck. I was very, very conscious of my overall "look." By this time I had been going out in public regularly for nearly two years, but every time I did, regardless of where I was going, I always took great pains to make sure that the image that was looking back at me in the mirror was ready for public consumption. Since that day it still has been extremely important to me that when people see me for the first time as my authentic self that they see a person that presents a womanly presence.

I pulled into the parking lot just like I had at the start of every other work day at Sleepy Hollow and headed for the front entrance. It was there that I met the gentleman who was in charge of what the company called "building services" for the entire location. He was my designated liaison to make sure that everything that was supposed to happen onsite actually went according to plan. He made sure I had a key to the officers' dining room bathroom (that I used just a handful of times), a new name plate outside my cubicle, and what was most important to me in that moment—getting my picture taken for my new company ID card. That needed to be done before anything else.

Gary met me in the glass enclosed lobby of the building at the security desk. We greeted each other cordially as we had already known each other for a while. I merely showed him a smile. I have always subscribed to the "lead with a smile" approach. In my quest to short-circuit as much BS as possible in public, I always made it a point to greet people with a pleasant hello and a smile. I figured that if they harbored any reservations about me that I could disarm them with my smile and a cordial greeting. Some would call it a defense mechanism of sorts. I call it being nice. What I do know is that it almost always works.

He escorted me to a room behind our security desk that up to that point I didn't even know existed. It was the room where our security department set up the camera for all new hires to have their ID picture taken. I really felt like a new hire, and rightfully so, I thought at the time. I was feeling a mixture of emotions that I suspect many new employees experience. It was a mixture of anticipation and excitement about what was about to unfold before me. I wanted to make a good first impression on everyone that I would come in contact with. It was my second "first day" at New York Life and I was determined to make the most of it.

A nice, but rather stoic man by the name of Jack was to take my picture and create my new badge. He didn't have much to say as he positioned himself behind the camera while I sat and posed properly for what was to me the most important picture taken of me in my entire life up to that point. It was more than just another "mug shot," like the kind that you get at your local motor vehicle agency. It just had to be right, as it would serve to commemorate that moment for the rest of my career at New York Life. In the years to come it would help me get through some tough times. A quick glance at my picture would remind me of what I have accomplished in my journey to my authentic self and provide the boost I needed to move on. In short, it was a big deal to me.

Sensing its importance, I suppose, Jack asked me if I liked the photo and offered to take another one if I didn't like it. I thanked him and told him it was fine, but to be honest, at that point I was getting kind of anxious and wanted to get upstairs to my office so I could deal with whatever was waiting there for me. I went back out to the security desk and had my new badge in a matter of minutes.

AND THEN THERE'S THIS . . .

So there I was. Standing all by myself in the middle of this fairly large and open lobby in a building that had about a thousand people in it—and no one was around. I was almost wishing that somebody, *anybody* would come through the lobby with their morning coffee just to break the silence. But it was not to be. Just me—and my thoughts.

Before me, right in the middle of this large, glass enclosed space, stood a large center staircase that went up to the third and top floor of the building. That's where my office was. In much the same fashion as I had done when I made my debut in New York City, I took a deep breath, collected myself, said a quick prayer, and up the staircase I went.

It is not, by any measure, a short staircase. It seemed even longer on this particular morning. But as I slowly made my way up the stairs, and got closer to the level of the floor I could start to see all of the cubicles come into my field of vision. To my right there were some of my staff's offices, but I didn't see anyone. To my left was where the remainder of my staff was, but again, I didn't see anyone. I thought for a second, "has everybody taken the day off and not told me?" It turns out it was the calm before the storm—of emotions, that is.

As I hit the floor I purposefully took the route to my office that I always did. Along the floor to ceiling windows I went until I came to the aisle where my office was, made a quick left, and—boom—there it was!

I was stopped dead in my tracks by what I could only describe as a sea of flowers staring back at me! And there were cards too! I felt like I had just won a beauty pageant or something like that. It momentarily took my breath away. Of all the scenarios that I had run through my mind, this was most definitely not one of them! I was absolutely floored.

As I turned around, seemingly out of nowhere appeared all of the women—my direct reports and one of our temps, too—that were responsible for the floral cavalcade. There were hugs and congratulations all around. And of course I began to cry, right on cue. I opened each of their cards, read their warm well wishes, and cried even more. I was utterly overwhelmed by their thoughtfulness. We were making quite the commotion.

I suspect this gave everyone else around us the okay to come by, because it suddenly seemed as if the entire department had descended upon my office. It turned into quite a scene. Such an immense outpouring of support that I have cherished every day since.

What I remember most is how heartfelt their good wishes were. I really felt like the new kid on the block being warmly welcomed into the fold. In particular, I remember our temp, Marcia—a huge Miami Dolphins fan—who, after giving me a hug said, "Finally, another woman I can talk football with!" How great is that?

As things quieted down, and I rearranged the flowers on my desk so I could actually plug my laptop into its docking station, I knew there was a phone call I had to make. I called Ann, the HR VP and my point person for everything, and thanked her profusely for all she had done to facilitate my workplace transition. She was very gracious in her response and told me that if I needed anything else, or if something didn't change over like it was supposed to, that she was just a phone call away. As I hung up the phone, it occurred to me that she remained unwaveringly true to the pledge she made to me at that very first meeting: that she "wanted to make my transition as smooth as we can for you."

I was smiling very broadly at that thought for more than a few moments when I suddenly was broken out of my mini daydream by the realization that I still had something very important that I needed to do.

Sometime the week before, my building services colleague had delivered my new name plate. If I have given you the impression that this was some large metal plate that had my name meticulously engraved in it then for that I must apologize. My new nameplate wasn't really a "plate" at all. It was more like a heavier than normal paper stock with my name printed on it in the block style font and color that matched everyone else's "nameplate." This could very easily be slipped into the bracket that was attached to one of the tall walls of my cubicle.

And now the time had come to do that. To just about anybody else throughout all of New York Life that day, nothing could be seen as any more routine than changing one's name plate when they switch offices. But I wasn't just switching *nameplates*, I was switching *people*. This was not something that I could ever imagine taking so lightly. Like my ID badge, it was symbolic of everything I had accomplished up to that point in my corporate life. I know that's a lot to put on a couple of mere corporate artifacts, but to me they were treasures.

As I removed the old card with "Michael Battaglino" on it, and replaced it with the new one that would forever say "Stephanie Battaglino," an immense sense of satisfaction washed over me. All I could do was stare at it and smile. I suddenly felt a presence close to me. One of my colleagues, Carmen, who was just a couple of offices away, was watching me and smiling back. I could feel the warmth of her smile from several feet away. I could tell she was genuinely happy for me.

MAKING THE ROUNDS

The rest of the day was a bit of a blur, a wonderfully satisfying sequence of individual exchanges with the various individuals in my department that I worked with in various capacities. I didn't get a lot of work done at all that day. I'm sure I had lunch at some point during the day, but what I remember most is how each person reacted to me in-person. What I had forgotten about in all of the hoopla was that they all attended a department-wide meeting the day before and were advised by HR what was happening and reminded of the company's **non-discrimination policy**. It's not that I expected any sort of blow back at all, but if there were any misgivings about my transition they did not manifest themselves in any outward confrontations.

First there was Mark, a peer of mine who I had a nice rapport with. We'd often talk about New York sports and life in general while going about our daily routine. He and I even had gone out for runs at lunch in the state park that was next to our office grounds on several occasions. His office was just at the end of the aisle mine was on. I popped my head into his office to say hello and he invited me to sit down. As I thanked him for being a colleague and friend and as he acknowledged that, I could see that he was trying to wrap his mind around what and who I was.

He kind of blurted out, "But you're still Mike, right? I mean, you're still, will always be, Mike on the inside, right?" It sounded like he thought he was losing someone, and perhaps that was exactly what he was thinking. I assured him, in almost the same manner I assured my son months prior, that I was still the same person, I still had the same interests and same allegiances to the Yankees and the Giants, but I was happier—and a *complete* person now. He seemed relieved. I think my reassurances really helped him grasp, in his own way, that we could still be colleagues and friends.

My boss, Ben, was next. This is the Ben of the "transitioning to what?" line that my chief marketing officer Paula had shared with me when I came out to her. Actually, I think we had a meeting scheduled to discuss business at-hand. So I showed up at his office door right on time as always. He invited me in, I closed the door behind me, and before we got down to business, Ben looked at me with a smile and said, "So this is the real you?"

"Yes it is," I quickly replied. He then mentioned something about being glad that I was happy—and that was it.

It was time to get down to business, and there were a few things he needed to update me on. I did not find his attitude that surprising at all. Ben and I had a very good working relationship. He was my boss. I was his direct report. No more, no less. Clearly, my first day at work as me was just another item on the day's agenda. And that was fine with me. Ben never missed a pronoun or my name for the entire time I worked for him, which was another two years.

I had other meetings, beyond my first day, that were very much like the meeting I had with Ben. When I would enter someone's office for the first time, I'd sit down and invariably I would start the conversation with something about the "new" me. I always felt like I needed to break the ice and to address the proverbial "elephant in the room" right up front so that we could get it out of the way. In that sense, I took it upon myself to come out individually, yet again, to each and every person I interacted with. It was completely unavoidable as far as I was concerned. I just wanted everybody to be as comfortable as they could be with me, and I thought that being upfront about it, yet not in their face—there is a difference—would make things easier for all parties as we went about our work each day. Truth is, I wanted everyone to like me. I didn't want people to be repulsed by me.

I was fortunate that each person I talked to, in their own way, got it. In particular, I remember having a meeting with an internal client of my team's services. He was an older gentleman by the name of George, who had a lot of years in with the company in all kinds of roles by that point in his career. I honestly didn't know what to expect, but he could not have been more gracious and understanding in our conversation about my transformation. Some people totally surprise you sometimes, and in a really good way.

I got a major surprise when I met with Mark, who was our numbers guy in Ben's unit. He and I were peers and we were always meeting about one budgetary item or another throughout a given work week. In our conversation, which went very well, he revealed to me that he had a cousin who was an out gay man. He didn't have to tell me that, of course, but I can't help but think that was his way of saying that he understood because of his experience with his cousin. I really appreciated that he shared that with me and I made sure to tell him so.

I have since learned that happens somewhat frequently as trans people come out to coworkers and other people in their lives. They will tell you about the LGBTQ people that you never knew about who are in their lives in one way or another. I honestly think that has everything to do with human nature. In this context, people can feel more comfortable if they can establish some sort of common ground with you. And this can be a way to do that, you just have to allow for it to happen within the conversation. You certainly can't *make* it happen, but if you approach the interaction by being upfront about who you are, if they didn't already know, it gives them permission to reveal it to you. In a sense, they are coming out to you in return.

You can file that under "expect the unexpected" I suppose. But here's the thing: You can never really predict how people are going to react when you come out to them. If you think you can then you're just kidding yourself.

Case in point, my brother-in-law Bill.

He's the epitome of a tough, streetwise guy, who has seen everything you could see on the streets of New York. I figured coming out to him was not going to go well at all. But when I did, he just turned to me and said in his New York accent, "Look, ya gotta do what ya gotta do." And that was it! There was no way I could have ever predicted that.

I learned a valuable lesson from that experience, as well as each one of the individual meetings I had on my first day; you have to make the effort to meet people where they are. It was on me to put myself out there in the first place, but I needed to be very aware, to the extent that

I could, of where the other person was coming from. I had no idea if they had even met a transgender person before (none of them had), but I couldn't assume that they did. That would have been a recipe for disaster. And besides, I had to work with all of these people beyond that first day.

As the "new employee" I had only one chance to make a good first impression, and I had to make sure it counted.

WE ARE GATHERED HERE TODAY . . .

Of all the "meet and greets" I had on my first day, there was one meeting that was very important. That was the team meeting that I had scheduled for that morning, just before lunch. Everyone in my unit, all twenty-five or so of them, was required to attend. What set this apart from any of the other meetings I had that day was the simple fact that these were all *my* people. This unit was *my* responsibility. These were the people that I worked the closest with each and every day. If I had any chance of keeping that relationship intact in the future it was critical to me that I had the chance to look each one of them in the eye and *connect* with them.

I just wanted everyone in my group to *see* me. That was my only agenda item.

We gathered in our conference center one floor below. Everyone filed in rather quietly. This was the second meeting for them in two days where I was the subject matter, so I suspected that they might have been getting a little tired of mandatory meetings. Once I saw that we were all together, I simply stood in front of the group and said the following:

"This is me. Does anyone have any questions?"

There was silence for what seemed like an eternity. I looked everyone in the eye, from one side of the room to the other. I thought to myself, "Well, this is going to be the shortest meeting of all time."

It was just then that one of the group's copywriters, Margot, said in a somewhat confused tone, "So what do I call you?"

I just turned to her and said, "Stephanie is fine. Steph can work too, if you like." I then made a joke about how I'd respond to just about anything, like "hey you." Thankfully, that got a laugh and—*voila*—the ice was broken.

I thanked them all for their understanding and I ended the meeting by reiterating my closing statement in my email about how I hoped I could count on their support—and their continued contributions to the team—as we moved forward together. I even got a round of applause.

With that, the meeting was over, and everyone went back upstairs. There was work to be done—by them and by me.

AND SPEAKING OF WORK . . .

So there I was, the newest "Flavor of the Month" at New York Life. As I settled in to get some work done, I began to notice that throughout the afternoon there seemed to be a steady stream of "drive by" visits to my office. People who I did not know, usually in groups of two or three, would just buzz by my office, take a peek, and move on. Try as I might, I could never make eye contact with them because I was usually involved with something in front of me that by the time I heard them or felt their presence and would look up—*poof*—they were gone.

I mean, they could have stopped in and introduced themselves. I'm not sure what they were expecting to see. I certainly would have welcomed them. After all, I was already in "outreach mode" by sheer default. In the final analysis, I didn't dwell on it all that much. I figured it just came with the territory.

What I mean by that is, I was the only one of my kind—that I knew of—who existed publicly in the entire company. Just by showing up as myself made a statement to those around me. I was cognizant of that fact from the moment I set foot in my building that day. Given the opportunity, I would certainly share my views about the issues in my community or in the workplace. But it's not like I was forcing myself or my community's issues on any colleague that would listen. That was never my approach. Certainly not on my first day.

I freely admit to enjoying the sound of people saying my name and using my preferred female pronouns for the first time in my workplace. That was beyond gratifying to me, as was the fact that I could now bring my whole self to work. It was very debilitating both mentally and physically for me to attempt to exist in parallel universes in all of those months prior to my coming out. All of the switching back and forth—all of that plate spinning—took an emotional toll. Simply put, it takes a lot of work to hide your true self in your workplace.

But at the end of the day I am there for the job that the company hired me to do. They are expecting that of me. No matter how supportive your employer may be of you in your transition, they still expect you to fulfill the requirements of your position.

From the company's perspective, by virtue of the policies and processes they have in place to make your transition as smooth and seamless as possible, they have made an investment—albeit a very wise one—in you. The return on that investment is you doing your job to the best of your ability, which, I hope would be something that would come to you naturally given that you are now bringing 100 percent of yourself to your responsibilities.

As the day was coming to a close and people were wishing one another a nice weekend, I wasn't really thinking about what was waiting for me in the weeks, months—and years ahead. I was simply focused on what had been an absolutely triumphant day for me. I just wanted to take a well-deserved victory lap. I had more near-term concerns to deal with like how was I going to get all these flowers home?

At that moment, I did not really care about what was next. This was such a huge milestone for me that it was virtually impossible to see past the bottle of wine and phone calls to my girlfriends to relive the day that was waiting for me when I got back home.

In the final analysis, I guess you could say that my first day was actually the end of one phase of my journey to my authentic self. It did *feel* like it. It certainly wasn't the end of my *entire* journey. That journey never truly ends. One plate may have stopped spinning, but it would eventually be replaced by another on the same stick soon enough. There was *always* another phase of some sort. Always another plate to be spun. For me they always tend to run together.

The truth is, as I was fighting the evening rush hour traffic over the Tappan Zee Bridge back to New Jersey, I had no idea what the next phase was, or what the next plate would look like. I didn't know it then, but I had already begun another transition. From one side of the glass ceiling to the other. From looking down, to looking up.

CHAPTER NINE
A BRAVE, NEW WORLD

One is not born, but rather becomes, a woman.

~ Simone de Beauvoir

I ONLY HAD A PASSING IDEA OF WHAT I WAS IN FOR AS I began my new corporate life as my true self. I had expended so much of my emotional and mental energy to come out in as smooth a fashion as possible that it left me with precious little capacity to prepare myself for what the daily workplace experience was going to be like once all of the "new car smell" faded away.

I had given 110 percent of myself to make sure everyone was happy and that I conducted myself in as professional a manner as possible, despite the fact that what I had just done was a deeply personal endeavor. True to my athletic roots, I put all of myself out there expending every ounce of energy I had to make sure that nothing went awry at any point in the entire process. I stood guard over each of those spinning plates twenty-four hours a day, seven days a week. I'd be damned if I let any of them begin to wobble—even for just a moment. Not on my watch. It left very little, if any, gas in my tank for the journey forward. In hindsight I think that made me more vulnerable than I would normally have been to my inner voices.

I could tell you that I triumphed over it all and seamlessly blended into the flow of the office and that there was nary a hiccup along the way, but I'd be lying and that wouldn't do anybody any good. Maybe to some it looked like I had it all figured out, I had become very adept at "putting up appearances," but something very different was going on inside my head. I was caught more than a bit flat-footed by my new world. How could a space that physically looks exactly the same from my pre-coming out days to my post-coming out days feel so completely different? It almost felt *foreign* to me. I was having a hard time reconciling all of it in my mind.

As I grappled with these dissonant feelings and tried to make some sense of it all, I quickly began to realize that there was a strange, new *presence* that kind of swirled around me like some strange ethereal being. Turns out it wasn't that strange at all; it was the glass ceiling making itself known to me for the first time in my life.

"Well, this is new." I said to myself. I had heard about it, read about it, and saw it on television and now, evidently, it was taking up residence in my world. It was right at that moment that I heard this little voice inside my head say, "Stephanie, you've crossed over, my dear. You're on the other team now. You know the one—with all of the other women. This comes with the territory over here, better get used to it."

As I began to absorb those words it became increasingly clear that this was to become the reality that would forever define my workplace. One that never existed in Michael's world.

And how I dealt with it, worked my way around it, and how I *danced* with it would boil down to how I felt I was being perceived every day by the world around me and how I processed that in my mind.

10,000 SETS OF EYES

What complicated matters for me on a daily basis was my intense preoccupation with my appearance. I guess I was always running from the "guy in a dress" imagery. At this particular point in my life it was very important to me that I be *seen* as a woman, not just *passing* as one. Everywhere. And that, of course, included my workplace, which was only just getting used to seeing the real me on a daily basis.

And therein lies the rub. The vast majority of people I was working with knew me and worked with me as my former self. They would always have some memory or image of Michael that they could draw a reference to. I was waging a battle inside myself that I could never win.

It was an *easier* deal when I would meet colleagues that I had never worked with before. They never knew Michael. They might have heard of him, but they never actually *saw* him. And they never experienced what it was like to work with him either, although how I approached my work became very different after I transitioned.

When I first started on hormone replacement therapy (HRT) which was over a year before I came out, I remember someone in my support group telling me that once the majority of the testosterone in my body was replaced with estrogen I would start seeing my world differently. Colors would be more vibrant. My demeanor would soften and, most important for my work life, I would reach decisions differently. I would be more thoughtful, more discerning, rather than the more abrupt way I had made choices before. I initially thought it was just nonsense I'm really not sure if I ever saw colors any differently. But I did find that over time I did approach my work more thoughtfully. At least it *felt* that way to me.

This all played into my thinking that I was working with a clean slate. I had a much greater chance of being seen as a woman from the very first interaction because they had a much narrower frame of reference with respect to how I was approaching my critical thinking each day. It all made sense to me and helped quiet whatever misgivings I had about my own appearance.

It was a much different kettle of fish, however, with those colleagues closest to me. They had a work history with my former self. They saw how I ran meetings, managed projects, and conducted myself during their annual performance reviews. And I thought that had a direct bearing on how they would approach the new me, if they would *accept* me.

In my mind I felt that I went about the running of my unit in the same way as before I came out—with one major difference: I was happy and relieved that I no longer had to hide my true self from my colleagues. I may have had my own inner struggles to deal with, but that never changed the overarching fact that I was absolutely delighted to finally be bringing all of me to the office every day.

But as happy as I may have been, I still had moments where I would conjure up all sorts of negative imagery in mind: my coworkers secretly making fun of me behind my back, mocking me for making the mere attempt at trying to pass myself off as a woman. And maybe they were. I'll never know for sure. I suspect that for those that had known me before I transitioned, the new me was a lot for them to process. And I had to cut them some slack and give them time to adjust.

But I was the boss. On some level they *had* to accept the new me. But that doesn't get around the fact that one of the more disturbing elements of the culture of my department was its passive-aggressiveness. For all I know, I'd leave a staff meeting thinking everyone was on board, but as soon as I left the room they were going off on what a wacko I was.

I've never had the greatest self-image and it was really rearing its ugly head at absolutely the wrong time. While I did celebrate the fact that I was now bringing my entire authentic self to my workplace, there were days—many days, in fact—where my self-consciousness got the better of me.

On the worst of those days, that same long center staircase that I traversed on my first day was merely a vehicle that transported me to where I would be confronted with what seemed to me like 10,000 sets of eyes watching my every move to see if I could actually pull off the whole "woman thing."

My friend Scotty had a similar, if not even more real, experience:

"There were a number of people watching me all the time. There were times I would walk into a lab and everyone would suddenly go silent. I knew they were talking about me. I could feel the hostility. I had to just keep swimming, and not give anyone an excuse to have an issue with me. It was a very stressful tightrope."

For my friend Shawn, a former Navy pilot and Obama administration appointee who also happens to be a trans woman, she too had her own share of personal demons to deal with. When the first meeting was called after her work transition, everyone already knew and it was business as usual. Some people held their gaze at her a little longer to adjust to the change, but everyone acted as if nothing was different.

One of the greatest things that happened was that people within her company went out of their way to say, "I am happy for you." Even people she only knew by sight. It helped her so much in her transition to know she was supported in work, after being so afraid for so many years that her secret would be revealed and her career would be over.

One day, Shawn walked past a general she had worked with when she was still in the military.

"Every time I see you, you look hurt," he said.

"It's nothing you have ever done," Shawn replied. "It's me I am uncomfortable with."

"You shouldn't be," he said with a smile.

Sometimes we can have a vision that others are judging us, when what we are really doing is judging ourselves. That encounter had a profound effect on Shawn, for it helped her to realize that and she learned to accept that she was, in fact, accepted.

Like Shawn, all of my paranoia and angst were mostly self-imposed. Other than the pressure I put on myself to conform my presentation to my own image of womanhood, I never felt that the degree to which I "blended" was directly tied to retaining my employment. Out of all the things that entered my mind, that was not one of them. I never approached my work life like the next episode of *Survivor: Corporate America*.

Quite the contrary. I was extremely grateful to New York Life for working so collaboratively with me on my transition. They certainly didn't have to. They could have just as easily let me go, or thrown money at me to make me disappear and washed their hands of the whole thing. But that's not what happened. I was celebrated and I felt it—every day from when I first came out to the day I retired some fifteen years later. And I was—and still am—so very grateful. It was that deep sense of gratitude that energized my work ethic and led, in part, to my encounters with the glass ceiling.

But let me be very clear here: this is *not* how it goes for the vast majority of trans people who come out at work. Many, sadly, are fired on the spot, and companies get away with it. It's the ultimate catch-22: by embracing your authentic self for the first time in your life, you suffer the loss of your livelihood. And that loss of income creates a downward spiral. Suddenly housing, healthcare, and the ability to feed yourself and your family are threatened. And that is wrong and hateful no matter how you look at it.

WELCOME TO THE WOMEN'S CLUB

From the very beginning I felt warmly embraced by the women of my workplace. I never felt shunned or excluded. Perhaps it had something to do with where I stood in the organizational chart, or—I hope—it had more to do with my being a nice, dare I say "cool," person to work with, but I found myself welcomed to the sorority and I couldn't have been happier.

They helped me find my balance and achieve a sense of stability that carried me forward with my career. Many of them served as my mentors on the ways of being a woman in the office, most without ever knowing it.

Once such moment came when I was attempting to navigate the women's locker room of our fitness center for the first time. I had absolutely no idea what was going on in there. *What do I do? How do I act?* I was more than a little freaked out by it. I had plenty of experience on the men's side, but none of that was going to help now.

One of my closest colleagues at the time, Carmen, rose to the occasion. I knew she worked out regularly, so one day I just asked her, "So what's the deal with the women's locker room?" Without hesitation she just looked at me and said, "I *never* let anyone I work with see me naked!" I responded, "Okay, good talk, very helpful." But she continued with some very instructive advice with respect to what to do with my towel and my underwear when I use the shower. Equipped with this knowledge I was able to pass the challenge of the women's locker room with flying colors. For me it was a much more private, and decidedly more modest, experience. And that was perfectly fine with me.

My locker room experience notwithstanding, there were countless other times when I received the unsolicited guidance of the women around me—about a whole host of things—from dating advice to my wardrobe choices. It gave me the sense that they were looking out for me. I suppose you can chalk it up to being somewhat of a cultural thing among women. Whatever its origin, it made me feel like I was now a member of the sorority, so to speak. One thing is for sure, in the years prior to my coming out I never got any wardrobe advice from my male colleagues!

One time, my friend Cindy just plopped herself down in my office and asked point-blank, "So when are you going to lose the wig?" I was dumbstruck. "Uh, Uh . . . I don't . . . know" was all I could muster in response. I confided in her that I was waiting for my hair to grow out a little longer, so that I would be more comfortable with its length, but that perhaps it was time to leave my wig behind. She understood and told me that it would be fine—whenever I was ready. Not long after that I did go with my own hair never to return to the world of wigs again.

I was invited to lunches with the other women and I most definitely had my share of trips out for cocktails on a Friday night after work. Besides, it was a great way to avoid all of the weekend getaway traffic on the Tappan Zee Bridge. It was fantastic. I had a lot of fun and I became friends with many of the women I socialized with. But more than that, I really felt their acceptance. It was tremendously validating and helped me overcome a lot of the insecurities I might have had about my appearance.

All in all, it helped me assimilate into the fabric of my workplace as a woman. And it came to my aid when all of the buzz had died down after my first day. I will admit to dealing with an odd mix of emotions over that. Part of me enjoyed all of the notoriety and attention. How could I not? It was so overwhelmingly positive that it didn't take very long to embrace its incandescence. The other part of me was content just to sit in the warm afterglow of the moment and envelop myself in the return to some semblance of normalcy.

Ultimately, the latter won out and I'm glad it did. It was humbling in the sense that it made me realize that, in the end, it wasn't all about *me*. I had my moment in the sun and now it was time to get over myself and get on with what the company was paying me to do.

THE SOCIAL EUPHORIA OF DELAYED ADOLESCENCE

There's an interesting phenomenon that occurs with some, but not all, trans women who transition later in life like I did. It's called delayed adolescence. I never experienced what it was like to be a teenage girl, or for that matter, a young woman in my twenties. Despite my sister telling me, very pointedly, that female adolescence was "overrated," I had all of this pent up female adolescent energy inside of me just waiting to burst out. So when I finally came out in all aspects of my life and to everybody this energy was released. Some of it had seeped out when I was out with my girlfriends prior to coming out at work, but now the faucet was wide open and I had to deal with it at my job.

While there is no precise definition for this condition, one look at its name and you can kind of guess what it is. It's when this euphoria spills over from your social life and *becomes* your work life that trouble can occur. That's what happened to my friend, Terri, and it served as a cautionary tale for me. She let herself get distracted by her newfound social status and she lost her focus. Her work performance began to suffer. Worse yet, it was noticed by her management, and they were not very happy about it either. She took her eye off the ball and she was reprimanded for it. Thankfully, it served as a wakeup call and she no longer had any issues with social/work balance after that.

Terri's story makes a point that I think is very critical to emphasize: You may be transitioning and busy spinning all the plates that comes with, but you are still expected to do your job and do it well. In fact, some employers might even be watching your performance and work output just a little more closely in the days and weeks after you come out. Whether they do or not, the thought can help keep you grounded amidst all of the excitement.

It's normal to embrace the moment, you deserve it. You made the immense decision to be true to yourself and embrace who you are and you should relish the spoils. However, things do die down and your job awaits—where it always was to begin with.

TALKIN' BASEBALL

According to the *Encyclopedia of Gender and Society: Volume 2, male privilege* can be defined as:

"the system of advantages or rights that are available to men solely on the basis of their sex. A man's access to these benefits may vary depending on how closely they match their society's ideal masculine norm."

For the first twenty-five years or so of my career, I was a beneficiary of this phenomenon, although for most of those years I never even really thought much about it. I just went along on my merry way, letting it work to my advantage. And certainly my being white didn't hurt. The system was already designed, some would say *rigged*, in such a way that it essentially ensured that I, as a white, college-educated male would be first in line. My name was always on the guest list to get into the cool kids' club before everyone else. And I relished it, even if I was oblivious to it. The way I figured it, it was always supposed to be this way. I had dealt with so much frustration, pain, and angst just to survive in the wrong jobs at the wrong companies that this was simply good karma.

I was getting opportunities to lead projects and get promoted in the process while most, but not all, of my cisgender female colleagues did not. I was basking in the limelight of my career successes and I will admit to not ever thinking once about what my cis female counterparts were going through, and the challenges they were dealing with, just to be *seen and heard.*

You might be thinking that because we live in an enlightened age now, companies aren't like this anymore. From my experience, I would have to say that while "individual results may vary," you'd be mistaken. The machinery has been in place for far too long for it to simply just fade away. Sure, times are changing, but certainly not nearly as quickly as they should.

For most of my work life, this was never even on my radar. I did not benefit from privilege. Or did I?

Just because I *believed* that I benefited solely from hard work and dedication doesn't mean that my white male privilege wasn't working on my behalf in the background. I might have acted differently if I was more aware of its presence. I can see a scenario where I would have leveraged that as much as I could because my drive to succeed and erase all of my past business failures was so strong. Maybe that actually is what happened, but I am conveniently remembering it differently.

For years I had believed that my successes were always of my own doing. I paid no mind to the context within which I was working. I was much too focused on the next project, the next opportunity to shine, the next promotion. And that's the thing. I *had* opportunities—in abundance. They always came my way. Was it the same for my cis female colleagues? Not that I was ever *aware* of.

Blithely unaware I lived my work life before my transition above the glass ceiling, treating it as my own personal springboard to success. This isn't to say that all my days were filled with nothing but lavish praise—far from it. But what was inescapable was that my starting point, my *floor*, as a man was higher than that of a woman's, which also meant that my ceiling was higher too.

Well, first of all, I never really knew I had male privilege to begin with. So it wasn't like I went kicking and screaming when faced with its loss. The other dynamic at play here was the fact that I had been living a lie—hiding from my true self at every turn. Once I had made the decision to live my life authentically and put my gender issues to rest, there was no turning back. Even if I had been concerned about losing my male privilege at that time I would have been helpless to stop it. There were much more powerful forces to contend with that had been kept at bay one way or the other for nearly forty years, and the loss of my male privilege could never hold a candle to that.

The way in which I first became aware of my newfound status on the other side of the glass ceiling is uniquely my own and had absolutely nothing to do with work.

At New York Life, one of the hallmarks of its culture is its *collegiality*. As such, we tended to celebrate, well, *everything*. Birthdays, anniversaries, baby showers, engagements were all met with cake, ice cream, and other assorted goodies. It was at just such an event where I first felt the cold underside of the glass ceiling.

I was sitting at the conference room table munching on birthday cake and two of my male colleagues who I knew quite well were engaged in a healthy debate over which team—the Yankees or the Mets—had the better bullpen. My ears perked up. I am a self-described baseball nerd and was eager to jump in and offer my opinion—backed by a healthy dose of statistics—on how my beloved Yankees and Mariano Rivera were leaps and bounds better than anything the Mets could ever muster.

So I tried to enter the conversation, and I tried, and I tried again. But neither of the men would let me in. Every time I uttered a "you know" and "but come on" or made a gesture with my hands I was immediately cut off and they just continued talking and not even acknowledging my presence. But here's the thing. I wasn't trying to do this from the other end of the table. I was sitting right next to them! It became very obvious, very quickly, that they did not want to include me in this debate.

So I did something that was not at all what I would normally have done in that situation—I backed off. I demurred. How ladylike of me. Truth was, I was more than a little pissed off, but I wasn't in a place where yelling over these two guys would have accomplished anything or be seen as appropriate workplace behavior, especially for a woman. Besides, I wasn't about to make a scene over this, in the middle of someone's birthday celebration.

As I walked back to my office I couldn't help but think, "Have I suddenly become *invisible*? Man, I did *not* sign up for this!"

LOTS OF QUESTIONS AND NO ANSWERS

Given the struggles I was having with establishing myself as a woman in the *world*, not just in my workplace, this experience was more than a wakeup call for me. It triggered a whirl of questions and insecurities that emanated from the inner struggles I was already having with my sense of self. It fell into a period of introspection that lasted for years after I transitioned.

I looked at my world of work through very wary eyes. I was very hard on myself and questioned everything. Perhaps I was missing things that I didn't usually miss. Maybe I somehow lost my edge. I must have taken my eye off the ball. I might even be less *competent!*

I was conflicted. My degrees, my MBA, and my years of experience hadn't changed. I searched for answers, but there were none. Then one day as I was ruminating over what I thought was happening I blurted out to no one in particular, "maybe they're all *transphobic!*" It was throughout this time that I began to feel like I was being challenged more distinctly in meetings with my superiors. And I wasn't making it up, either. I was being questioned about my proposals, my projections, and my answers to questions much more than before. Was this some sort of test? I distinctly felt like I was being treated "less than" and I was not comfortable with that.

"They're just smiling and appeasing me," I thought, "while behind my back they are plotting how to get rid of me." My paranoia was reaching new heights. I think I may have been suffering from the PTSD of nearly losing my job as the "internet marketing guy" just a few years prior. That was a very trying time, and it was only amplified by the fact that it came right on the heels of the attacks on the World Trade Center towers. It left a scar that this situation seemed to pick at.

That's when it hit me like a bolt of lightning from above.

These people were not transphobic at all! I was being treated this way because my performance was being judged within a totally new paradigm. Amidst all of my anxiety and distrust, had I somehow forgotten that I was now firmly on the other side of the glass ceiling? This had nothing to do with my being transgender, but had everything to do with the fact that I was now seen as a woman in my workplace.

I felt relieved yet very deflated all at the same time.

The *good news*, that acted as a salve to my overwrought concerns about my presentation, was that I was accepted as a woman in my workplace. The *bad news*, now that it was clear where all of the challenges were coming from, was that *I was accepted as a woman in my workplace.*

THE SOCIALIZED ART OF SELF-DEFENSE

I had reached the point where I could no longer just sit back and let this happen to me. Emboldened with my newfound place in the world,

184

such as it was, I drew on my athletic roots and prepared for meetings like I was a prizefighter. I *overprepared* and *to secure* my newfound standing in the organization.

One particular meeting stands out among many others. I was to present a readout of my team's performance to a number of higher ranking internal clients and discuss some new workflow ideas—all to better serve their needs.

Well, that was the original idea at least.

Clearly, our internal clients had a different agenda. I quickly found my proposals being attacked. But I was ready. I shot back with details and numbers and diligently, if not animatedly, defended my position. Something just kicked in and transported me to the middle of the football field with the score tied and the clock running out. I just reacted.

And that's the point.

I had my own *history* to draw from that brought out a frame of mind that had me acting like Michael would have. That never went away after I transitioned. While I may have looked physically different to the world, the *essence of Michael* remained. It was an unretractable part of my being.

On top of that, I had decades of socialization as a white male in the corporate world to pull from. There were many instances during my rise up the corporate ladder at AT&T where I found myself in similar situations. Like being the lead facilitator with much larger disparate groups of really smart people and getting them to agree on an approach to a seriously big project, for instance.

Take no prisoners. It never occurred to me for a second that "women do not behave this way in meetings." Screw that! If this is how I had to fight for respect then that's what I was going to do. It worked before and it would work again.

As I was collecting my things and heading back to my office, one of my cis female colleagues, grabbed me by the arm and said "You got a minute?"

"Sure, let's go back to my office."

Once we got there, she said to me with this look of shock on her face, "What did you just do in there?" I will admit I was taken aback by that comment.

I simply said, "I defended myself."

She looked me straight in the eyes and replied, "I could *never* do that. I wasn't *raised that way*. I was raised to be non-confrontational."

Talk about being in two completely different places for the same situation. Acquiescence of any measure was the furthest thing from my mind. I could not have reacted any other way. To even think of doing so seemed so very *foreign* to me. For a while I was concerned that my behavior could be construed as "wearing my male privilege on my sleeve." That is to say that I was worried that if I came on too strong people wouldn't be seeing Stephanie, they'd instead be seeing Michael. It was beyond important to me that I was always seen as my authentic self and not my former self.

It was one thing to defend my abilities, but I was concerned that perhaps I was acting "too male" for those around me. In my zeal to defend myself maybe I crossed the line and unwittingly attempted to exert male privilege that I no longer had. Old habits can, even when you didn't know you had them in the first place, die hard.

I really think it was a case of "muscle memory" kicking in. I was exhibiting behavior that I had learned over all of my years as a male in the corporate world. Regardless of its origin, my goal was to somehow meld that side of my management style into my new corporate persona.

After all, I didn't want my behavior to serve as a detriment to the rest of the women in my department. I had just joined the team. The last thing I wanted to do was get tossed out of the clubhouse.

It was different now. I was not on the opposite side anymore. We were all on the same squad. I began to think about the cost that my cis female colleagues had to deal with to have a career—and a family, for example. Again, not every woman I worked with was dealing with that specific dynamic, but many were.

What sacrifices did they have to make that their male counterparts didn't? I can answer that question: plenty. As I slowly began to feel more comfortable with where I was with professional life as the real "me," I felt a growing sense of empathy and respect for these women. I was in a new place, a new situation, but I was certainly not alone. As each day passed, it became more evident that "me being me" was not going to be an issue with any of my newfound sisters.

And as for "me being me" it was really a function of living into myself a little bit more as each day in the office came and went. As I became more comfortable in my own skin, that confidence radiated outward to everyone I came in contact with. Eleanor Roosevelt put it much better than I ever could:

"People grow through experience if they meet life honestly and courageously. This is how character is built."

And I really tried to meet each day honestly. I resisted the temptation—and it was there every single day—to fall back on the old habits of years ago when I would live my life solely to fulfill the expectations of others, rather than my own. I was not about to sacrifice my self-worth just to meet the expectations that others may have had of me. I was not play-acting. This was my *life*.

And that's not an easy thing to do in corporate America. You are judged every single day—by your superiors, peers, and subordinates. It's the nature of the beast. I was working in a very hierarchical culture and that was the way the game was played. But I had been through enough in my life just to get to a place of happiness, and I wasn't about to compromise on that. The dynamics of my transition aside, where I was in my career when I came out was very different than many of my cisgender female colleagues. While sacrificing aspects of themselves to advance their careers may have been a part of their corporate life that came hand-in-hand with their ambitions, it most certainly was *not* a part of mine.

I came to New York Life later in my career. I had already been working for twenty years. I started out at an officer level. Making the move from AT&T was already a big step up for me. I saw it as a major achievement in my career. As a result, my expectations of moving up the corporate ladder were tempered from the very start. A fact that was further galvanized by almost losing my job less than two years in. I wasn't about to compromise on what I had already accomplished so that I could position myself at the top of some imaginary promotion list.

I was determined to do my job to the best of my ability while at the same time living my truth.

THE REAL PLATE SPINNERS

It all served to put me in a place where I could, finally, turn my gaze from inside to outside. Much like my friend Kate had shared with me a few years back, I began to observe the workplace behaviors of my cisgender female colleagues much more closely.

I watched in amazement as some of them worked tirelessly while pregnant without missing a beat—well into their ninth month—and then returned a mere two months or so later to pick up where they left off. I listened to their tales of how they managed it all: work, school, homework, after school activities, and just marveled at the notion that they made it all look so effortless. I had my own responsibilities to juggle as well given that I was a single parent with joint custody of my son. I had to balance all of the trials and tribulations of his middle school and high school years after I came out.

So I understood what their version of plate spinning was all about. All of the juggling of multiple responsibilities and commitments while still remaining dedicated to their jobs and careers…at least to a point.

I'll never know what it is like to carry your child to term and give birth to them. While I cherish the relationship I have with my son, I know that it is very different from the bond he has with his mother. I don't think that one is necessarily better than the other, they're just different. Either way, it didn't diminish for a moment the amount of respect I had for their nonstop balancing act. It spoke volumes to me about the content of their character as *human beings.*

It's about the sacrifices these women made every day and their determination to make it all work. Their commitment to their kids, their families, and their careers was, and is, exemplary. And it wasn't just the women who had children. All of my cis women coworkers at all levels of management exhibited vast amounts of all of these qualities and then some.

I became a student of their management styles, too. Some seemed to consciously emulate the behaviors of our male colleagues, while others seemed to take a less abrasive, more collaborative approach. I often wondered if they were making a conscious decision to act that way, thinking that the only way for them to "get ahead" was to act like "one of the guys." And it felt like that was most certainly the case for some, but not all, of the women I came in contact with. I think that for some women—driven in part perhaps by their own career aspirations, drive, and insecurities—they felt the need to overcompensate, torn by their responsibilities to their jobs and to their families. The truth is, there were elements of all of that at play. It wasn't until I was on the other side of the glass ceiling when I became aware of, or to quote the vernacular, "woke" to how hard my cis female colleagues had to work just to get a seat at the table of opportunity. They are wicked smart. They are driven. They are empathetic. They are committed. They are hilarious. They are multitasking machines.

The way they handled it all was beyond inspiring to me. I was, and am, proud to be counted among their ranks.

MIND THE GAP

You might be wondering what the differences might be between me and any other cisgender woman are.

To me the answer is very simple: Trans women are women. Period.

I get that my lived experience as a woman may have more twists and turns in it than a cis woman's, or that it's somehow been shorter in duration. But that doesn't make it any less *valid*.

Within the dynamic of the workplace my cis sisters and I have arrived at the same place. We all need to function within the same organizational construct, the same culture. We all must work together. What I saw and felt every day was the bond created by our shared experiences in the workplace. We all were fighting our own battles and dealing with our own challenges in one way or another, whether they were brought about by the existence of the glass ceiling or not. Sometimes they were a result of issues we had with each other.

But despite all of that I felt a tangible sense of *community* with these women that I considered myself fortunate to be a part of. And we needed that space as we worked beside our male counterparts each day, because in order for the work to get done, we had to do it together.

My hope is that this exists at other companies too, but it's hard to say for sure. It's really a function of the culture and the women—all the women—who work there. Over the years, and New York Life was no different, very vibrant and effective women's employee resource groups have been formed to create a space for conversations about gender inequity in the workplace and what can be done about it. Many of these groups can count male allies among their ranks. The more that happens, the more robust the conversation can be.

But like any equality movement we're not there yet. I suspect that there are companies of varying sizes in all kinds of industries where much work needs to be done. Cultures have to evolve and systems of ingrained inequity have to change in order for *all* women to truly shatter the glass ceiling, once and for all.

CHAPTER TEN
NURTURING MY SPIRIT

No one is a prophet in one's own country.
~ Luke 4:24

AS THE MONTHS AND YEARS PASSED AND MY FIRST day disappeared into the rearview mirror, the prevailing sense of gratitude that I felt for the company was gradually replaced by a growing sense of restlessness and unease. Part of it had to do with the fact that I was feeling particularly unchallenged at work. Sometime after my transition, my department went through a reorganization and I no longer had a unit of people that reported to me. In fact, the entire group was moved out of my department in its entirety. Suddenly, I became a "unit" of one. The phenomenon of reorganization, a staple of corporate America, is something that I had to weather several times throughout my entire career, so the fact that it actually happened was not a shock. That it created such a vastly different workscape for me sure was.

I enjoyed leading a team of people, and having them come in and out of my office with problems to solve and challenges to be mitigated. Every day, no matter what I might have planned, was different than the next. It made coming to work an adventure and I thrived in that environment. Then overnight it all changed. I became something called a "communications planner," orchestrating the communications mix to our agents for all of our life insurance products. And then after a couple of years or so, I switched over to doing the same thing for all of our annuity products.

In the beginning, it was a refreshing change and I liked working with an entirely new group of people who were seeing the real me for the first time. There was one internal client, Phil, who stood out. He led a project team that was responsible for bringing to market one of the most innovative whole life insurance products to hit the industry in a long time. It was a big deal. I had never seen Phil until our first team meeting. He was a complete gentleman, treating me with respect, and he openly acknowledged my contributions to the effort every chance he got—all with a hilarious sense of humor. If there were any reservations among the rest of the team members about me, Phil's embrace put them all to rest. Compared to the borderline misogynistic behavior of some of his peers, Phil was a renaissance man. And I really appreciated that, because all I ever wanted to do was contribute my talents to the team's success. And, of course, fit in.

I didn't sense any glass ceiling holding down any of the women on the team, myself included. There was no time for any of that nonsense. We were there to get a groundbreaking product to market, and there wasn't any room for any larger-than-life egos or condescending behavior. Unfortunately, that experience was pretty much the highlight of my five-year tenure as a planner.

MY CALLING WAS CALLING

There was something much more profound happening during that entire time. With each day that passed, I became more and more aware that something else was stirring inside of me. It began in a very non-descript sort of way. I felt a sort of pang that made me feel like there was something else I should be doing with my life. As that feeling began to grow, it spoke to me in a way that my work as a planner never did. I thought back to one of the meetings I had with the HR VPs when I told them, "I may be the first, but I certainly won't be the last." And that's when it all sort of clicked for me. I never really thought of myself as a trailblazer, but in fact, that's what I was. To my way of thinking, if you are going to refer to yourself that way, then you have to be willing to put in the work that goes along with it. And that ethos would one day get me into trouble.

I've heard many people talk about how their work in employee resource groups (ERGs), for example, was their "true passion," as if that somehow was a mechanism for them to keep their two work worlds from interfering with each other. I saw it more as an effort to keep the "day job"—the thing that paid the bills—separate from the "side hustle"—where I could unlock a source of energy and inspiration that fulfilled my life. To be fair, maybe they were perfectly content with having a sense of equilibrium with each of those worlds, and if that was the case, good for them. But given my perspective, my only conclusion was that they must not be all that passionate about the job that they were being paid to do in the first place.

Call me jaded, or even cynical perhaps, but that's how I saw it. I struggled mightily with that separation. It was never easy for me. Because the scope of that feeling inside of me just felt so much larger, like something more divine was happening. No matter how much I loved my day job—and toward the end of my career at New York Life I really did—it could not hold a candle to the other work that I knew I was put on this earth to do. That's why I refer to it as my *calling*.

And at the beginning that notion provided a measure of relief as my planning role began to feel much less strategic and decidedly more rou-tine—mind-numbingly routine. My calling nourished my soul in a way that my day job never could. In part because it had everything to do with the essence of my being—of being a transgender woman. It connected directly to my heart and to my soul. In those days my job was anything *but* the essence of my being.

I'm not sure what came first, either, or that it even really mattered. Whether its existence brought about my feelings of discontent and in-congruence with my job, or if it was the other way around. But what I did know was that I needed to somehow establish equilibrium between the two. In that sense what I was feeling wasn't all that different from ac-knowledging my authentic self for the first time. But instead of changing genders—making a complete shift from one to the other—this time I decided it would be better to keep my feet in both worlds simultaneously. There was more for me to do, I concluded. As it turned out, that wasn't the wisest decision I ever made in my life.

THE EMERGENCE OF MY SIDE HUSTLE

I first sought to bring this energy, this light, to where I worked. That seemed like a logical place to start. And that's really how I became involved in the launching of the first-ever LGBTQ employee resource group at New York Life. I was one of the original group of seven found-ing members who came from many different areas of the company. It seemed as though we all shared a common vision of creating a place where the company's LGBTQ employees could feel safe being their au-thentic selves. We had all come to the same realization and arrived at the same place at essentially the same time. Our individual journeys may have been different, but we all shared the same desire for inclusion with-in the company. Our first executive sponsor was our chief technology officer, who just happened to have a gay brother. We called it NYLPride (pronounced "*Nile*Pride") and as it grew it became a powerful force for change and inclusion within the company.

And in the beginning, of course, I was involved—*very* involved. But there was a problem. I was not working at our headquarters location in Manhattan. Twenty-five miles or so north in the Sleepy Hollow, New York campus, I felt disconnected, even exiled. The company had developed the site in the years after 9/11 in effort to have less of a Manhattan-centric workforce. And it created all of the logistic—and mental—hurdles that you might imagine. I felt isolated from all of the action. I missed the human connection with my peers in the group. And I was worried that I would somehow become irrelevant.

We soon reached a point in our development as an ERG where we had to consider appointing co-chairs. A number of members reached out to me privately asking me to consider throwing my hat in the ring. I was more than flattered by their heartfelt appeals. But in the end I thought that if I were chosen it would have been difficult to lead the group remotely since the majority of our members worked in Manhattan.

But more than that, if our group was to truly thrive it needed co-chairs who were no more than a few floors away from our executives so that if any in-person appeals needed to be made on the policy or budgetary fronts, for instance, they could be done much more effectively and efficiently. I came to the somewhat reluctant conclusion that I could not properly advocate for the company's LGBTQ employees from afar. Whatever personal ambitions I may have had I needed to put aside for the greater good of our small, but mighty band of pioneers. And with that I pledged to come into the City as much as I could for key meetings and to be the point person in my building for the group. I tried to convince myself that it would compensate for the fact that I wasn't "in the mix," but it proved to be as much of a failure as it sounds.

My friend Jenna, who successfully transitioned while in her position at Johnson and Johnson, played a key role in devising a novel idea that, if it ever had existed at New York Life, might have changed how I dealt with my restlessness. To her credit, what Jenna realized, much like I had, was that there would be other trans employees that would be seeking to transition after her. And sure enough, there were. Soon after she came out to her boss, she found out that there were two other transpersons embarking on their transitions at the company as well. Each of them had created their own transition plan and when they connected, they decided to combine notes, ideas and experiences which led to the creation of first internal guidelines for anyone transitioning at Johnson and Johnson.

Working with her colleagues in Human Resources, among others, Jenna had a hand in transforming the narrative and policies at Johnson and Johnson as they pertained to their transgender employees. So much so that her LGBTQ employee resource group created the position of Gender Liaison, a role that Jenna ultimately inherited. This unpaid position serves as a designated advocate for transgender employees - and their dependents - going through transition, as each has unique circumstances and need support to help them through the various logistical issues that accompany a workplace transition. In the absence of such a position, I began to search for other ways that I could make a difference on the LGBTQ front.

One day while I was sitting in my office with not much to do in between meetings, I glanced over at a copy of the New York Life Foundation annual report. It was something that was distributed throughout the company each year. As I started to thumb through it I had a thought: does the Foundation contribute to any LGBTQ community causes or organizations? I went through all of its contents and couldn't find a single one. That gave me the idea to see if there was a way that I could create a connection with the Foundation and a deserving LGBTQ organization that had programs that specifically benefited children. This was because the mission of the Foundation back then involved "nurturing the lives of children."

Around that same time I was becoming more involved with the LGBT Community Center of New York, commonly referred to as "The Center." Since I had been going to their trans drop-in support group for a while, it seemed like a logical first place to look. That, and I had developed a deep affinity for the place. It had its own energy; I felt it every time I walked through its doors. At any given time, there was always something going on that supported various segments of the City's LGBTQ community. It was a safe space for people like me and for so many others to be free to express themselves in any manner they chose. Sometimes I felt like the building was giving everyone who went there a collective hug.

It was there at times when I really needed it, and the other trans women I met there—from all walks of life—taught me a lot about what our community is all about, from a perspective that I couldn't even imagine. Some spent portions of their lives out on the street, homeless, and doing sex work. Others had been a part of the ballroom culture scene that was popularized by the television series *Pose*. Through them I learned so much about what was really going on in our community. The trials, the pain, the hate, and the violence. And I felt it inside too because we were sisters, after all. I carry their stories with me to this day.

So, of course this was the first place I looked. There was never any decision that needed to be made in my mind. As it turned out there was a program that existed there called "YES" which stood for Youth Enrichment Services, that seemed like it might be a good fit. Armed with that information, I set up a meeting with the head of our Foundation.

Her name was Linda and I was impressed with her from the start. A smart, together woman with a long career as a philanthropic professional, she was very open to our conversation and to the possibility of expanding the Foundation's support portfolio into the LGBTQ space. I might have been a little nervous at first, as I introduced myself and gave her my pitch. But Linda was very disarming and I could see right away that she got it. Our conversation flowed smoothly and it became more about making sure whatever program I found fit the mission than that it would be for an LGBTQ-identified non-profit. I had prepared for pushback, but what I got instead was understanding and a sincere desire to collaborate on a solution. I honestly didn't think the culture allowed for that. But in her vision and demeanor, it did. I had found a collaborator, or some might say a co-conspirator, and it was beyond refreshing.

Fast forward to a few months later and after all of the appropriate introductions were arranged and paperwork filed, the YES program received its first two-year grant from the New York Life Foundation for $50,000. Over the life of the relationship, the Foundation supported the Center to the tune of approximately a quarter million dollars. It was very rewarding to be able to make that connection on behalf of the LGBTQ kids who benefited from that program. I am very proud of that accomplishment, and that it was able to happen within the existing culture of the company. And if that's what making a difference felt like, then I was all in for more.

Linda and I teamed up again to support my next "target"—the Hetrick-Martin Institute. "HMI" as it is also referred to, is an amazing non-profit organization whose mission is to serve all young people, regardless of sexual orientation or identity, to create a safe and supportive environment for them to achieve their full potential. In 1985, with funding from the New York City Department of Education, HMI established the Harvey Milk High School, the first high school in the United States that specifically catered to LGBTQ students.

Equipped with what I now knew about the Foundation's mission of "nurturing our children" it seemed like a strong fit. But here's the thing: I did not have any prior association with the organization. So I essentially cold called them. When I first showed up and said that I'd like to create a connection between it and my company's Foundation, they looked at me like I had just flown in on angel's wings. Once all of the connections and appropriate paperwork was submitted, the New York Life Foundation issued a grant to HMI for $100,000 which was used to create a new companion operation in Newark, New Jersey. From that humble beginning, the New York Life Foundation continues to support the organization to this day at a level in excess of $500,000.

All of these developments had nurtured my spirit and certainly increased my network within the community throughout the New York metropolitan area. And it all came at a time when I really needed it. My day job was totally unfulfilling, but it afforded me with the opportunity to manage my own schedule. That meant I could work out of our Manhattan office from time to time so I could do my work and meet with my internal clients who worked there and also explore all of these connections. Soon opportunities for deeper involvement came to pass.

It should come as no surprise that the first opportunity came to me from The Center—and it had everything to do with this "thing" I have for reading annual reports. I was at The Center for a meeting with the Foundation and I saw copies of their annual report fanned out on a coffee table. Of course I picked up a copy and stuck it in my bag so I could read through it once I got home that night. When I sat down with it that evening, I couldn't help but notice that right on the inside cover or on one of the first pages they had included an appeal for new board members. "Hmm, I could do that," I thought.

Through a series of conversations I found myself at one of the premier fundraising events The Center staged each year called "Women's Event." It was billed as the largest lesbian-focused event on the east coast. As I was mingling in the crowd, I felt like I was the only trans woman in the entire room of 500 or so guests. And believe me, I had my radar out. "There just has to be another trans person here," I thought to myself as I made my rounds. "I can't be the only one, can I?" But apparently on that night, I was. That's when I realized that the vast majority of trans people who lived in the area couldn't afford the cost of the ticket to begin with. It was at about this time that I was approached by one of the board co-chairs who was evidently searching for me. He mentioned that he had heard I was interested in joining the board and I told him that yes, it was something that I'd be honored to do. I explained to him what I had done with the YES program and he said he'd be in touch.

A few weeks later I found myself at the end of a very long rectangular table in one of the more cavernous meeting rooms of The Center being interviewed by the nominating committee of the Center's board. Leading the conversation was Gina, one of the board co-chairs and a very prominent corporate lawyer in the City. There was a lot of talk about what would be required of my time, etc., but the one question that I will always remember was when Gina turned and looked at me with a bit of wry smile and said, "How did you get a large company to out of the blue just up and give $50,000?" She seemed genuinely stunned by that. All I said in response was, "I asked." And I think that answer, more than any other that I had given that evening, was the one that sealed the deal for me.

What followed was three terms, six years in total, of service to the Center board that I will always hold so dearly in my memory. I had the opportunity to contribute to the task force that re-branded The Center's image and marketing, the result of which is still visible today. And I actually became one of the co-chairs of the Women's Event. It was such an honor and a privilege to serve in that capacity for several years. And it was personally satisfying, too, going from the first time I went all by myself, watching all of the people that spoke from the podium that evening and saying to myself, "I am going to be up there one day," and then to make that happen just a couple of years later. I am beyond blessed.

Ever the overachiever, I also joined the board of an amazing organization called the Transgender Legal Defense and Education Fund (TLDEF) a few years later. It was the complete antithesis of the Center's Board: we were a small but mighty group of six or so that met in the organization's rather spartan offices to conduct business and review the wonderful outreach and legal support work the organization achieved through programs like their groundbreaking Name Change Project, which brings together low-income transgender and non-binary people with pro bono attorneys to assist with legal name changes. It is very satisfying to see how the organization has evolved over the years since my board service as it continues to fight for the rights of trans and non-binary people across the country.

PUSHING THE BOULDER UPHILL

Because of the network I had created within the LGBTQ community in the New York area, I found myself with opportunities to speak at companies and at conferences—always on my own time and on my own dime. A shining example of this non-support came about after I had won a scholarship from Out & Equal Workplace Advocates for my work in the community to the UCLA Anderson School of Management's LGBT Leadership Institute. It was a very intensive leadership development program exclusively for a hand-picked group of LGBTQ leaders from a variety of companies and industries. I was honored to be a part of it. Trouble was, I was the only one that seemed to care about it in the entire company. At the risk of sounding boastful, I talked it up to my boss and on up the line. I was congratulated, of course, for winning the scholarship, but when I asked them to fund my trip out to Los Angeles for the on-campus portion of the program, it fell on deaf ears.

"But surely there must be a budget line for training programs that you can pull it from," I said, valiantly trying to hold back my anger and frustration. But there wasn't any—or so they claimed. "Oh, we support you," they said, just as long as I used my vacation and personal time to fly out there, pay for campus housing, my meals, and airfare. By that time in my career I wasn't necessarily trying to leverage this to become the company's next vice president, but that the recognition of my leadership in the LGBTQ community and its potential transfer into my current role within the company didn't seem to resonate with them at all just hurt—a lot.

The coup de grace came while I was having lunch with one of my fellow attendees from Pepsico. He told me that he and every one of my peers in the program had been nominated by their ERG leadership and executives to represent their respective companies at the program. It was a huge deal inside their ERGs and in their companies too. It seems as though their companies thought highly enough about their LGBTQ employees and how the leadership program could nurture their growth that they signed on with UCLA. So, of course, they were all there on their company's time with all of their expenses paid. I was envious of the commitment their companies had made in them. He was more than shocked when I told him I had to pay for everything—except the tuition, of course—to attend. I walked back to our lecture room in a state of shock. I felt like I just had the wind knocked out of me. I was deflated. It took everything I had to shake of that revelation so I could concentrate on the remainder of the day's work and the rest of the program.

The next day, as I was out on my morning run through the beautiful Westwood campus I came to the conclusion that I was basically on an island at New York Life. And that whatever difference I was going to make in my community and the LGBTQ community at-large would have to happen outside its walls. I could try to bring people along at the company, but in terms of bringing my own energy and vision to the movement, that would be something that I would have to do on my own.

The whole UCLA experience really shouldn't have surprised me all that much. I had been attending the annual Out & Equal Workplace Advocates Workplace Summit gatherings—at my own expense—for a number of years already. In fact, when I went to my first Summit in 2007 in Washington, D.C. I was the lone representative from my company. I told the folks at NYLPride, but it wasn't like we were in a position to gather up a delegation of attendees like so many of the other companies there did. We just weren't there yet. It was mind boggling to me what I saw there. Fortune 100 companies, just like New York Life, with delegations that numbered close to a hundred people. I was just embarrassed and frustrated that what seemed so obvious a thing to support and have your company associated with, was such a heavy lift for my company. It wasn't until a number of years later, in 2014, that I was actually a part of a delegation—of eight—who attended the event.

But wait, there's more. There was another element beyond the lack of budgetary support that became just downright annoying. It was not being allowed to identify myself as an employee of New York Life in any external gigs that I found myself speaking at. If it sounds a bit strange, that's because it is. But that's precisely what happened.

One of our first chief diversity officers told me that I really shouldn't mention the company when I would speak externally. I remember being more than flabbergasted by that because it wasn't like I would ever say anything bad about the company. If anything, my remarks about how they supported me through my workplace transition cast them in a very favorable light. It was mystifying to me. But not wanting to make any waves since I was, after all, wanting to stay gainfully employed so I could pay for my son's college education, I just kept my mouth shut and went along with it.

It wasn't until a few years later, when I had a conversation with someone who worked in the area that oversaw the company's code of ethics, when it became very clear to me that my speaking and any consulting work I was doing on my own time did not create any conflict of interest whatsoever with the company's business. Every year, I diligently completed the company's conflict of interest questionnaire where I outlined all of my board service and the speaking and consulting work I was involved in through my LLC, Follow Your Heart. For years in any bio that I ever wrote, or even on my first website after I formed Follow Your Heart, I would use the words "financial services company located in New York" to describe where I worked.

But lost in my acquiescence was the larger message the company was sending to me about its culture as it related to me. For reasons that are unknown to me to this day, they didn't want other people and by default, the companies that they worked at, associating me—the trans woman who was speaking at their company event—with New York Life. It was obvious that they wanted my coming out story to remain *inside* the company. How could I have been so blind? But the truth is I was. I was so focused on the opportunities to speak that were coming my way that I lost sight of the fact that it was impossible for me to feel completely supported by the company when I couldn't even publicly acknowledge that I was an employee in the first place.

But there is a silver lining to this story, because the good news was that each time I did a keynote speech or conducted a workshop, I felt like I was having an out of body experience. Time became irrelevant as I locked in to my subject matter and to the faces in my audience. I could feel the energy well up inside of me as I told my story and what I had learned from the journey. I could feel and see the connection I was making with people. I was changing hearts and minds. It all served to reinforce the feeling that this truly was a calling for me, and that perhaps I could make another career out of it.

But even that was a double-edged sword. At the majority of companies I spoke at, and especially when I would do a workshop or panel at a national conference, like at the aforementioned Workplace Summit, where I did several over a period of ten years or so, I would see how much further ahead many companies were with their transgender and LGBTQ inclusion initiatives. And that really frustrated me on multiple levels.

For one thing, it provided context for what was really happening at New York Life. We all thought that we were moving at light speed, and within the context of the company's LGBTQ history—which was essentially zero prior to NYLPride being formed—we were. But the reality was that the bar was set pretty low for us from the beginning. It was all great work, but paled in comparison to so many other companies.

THE ENVELOPE CAN ONLY STRETCH SO FAR

But that fact didn't stop NYLPride from trying to sustain this progress. And one of the big initiatives we embarked upon was getting the company to establish transgender-inclusive healthcare benefits. I can remember it always being at the forefront of our discussions as a group. In fact, we even mentioned it in our remarks when we had our introductory reception with all of the executives. And I will admit that from the start

I had a much different level of expectation about how quickly the company should make these vitally important benefits available. Obviously, as the only out trans person that anyone knew of in the entire company, I had a personal stake in making this happen, even though they wouldn't apply to me because I had already had my gender reassignment surgery.

But it wasn't just that. In all of my travels to other companies that my side hustle took me to, I saw firsthand how many other companies were instituting these changes to their employee benefit plans in a much swifter way than New York Life was doing. That, and I allowed my overall sense of restlessness with my unchallenging role to seep into my growing sense of frustration with the entire process. In hindsight, I was being selfish. Through no one's fault but my own, I was feeling left out and left behind—in everything that was happening in my work life, I went off like a precocious child and it almost scuttled the effort entirely.

I was contacted by a reporter for the Associated Press who was working on national story regarding the effort that many companies across the country were taking to establish transgender-inclusive health benefits into their benefit plans. In the course of our wide-ranging phone interview I *may* have mentioned (wink, wink) that New York Life was well on its way to instituting these benefits in a matter of months. Well, as it turned out, my quote made the story that I can only imagine appeared in newspapers across the country that picked up the story. From a side hustle perspective, I actually was pleased to get the coverage but I conveniently *forgot* to do one very important thing: get the company's permission to talk to the national media in the first place.

A day or so after the article was published, I got a call from our senior vice president of communications. When I first made the switch to a planner role, it was in her organization so we knew each other well. To this day I consider her a friend and ally (and fellow Bruce Springsteen superfan). She summoned me to a meeting in her office in Manhattan the following day. I knew I was in trouble. It wasn't a very long meeting.

She looked at me, shook her head and "Steph, you know you are supposed to clear any interview requests with me first, don't you?" But before I could answer, she continued, "Every one of the senior executives in the company have to have their media interviews approved by me first. You know that, right?" I sheepishly shook my head "yes" and explained that in my zeal to make this happen I did not go through the proper channels. We both agreed that this would never happen again—it didn't—and with that the meeting was abruptly ended. I left her office in a flash, and as I waited for the elevator I had to take several deep breaths to keep my heart from beating out of my chest. I knew I had dodged a serious bullet.

I'm lucky I didn't lose my job. I know I pissed off *a lot* of people. No one ever approached me directly, other than my meeting with our communications SVP, but they didn't have to. I'm sure my little escapade with the national media created a serious setback to the effort that my colleagues in NYLPride had put forth up to that point. From that point on, I just kept my mouth shut and made sure I didn't speak on the record to any reporters.

In the weeks and months that followed, I helped out with various data requests that the working group had as they were preparing their presentations to our executives, but that was about it. No one asked me to personally attend any of them, and it's just as well. I knew I needed to just lay low and let them execute their plan. It seems they were much more adept at navigating the company's culture than I was.

And we did finally achieve our goal. Trans-inclusive health benefits were put in place. It was a triumphant moment for NYLPride and for me personally, despite the major wrench I threw into the proceedings what was now many months prior. There were no major public pronouncements about it either, that I can recall. It seemed to me that the company wanted to keep this newest development to itself. And yes, part of me was not overjoyed by that, but the much larger part of me was just very thankful that it finally happened.

BE CAREFUL WHAT YOU WISH FOR

Of all the bosses I had at New York Life there was only one who embraced the same sort of job movement paradigm that I had experienced in my years at AT&T. It should come as no surprise at all that Jane was not a long time NYL employee. An engineer by trade, she had joined the company just a couple of years earlier as a client of my area, but not of mine specifically. In one of our one-on-one meetings I just started to speak very candidly about how stale I felt I was getting in my planning role and that it sure would be nice if I could do something else. And to her credit, she understood what was going on and was receptive to what I was saying. She then looked at me right in the eye and somewhat nonchalantly asked, "So what do you want to do next?"

My jaw must have hit the floor with a thud. That was a question I had never heard uttered in the nearly ten years of employment I had logged by that time. I thought about it for a few seconds and said, "Well, I think working in our external meetings area would really round out my marketing experience."

Truth is, I had eyed that area from afar for a while, as the unit that I had managed when I came out produced a lot of material for them. That, and the idea that I would also be traveling again—and to some pretty nice places—certainly had its appeal. But from a glass ceiling perspective, I doubted that this even created a small crack given that it was nothing more than a lateral move for me on the organizational chart. But that said, I embraced the move with renewed energy and commitment.

But that faded fairly quickly, because the man that I began working for turned out to be, without question, the absolute worst boss I have ever had in my entire life. He was the textbook example of the insecure boss, and in lieu of a proper name, I call him TWBE—The Worst Boss Ever. So much so that it is very difficult for me to describe the myriad obtuse ways this person conducted himself. In fact, for my own mental health I will only say that those eight years made me feel like Bob Cratchit of *A Christmas Carol*, intentionally and blatantly harassed. Admittedly, there was a lot that happened inside of these margins over those years, but I do not have the desire nor the inclination to waste the precious ink on these pages on the never ending examples of TWBE's utter ineptitude. I made a pledge to myself that I would never again give him the power that I gave to him during that time. I wouldn't be honoring that pledge if I relived each of his many indiscretions here. Suffice it to say, the times where I felt disrespected, degraded, unappreciated, and condescended to were multitudinous.

To this day I have absolutely no idea if he was transphobic, homophobic, or just so self-absorbed that the people that worked for him existed merely to satisfy his own end game—whatever it was. And I put up with it because, to be blunt, I needed the job. My son was preparing for college and I needed to maintain the status quo so I could pay for it. That's where the transfer of power comes in. I swallowed hard and bit my lip so much that I thought for sure I'd wind up in the emergency room—or the psych ward—of the local hospital.

I had my share of sleepless nights and anxiety attacks. At one point a number of years later, I was taking so much Xanax every day that I thought I might have a problem. So I explained what was happening to my doctor and she suggested that we try something else that worked great "for dealing with asshole bosses." And it worked, it ratcheted down my visceral reaction to all of the insanity, and I stopped taking all of that Xanax. I essentially became numb to all his shenanigans.

The glass ceiling for those entire eight years couldn't have been any thicker. You could make the case that I actually added to its depth because I didn't push back on TWBE's asinine behavior. But the last thing I wanted was to be fired. At the very beginning of my tenure in this role, I remember thinking that I actually could learn from him and grow to the point that I could become the point person on meetings of my very own, thereby taking some of the burden off of him. That idea crashed and burned before it could ever get going.

What I didn't realize is that in all of his insecurity he saw my honest overture to learn from him as a threat and kept putting off any conversation remotely related to the topic. And here's the thing: When I finally discussed what was happening with his boss—who claimed he had an "open door policy" for such things—all I got was a lot of happy talk about how I needed to earn that and that my crazy boss himself would be the one to make that determination! For the first time I felt the glass ceiling pushing down hard on me, really hard. I was going nowhere fast. Its downward pressure squeezing out any last hope of moving my career in an upward direction. And it wasn't like I was demanding to be promoted. I just wanted to have the opportunity to "develop in place" as some of my friends in HR like to call it. But there was precious little room for that.

I concluded that any "growth" that I would experience would have to be created on my own because my boss was simply incapable of providing it. I was trapped between a beyond incompetent boss and his superior who was totally blind to what was happening. And it went on like that for years. Frustration and anger morphed into just becoming so jaded to the fact that no one up the line saw the daily insanity like I did. I began to realize that I was looking at the back-end of my career. There was no next role, next opportunity, or—perish the thought—next promotion. I had reached the end of the line. That's what my glass ceiling looked like.

So I soldiered on, gaining strength from aspects of the job that brought me joy. These were incentive business meetings that ranged in size from 1,000 to well over 5,000 guests—and they were an integral part of the sales culture of the company. I so enjoyed being "on-site" as we called it, getting to personally know our top agents, managers, and their families. Who, by the way, came from all walks of life from nearly every state in the country. And for every one of them this was a hard-earned celebratory trip. I admired their achievements in what can be a very tough, what-have-you done-for-me-lately, results-driven sales environment. In the beginning I had my concerns about how these people were seeing me, but that didn't last for very long because I simply didn't have the time to think about it. I was busier than I ever was and I had commitments to the other members of my team. And I just told myself, "Stephanie, you just do *you* and do your job and you'll rise above it all."

It helped that I was blessed to work with some amazing people who over time, became what I like to call my "road family." We all were away from our loved ones for days at a time and as I got to know everyone better and they got to know me, we all just embraced each other as one big collective. We had contractors called travel directors who had been working with us for years before I ever showed up. They were all an integral part of the fabric of these events. And it just so happens that a number of them were gay, which made my transition onto the team that much smoother. I'm sure they got the word ahead of time that I was coming on board, but all of them, regardless of their sexual orientation, made me feel right at home from day one. I count each one of them among my friends to this day and I always will. They were my buffer and my shoulder to cry on when working for TWBE became, as it often did, too much to take.

I learned some very valuable lessons during those eight years working for TWBE. First and foremost was to never give anyone more power than they deserve, if any at all. I had so many people tell me that they all knew who was really doing all the work—and it wasn't him. I never stopped believing in myself. And I learned a lot about the value of one's reputation. In the end, that's all I really had to hold on to and I fiercely protected it, especially when the TWBE would attempt to take shots at it, which usually happened around annual review time. It was his twisted way of trying to assert his superiority over me.

I never allowed it to work because I never stopped believing in myself, especially when it felt like I was the only one who did. It was my determination and perseverance to see things through, and my unwavering belief that there were better days ahead that kept me from giving up. I found my joy and positive energy wherever I could, and more and more it seemed that those sources emanated from places outside the company.

FEELING BOXED IN

So I found solace in my side hustle. At least at the beginning I did. I took on as much speaking and consulting work as I could, within reason. I was always very mindful that I couldn't let the two worlds come in conflict with each other. As time went by, and my community involvement increased that became harder and harder to do. And not just logistically, but mentally as well. I found all kinds of ways to find time to work in the City to go to appointments with clients over my lunch hour. I used vacation and personal time too. There were many days when I felt like I was teetering on a see-saw between both worlds, but I made it work. Or so I thought. I actually found that I was putting out more effort to keep the balance between the two and that was slowly beginning to take its toll on my peace of mind.

But like a moth to flame I was drawn to the outside work because it so nourished my soul and my spirit. It enriched me in a way that my day job could never do. For my own sanity I suppose I said "yes" to some opportunities that I would have been better off saying "not right now" to instead. But when I spoke at a company or worked with a client on their trans-inclusive policies, or was involved with my board work, it tapped into a part of my energy that my day job rarely did. I was uplifted by the people I was connecting with who, unlike back in the office, very much wanted to hear what I had to say. Sure, it stroked my ego, too. But if feeling valued and recognized for my experience and expertise meant that I was somehow egotistical, then I'm guilty as charged, I suppose. But it was never about my ego. I was about changing hearts and minds around what it meant to be transgender and why workplaces needed to protect and celebrate their trans employees.

After a while it all reached a point for me that I just had to find something else. The daily abuse working for TWBE was just unbearable. And for every lousy day at the day job I had it seemed as though something terrific was happening in my other world. So it should come as no surprise that I actively began searching for jobs in the LGBTQ non-profit community and in the quickly emerging field of diversity and inclusion on the corporate side. And over a space of nearly four years I tried my damndest to do so. I absolutely networked my brains out. I called and emailed everyone I knew to try to get the inside line on openings that I would apply for. I came very close in a couple of instances, but in the end I was either making too much money or I lacked something specific they were looking for, whatever that meant.

I even started applying for internal job opportunities within New York Life. In a variety of roles that I felt at least partially qualified for. I even interviewed for diversity and inclusion jobs twice, but every single one of them came up empty. Of course I was crestfallen. I got so emotionally invested in each and every opportunity. I prayed incessantly for an offer. I lost sleep worrying about what the outcome would be and why it was taking everybody so long to reach a decision. In the end it was always someone else's job to get, not mine. Each negative outcome had me drowning in a pool of my own tears. I so wanted to get away from this toxic boss of mine that I tried just about everything. Some of these positions would have required my relocating to another part of the country or taking a fairly substantial cut in my compensation. But I always thought the reward far outweighed the risk. But in the end it didn't really matter. All that was left was my bruised and battered psyche.

And I never really stopped to think if it had anything to do with my being trans or not. I couldn't allow the thought that I might have been the victim of some level of transphobia to seep into my consciousness. This was all about my credentials and my experience. That I also happened to be transgender just came along for the ride. Besides, all of the non-profit jobs were openly courting trans candidates. But I learned very quickly that there's a difference between encouraging trans people to apply and actually hiring one.

In the end, I just had to stop the madness that I had created by trying to live in two worlds simultaneously. While that might have been okay back when I was doing the planner job, once I switched over to the meetings job, my workload increased dramatically and the plate spinning that was my side hustle quickly became difficult to maintain. That only got worse when I added yet another spinning plate—looking for another job. In the blink of an eye I now had two very big plates wobbling over my head. You might have thought I would have learned from all of the plate spinning I did during my transition, but much like my own life's journey never ends, so too with the plate spinning. So I made the decision to step away from my side hustle work and I stopped looking for other jobs. Besides, it had all become entirely too debilitating for me—physically, mentally, and emotionally. I had learned a valuable lesson—that they don't call them "side" hustles for nothing.

ON BEING VANNA WHITE

There was something about my work in the meetings area—and at the company in general—that I could never quite reconcile in my mind. I was in a very public facing role. I was seen by and interacted with all of the top executives of the company and our highest performing agents and managers at every meeting I worked on. I couldn't be more out than I already was. I would even be positioned at the side of the stage at each meeting's honor dinner program to congratulate the award recipients and help them exit the stage with their awards in hand. I had to get all dressed up and I would occasionally appear on the large video screens that were on the sides of the stage. I used to joke with my colleagues that I felt like Vanna White, of *Wheel of Fortune* fame. I just wasn't turning any letters.

It just seemed at odds with what I had come to understand was a culture that had its limits with respect to how far it could go in supporting LGBTQ-focused employee initiatives. Because for all of that positive movement, it was still in my view a traditionally-minded company. Despite people, including my wife Mari, basically saying, "there's nothing to be concerned with, just go with it," I was puzzled.

So much so that during one of my sessions with my therapist Margie I brought it up. The incongruence was still annoyingly poking at me. After I had finished my explanation of how I was feeling, she just looked at me and pointedly asked me, "Steph, did you ever think that you might be a *token*?" Her statement hit me like a ton of bricks. Of all the possible explanations I had conjured up, being seen as a token was most definitely not one of them. I drove home from the session in a bit of a fog as I ran that notion through my mind over and over again. When I got home I felt compelled to look up the definition of the word—and courtesy of Merriam-Webster there it was, plain as the nose on my face:

1.a.: representing no more than a symbolic effort

1.b.: serving or intended to show absence of discrimination

Maybe Margie was right. Perhaps that was the answer to the riddle after all. It sure explained a lot of things. The more I pondered it, the more it made sense to me. I was good at my job and seen as a key member of my team, but perhaps there was something else going on that had been kept from me the entire time. Regardless of whether there was something surreptitious going on or not, pursuing conspiracy theories seemed like a colossal waste of time and effort. I concluded that if that was the case, then I would completely own it. "If I am a token, then so be it. I am going to be the best damn token that anyone has ever seen!" I thought.

And that's precisely what I did. Each June, when Pride Month rolled around, NYLPride would always be front and center with programming that was meant to shed light on the LGBTQ community and our LGBTQ employees in particular. One of the most popular events we ever did was something called "Coming Out Stories." It began with members of our group getting interviewed by an executive sponsor about what our coming out experiences were like. It was a wonderful way to put a very human face on what it meant to be an LGBTQ person and an employee of New York Life. I was honored to be a part of the first-ever panel that we had at the company. And I told everyone who was in the audience and who was connected by videoconference exactly how it went for me on my coming out day. All of our stories, when taken together, made such a powerful statement to all of our colleagues and it changed hearts and minds in the process.

A number of years later, a year before I retired, they asked me to come back and do another panel. But this time my co-panelist was an amazing trans kid who also happened to be the nephew of one of our HR executives. My little brother told his wonderful story and I had the chance to tell mine, but this time to a whole group of more recent employees who had never heard it before. It was such a wonderful experience and I was honored to be a part of it. And the executive who was the panel moderator was my friend Elaine, the communications SVP, who years before dressed me down for my unauthorized escapade with the national press.

It's opportunities like these that made me realize that perhaps "being a token" wasn't really such a bad thing after all. I began to see that I was being given the chance to change hearts and minds by simply being my authentic self. I treated each opportunity that I had to share my story as a chance to move the needle in a positive direction on trans equality throughout my company. It provided a forum for me to share my journey with so many people, some who no doubt were seeing a trans person up close and personal for the first time in their life. My hope is that through it all they were able to connect with our shared humanity. Because even though our life journeys have been traversed on decidedly different paths, that is a cardinal virtue that we all share.

CHAPTER ELEVEN
POSTCARDS FROM MY CUBICLE

"Progress is impossible without change, and those who cannot change their minds cannot change anything."
~ George Bernard Shaw

MY LIFE'S JOURNEY BROUGHT ME TO A CROSSROADS. I could have gone on living my life as a total falsehood built on an ever-growing foundation of shame, guilt, and denial. Or, I could embrace my authentic self and move on with a new life, enriched by the notion that I am loved and celebrated for the person I have always known myself to be. I wear my choice proudly each and every day represented by how I conduct myself and represent my community. I am aware of my place in the movement for the fair and equitable treatment of all people in the workplace, including—of course—cisgender women and my transgender and gender non-conforming brothers and sisters.

It's no different for companies.

They have a choice, too. They can choose to proactively respond to shifting and evolving societal and marketplace forces that shape the context within which they conduct their business operations. Or, they can choose to put their heads in the sand and proclaim that their business focus does not include a more diverse workforce and inclusive workplace. They can choose to step up and be seen as leaders of diversity and inclusion in their industry segments and more broadly, in all of corporate America. Or, they can choose to follow, letting their competitors test the waters of inclusion first before deciding that they, too, should jump into the pond with everyone else, regardless if they are seen as laggards or not.

We all know where the source of that decision lies—in the boardrooms and the C-suites of companies. But what is harder, perhaps, to ascertain is, how did they get there in the first place? How did they arrive at the place where the script was flipped and suddenly they saw a diverse and equitable workplace as a strategic imperative? I suspect the answer to those questions are as varied as the companies themselves.

In the years since I transitioned I have seen countless companies make these choices, in myriad ways. Even at my company, New York Life—while I may not know exactly what their tipping point was, I have experienced firsthand what the tangible results of that choice have been. Perhaps my transition served as a catalyst for change. I'd like to think it did, but the reality is I'll never know for sure. But the good news is they did get there. Perhaps more slowly than I would have preferred, but they got there.

Like so many other companies, they began their journey toward full workplace equality for all persons by doing the more obvious things first: changing policies and procedures. It was a logical *first* step, but it certainly should not be seen as the *last* one.

YOU HAVE TO START SOMEWHERE

When I first became involved in the transgender workplace inclusion movement in 2006, many—but not all—companies were scrambling to get their houses in order by having their existing equal employment opportunity (EEO) guidelines and employee non-discrimination policies amended to include protections based on the additional dimensions of sexual orientation and gender identity and/or gender expression. It was the necessary first step for them to take as they embarked on their journey to full workplace equality for LGBTQ persons. And for many companies, changing their EEO and non-discrimination policies was a relatively straightforward undertaking.

Some were already well on their way, having achieved a perfect score of 100 on the Human Rights Campaign's (HRC) Corporate Equality Index (CEI) 2005 Report. In its fourth year of existence by then, this report and the survey that it is built on, was quickly becoming the barometer of LGBTQ inclusion in corporate America. But there were quite a few companies, including New York Life, that weren't quite there yet. The fact that they did not yet have protections in place based on gender identity or gender expression was certainly not lost on me. It was the first thing that I checked on the company intranet as I first began to think about coming out later that same year.

And it has now become one of the first pieces of information that many trans people turn to when they are making the momentous decision to come out at their place of employment. That's how I first found out about it. One of the folks in my support group mentioned it in one of our meetings right around the time that I was contemplating my transition plan. She was checking in on her company and said that this report was very helpful to her in determining what, if any, policy protections were in place for her.

The first report I ever looked at online was the one from 2004. The company came in at a score of 50 out of 100. Unfortunately, I didn't really know what that meant in terms of what policies they didn't have in place at that time because the report didn't go into the level of individual response detail that it does now. But suffice it to say, 50 percent didn't inspire a lot of confidence.

To be fair, every company that has a perfect 100 percent score today didn't start out that way. To get there, they had to embark upon their own journey of equality and inclusion for all of their LGBTQ employees. And New York Life was no different. They were just starting out on their diversity and inclusion work back then and the same time I was beginning my quest for my true self. In a way, they followed a parallel path. My story simply reflects how our two journeys found each other, how they intersected.

Much of the narrative in those days was centered on policy and procedure creation because they were the only metrics that were being put out there to judge how well companies were doing with respect to LGBTQ workplace equality. So, consequently, that's what I found myself thinking about most. Because it was the absence of policies that could protect me from discrimination that could directly affect me—and my livelihood. I wasn't even thinking about transgender-inclusive health benefits, for example. I was much too preoccupied with whether or not I would be fired on the spot if and when I decided to come out.

Trans inclusive policy development was evolving in many companies, and I was hopeful that it would arrive at New York Life in due course. But honestly, that was not my focus at that time. I couldn't have cared less about what questions were in the CEI survey. I was totally consumed with making sure all of my transition plates kept spinning and that I could blend into my workplace as my true self. Activism took a back seat to ensuring I stayed gainfully employed.

It wasn't until a number of months later that an intranet search revealed that, in fact, *gender identity* had been added to their non-discrimination policy. So maybe my coming out actually did have something to do with that after all.

I began to look at the bigger picture of how transgender workplace inclusion was evolving later, when I was actively involved with speaking at other companies and doing consulting work on my own time. My "side hustle" work gave me a much larger perspective beyond New York Life and the insurance industry. I was seeing firsthand how companies in different industries and different cultures were dealing with it in their policy development and internal training. And I saw how the CEI played a role in that development.

It was all happening so fast. More and more companies were getting perfect scores, which meant they were becoming more trans-inclusive, but I was hearing rumblings in the community that some companies were just doing it for "show"—that trans people were still not being treated with the dignity and respect that their policies were supposed to dictate.

Something was clearly missing. It was obvious to me that the policy piece hadn't made it into the actions of the managers and HR representatives who were supposed to enact these policies. That disconnect meant that the possibility still existed for transgender employees to be mistreated by their bosses and their companies.

MOVING FROM POLICY TO PRACTICE

That's how my mantra, "moving from policy to practice," began. As I worked with very well-meaning companies on their transgender workplace inclusion initiatives, it became very clear to me that they were struggling with how to "make it real" in the actions of their managers and HR professionals. The policy piece, they told me, was the easy part. It was the practice piece that would require some thought and initiative.

As I thought more about it and my own transition journey, the first thing that struck me was that how it all went had everything to do with culture. Admittedly, culture was always on my internal radar screen because I had become a bit of a "culture nerd" ever since I took my first organizational behavior class in grad school. I was fascinated by the work of the pioneers in the field, like Edgar Schein and Geert Hofstede, who were among the first to examine how values in the workplace are influenced by organizational culture. So it was a natural first step in my thinking.

But culture change doesn't happen overnight. And the companies I was working with then knew it—and how *macro* a task it really was. At one large advertising conglomerate that was particularly true. I was working with them on instituting a set of transition guidelines that was to be incorporated into the practices of each one of the agencies that existed under their corporate umbrella. And there were several, each with its own "culture within a culture." That was when I first had a conversation about how far-reaching transgender inclusive policies and practices were to the entire enterprise.

One of my clients pointed out that it wasn't "just an HR thing." And he worked in HR! He rightfully pointed out that it cut across every aspect of an employee's interaction with the organization, from talent acquisition, to recruitment, to onboarding, retention, and career development.

And that's why it matters. But how to make it all happen is another story.

Part of the answer lies in cultural transformation. As former HRC president Chad Griffin put it in his preamble to the 2016 CEI, "But we know that policies in and of themselves do not always translate into genuine inclusion of the transgender community. Critical cultural shifts need to take place to foster greater inclusion of the entire LGBT community." The reality for many companies is that the next chapter of the workplace inclusion story will involve focusing on taking the necessary rudimentary steps that will breathe life into their foundational policies. This happens when a company successfully unites its core values and its cultural landscape with these policies and procedures. That's how dry policy statements on the company intranet are transformed into "the right thing to do."

In some respects, New York Life was already there, because its culture had large doses of "the right thing to do" already in it. But also in play was its conservative element, which was a natural byproduct of the business it was in. As I mentioned before, life insurance, by its very nature, is conservative. It is built to be safe and be around for years until the time comes when it's needed. And the company has to take actions to ensure it will be around to honor those promises it makes to its policyholders. Last, New York Life has always been a mutual insurance company which means it is not a publicly traded company. Instead it is owned by every one of its customers. And that is baked into how it conducts its business each and every day.

What I came to understand was that policy and process are wonderful for addressing situations, but the practice piece gets to the heart of the underlying human interactions that are the lifeblood of doing business.

I distinctly remember having a conversation with a roomful of HR leaders at a large consumer goods company headquartered in the Midwest. We were specifically discussing what moving from policy to practice looked like in all of the divisions of the company that they represented. And they were diverse. Some were from manufacturing divisions, where assembly lines and warehouses the size of football fields were common. Others were from office environments where predominantly white collar employees worked.

But despite the rather disparate settings, we had a robust conversation around questions that were foundational to moving from policy to practice: has the manager, and HR for that matter, been properly trained on how to interact with the transitioning employee? Do they understand the basics of what it means to be trans? Are they knowledgeable with the vocabulary used within and in reference to the trans community? Do they simply know what to *say* to a trans-identified person, for perhaps the first time in their life?

Within a short period of time, I filled the conference room white board with their reactions to each of these questions. It was very cool to see how in their responses they were trying to fashion a practical solution to each of their specific workplaces—and to each of their specific workplace cultures.

Each person understood and embraced the belief that success happens when they are able to shift the conversation to what the *practical* application of their trans-inclusive policies look like in the day-to-day workflow of business in their division. They understood that it is language and engagement that address the employee-to-employee and employee-to-customer interactions that form the bedrock of a company's business processes.

When we were finished with the session, and they were sketching out their work plans, it was very obvious to me that they got the key principle I was trying to get across to them: that the practical application of workplace inclusion begins the moment that an LGBTQ candidate first interacts with your company website and continues throughout their employment. Every stage of the employee evolution—from applicant, to candidate, to new hire, to tenured employee—creates multiple touchpoints where their value as individuals and contributors to the company's success can be recognized and affirmed.

Think of it this way: Let's say I'm already out and living as my authentic self in the world and I am looking to make a change in my employer for better opportunity. I would immediately eliminate from consideration any company that isn't already "out" about its recognition and support of its LGBTQ employees. I would also check the aforementioned CEI to see if they show up at all, and what score they have.

And if I came upon a company that had a 100 score that was of interest to me from a professional perspective, I'd explore further. And upon visiting their website, if I see no visible signs on it that there is anybody working there I can identify with, or who "look like me," then I seriously doubt I'd even apply.

Because if the people I see do not express themselves in their outward appearance in the same way—or at least close—to the way I do, then I have a hard time believing I could ever be welcomed there to begin with. In the end, a company's reputation only goes so far.

And I haven't even gotten to any of the face-to-face interactions yet!

Whether it happens virtually or in-person, I would have an expectation that recruiting staff would be comfortable with having a conversation with a candidate like me. That's why language and communication is so important. You can't create a dialogue if you feel like you don't know how.

The same can be said for staff and local management that are involved with the onboarding/employee orientation process. From my perspective as a new employee, feeling welcomed at a new company makes me feel good about a lot of things, especially about the decision I made to join the company in the first place.

It sure made me feel good about my decision to join New York Life. My transition was handled with humanity and respect from the very beginning. And that created an awful lot of good will in my mind. Mostly because they didn't fire me on the spot.

All of that goodwill could have evaporated if they forgot about me. I made sure they didn't. After all the excitement had faded and I settled into my position, I worked hard and made sure that from a performance perspective I didn't slip up. That's not to say that I didn't have my moments of frustration with what was happening with my career post-transition. But that had more to do with me getting a handle on what it was that I wanted to do with the rest of my life, more than it did with New York Life providing internal opportunities for my continued career growth, and the realization that I wasn't necessarily seen as a "high flyer" in my 30s like I was at AT&T anymore.

I do think it would have been different if my transition happened when I was younger. Knowing me as I do, I would have had a much stronger desire to move up the corporate ladder than I did when I came out. Maybe it had something to do with the immense sense of relief I had after I transitioned. It was no less than the culmination of my lifelong struggle with my true self.

The absolute last thing I wanted to do was to seek employment elsewhere. I knew what it was like out in the job market for transgender people. I was fortunate and lucky that things went down the way they did for me. But that was not the experience of the majority of trans people that were contemplating a workplace transition in those days.

I realized that as long as I performed and worked well with those around me that I had a "safe haven" at New York Life. I was not about to test the waters someplace else. Not after all I had been through. I felt I owed the company my gratitude and my service.

But all of that said, it is not to suggest for one minute that I did not advocate, along with my colleagues in NYLPride, for LGBTQ employees to have equal access to any and all career development programs and to be considered for opportunities across business units whether they be promotions or lateral assignments. And that's why no less than *everyone* in the organization has a stake in this work and a role to play in its evolution.

BECAUSE THE GAME HAS ALREADY CHANGED

And lest we forget, the candidate pool is always changing, getting more and more diverse with each passing day. How a company responds to that changing dynamic has everything to do with how well they have prepared themselves as an organization *to meet people where they are* during the recruiting and interviewing process.

While the workplace has been a convergence of many types and generations of people for decades now, it's never been quite like this. For starters, more LGBTQ people, including those who identify as transgender or non-binary are "out" in much larger numbers than they were, say, in the '90s. And what's more, their emergence has led to much greater visibility in society and popular culture. Viewed through this lens, it should come as no surprise that these trends should have an impact in the workplace.

These younger generations of LGBTQ individuals are not as tied to the gender binary of male versus female than the generations that came before them. They have grown up in a space where a much more fluid notion of gender is more widely embraced. They have grown up not thinking of gender as a binary: male or female. Rather, many have embraced the notion that gender is more of a continuum, where the amount of "maleness" or "femaleness" one feels about themself can change from one day to the next. And this can be reflected in their gender expression, which for our purposes here is the external appearance of one's internal gender identity.

These individuals will be arriving at your company with a much different set of expectations than people of my Baby Boomer generation who came out later in life. They will have done the research on your company's non-discrimination policy, they will have looked up your CEI score, and checked to see if you have an LGBTQ ERG. They may even have reached out online to other LGBTQ employees at your company to find out how they have been treated.

A younger trans person once told me that she did exactly all of those things, because even in today's "more enlightened" times she felt very uncomfortable about revealing her history to her prospective employer. And she was very much the activist for our community outside of the work environment. She was concerned that it was all just a "show" on the part of the company she was interested in. She ultimately interviewed with them, but did not come out at work until months later when she felt more comfortable with her coworkers and the company's inclusiveness. She was decidedly not like me, and those of my generation, who came out later in life and were thrilled that they didn't get fired the moment they uttered the word *transgender*."!

And this is a perfect example of what we're seeing among the youngest generation. While being pretty visible with respect to the social issues that affect them before entering the workforce, they have a tendency to go into non-disclosure mode when they seek out employment and arrive at the workplace because they are uncertain about how they will be received.

My friend's story plays into the "meeting people where they are" point I made earlier. And it demonstrates the need for culture to rise up to meet this generation, as opposed to expecting this generation to rise up to change the culture.

WHAT IT REALLY IS ALL ABOUT

The point that I want to emphasize above any other is that there is so much more work to be done. On one hand, when I look at the latest CEI results and see that nearly 700 companies have perfect LGBTQ workplace equality scores it makes me think that so much has been accomplished in the decade and a half that I have been involved in the transgender workplace equality movement. And that's because it has! The needle has most definitely been moved in a positive direction on my community's workplace inclusion journey. But the work is far from finished. The raw truth is the work will *never* be finished. If the CEI can be used as a barometer of progress, it can also be used as a measuring stick for what still needs to be done. It has become a key tool that companies use to grow, to keep the work alive. I've seen it in action at New York Life. Because once we made it to 100, we had to stay there and the CEI facilitated that.

I know I startled many of my colleagues when I let out a shout of joy and triumph from my desk the day I got the news that New York Life had finally made it to a 100 score. All of the members of NYLPride were burning up our email servers that day. Everyone was so proud of what we had collectively accomplished.

And then we set our sights on what we could do next; on what we could do to be a catalyst for cultural change within the organization; on moving from policy to practice.

We never stopped or rested on our laurels. We went about the task of seeing what was next to be accomplished. Because we knew that the work of equality and inclusion never stops changing and evolving because the world we live in never stops changing and evolving. No one ever told us that changing ingrained behavior and culture was easy. But we knew the payoff could be huge. Because we all believed that when you successfully move your culture, you change it for the better.

As I reflect on my twenty years at New York Life I have an immense sense of pride in all of the "firsts" we accomplished as a group, and of how I contributed to them. To be sure, my own personal story adds color and depth to that feeling of accomplishment. And for that I am grateful that I was able to make a difference.

But there is one thing that rises above all of that. And that is how we created an environment—a culture—where it was seen as safe for LGBTQ employees to simply be their authentic selves at work. There were countless stories of people who were out in every other aspect of their lives except at work, because they didn't feel the environment—the culture—permitted it. But then once they heard about and saw how our group was creating change they realized that it really was safe to be their true self at work.

CHAPTER TWELVE
SO, WHAT DO I CALL YOU?

What we've got here is failure to communicate.
~ The Captain, *Cool Hand Luke*

THOSE WERE THE EXACT WORDS SPOKEN BY ONE OF my team members, Margot, when I gathered my team together for the first time on my coming out day at work. The conference room was completely quiet as I stood in front of nearly thirty people who were seeing the real me for the very first time. I didn't have much planned in the way of remarks. All I said to the assembled group was, "This is the real me. Does anyone have any questions?"

After what seemed like forever, Margot broke the silence with her question. I will admit to being taken a bit off guard, but I rebounded quickly to say, "Well, Stephanie, or Steph is good for starters, but I'll respond to just about anything; 'hey you' is fine." Thankfully, my attempt at humor landed and everyone had a good laugh, if not somewhat nervously.

From that moment on, I was always "Steph" to Margot and she never missed a pronoun. And I really appreciated that.

In one way or another for the rest of my career, language, and more specifically how people formed sentences to address me, was something that I always had to think about. There were many moments when I cringed while in the heat of an intense discussion one of my colleagues would fall back on the wrong pronoun. And, worse yet, there were a couple of times (thankfully, only a couple!) when they would revert to using my former name.

Within the first few weeks of my coming out I was misgendered and deadnamed with annoying regularity. To be fair, none of it, as far I could tell, was done in a deliberately malicious way. Regardless, it stung each and every time it happened. For most of the folks I was working with, they had only known me as my former self, so I cut them some slack. They all felt badly about it and would try to correct themselves, all of which I appreciated. But even with that, I had to do my share of politely, yet firmly, correcting those that repeatedly had problems.

To return briefly to "Transgender 101" for a short lesson:

◊ Simply stated, when you *misgender* someone—especially a transgender person—it means that you refer to that person using a word, typically a *pronoun*, that does not correctly reflect the gender with which they identify.

◊ *Deadnaming* occurs when someone, intentionally or not, refers to a person who is transgender or non-binary by the name they used before they transitioned. Generally speaking, this is not very cool to do at all—at any time. Unfortunately, it tends to crop up a lot in the media when a less-than-informed writer is reporting on a story involving a transgender person.

USE YOUR WORDS

Being misgendered *always* hurt. Pronouns are a funny thing. They are among the smallest of words in the English language, but when they are used incorrectly they can cut like a knife. And the cut is deep. That's how it felt to me every single time, whether it was in the office or in some other public setting. When someone would use the wrong pronoun when they were referring to me it immediately knocked the wind out of my sails, momentarily taking my breath away.

When I first came out I will admit to being somewhat sheepish about correcting people. It had much to do with how I was raised—to not make a scene and avoid conflict. As I think back to those times I get angry with myself for not defending myself more vociferously. I had this disturbing tendency to give people the benefit of the doubt. Even at times when they didn't deserve it. And that's on me, not them.

Over time I learned how to correct people in a way that got my point across and ruffled as few feathers as possible. At first, I developed that defense mechanism as a way to deal with whatever misgendering took place at work. I had enough presence of mind to realize that I still had to work with these people. Flipping out at someone who perhaps made an honest slip up wouldn't have served me well. It evolved into a practice that I was able to use effectively outside of the office too. But there were more instances of botched pronoun usage at work, where many people had known me as my former self, than on the outside, where most of the time when people saw me for the first time—like a server in a restaurant—they saw me as a woman.

There was one woman on my team that repeatedly kept using the wrong pronouns, but then in the same breath corrected herself, only to do it again on the very next sentence. She was getting very flustered with her inability to get it right—she was trying so hard. I just stopped her and said, "Take a deep breath and calm yourself. I'm not angry or upset. I know you're struggling and it's okay. Just take a second to think before you start to talk." And from that moment on, with the exception of one or two slip ups in the days immediately following, she was fine. I think my recognition of her having difficulty—and that it was okay—made all the difference.

The basics of proper pronoun usage when interacting with a trans-gender or gender non-conforming person are actually pretty straightfor-ward. I think the thing that gets people flummoxed is the fact that they do not want to embarrass themselves. They get extra conscious about saying the wrong thing to someone who they are meeting for the very first time, perhaps in their life, and they freeze up. I get that. But you do need to move past that. And here are a few tips on how to do that.

1. *Always use a transgender person's **chosen name**.*
2. *Use the pronoun that matches the person's authentic gender.*
3. *If you are unsure, never assume, **JUST ASK!** And what can of-ten create a less stressful setting is if you **first** tell the person what **your** preferred pronouns are.*
4. *Some people use the singular **they/them** to reflect their non-bi-nary gender identity and/or gender expression.*

It's kind of funny in a weird way, but I can tell right away when someone I am talking to for the first time is still trying to figure out how all of this language stuff works. At the heart of their actions I am sure they mean well, but when they keep using different permutations of the word *transgender* incorrectly it sends an immediate signal that they still have some sentence structure work to do. And it's important to under-stand that because the last thing you want to do is to unintentionally send the wrong message.

For example, a trigger for me that someone who may mean well and genuinely wants to be supportive but isn't quite up to speed with how to use the language is when they use the term *transgender* incorrectly. It's a common mistake among many well-meaning allies. At one of my first speaking gigs at a large Wall Street-based company, one of their top executives began my introduction by passionately declaring his support for the LGBTQ community to the 200 or so employees who filled the room. As he turned his remarks to my bio he called me *transgendered* several times and topped it all off by referring to the larger transgender community as *transgenders*. Yikes! And I'm sitting no more than ten feet away from him while he's saying this. I just smiled and nodded my head in appreciation while the little voice inside my head was saying, "Wow, this guy has some more work to do on his language."

The primary English lesson to understand is that the word transgender is an *adjective*. So when we use the word transgender we use to describe:

◊   a transgender *person*

◊   transgender *people*

◊   transgender *individual(s)*

What you *don't say*, or risk being immediately seen by a transgender person as someone who hasn't quite gotten it yet, are:

◊   Transgender*ed*

◊   Transgender*ing*

◊   Transgender*s*

◊   *A* transgender

I have cherished every correct pronoun from the day I came out. That's because I have always viewed it as an affirmation of my authentic self in every conversation I had at work. It helped me cope with whatever insecurities I had about my presentation and about myself. In so many ways, my colleagues' use of the correct pronoun was the gift that always kept on giving.

Understanding all of this "language stuff" can be a daunting task for the uninitiated. It is understandable to a degree that if you do not have a transgender or gender non-conforming person in your life—be they relative, friend, or colleague—chances are you never have thought about any of this before. But it *is* vitally important that you do. Frankly, language is at the center of everything that happens in our world—both inside and outside the workplace. It's how we communicate as human beings. And our human family has expanded to include persons that identify as trans and non-binary. It only stands to reason that our language needs to expand as well.

I have seen this bewilderment firsthand at just about every training I have led. Many attendees, especially those who have never personally interacted with a transgender person before, have expressed frustration to one degree or another over having to learn a "second language" just to be able to have a conversation with a transgender or non-binary person. But it is a necessary building block of the workplace inclusion effort. When you think about it, the existence of a new lexicon of terminology and sentence structure is precisely what we need to communicate inclusively with trans and non-binary people. If you are serious about meeting people *where they are* and relating to your fellow human beings with mindfulness and respect—regardless of how much different they may look than you—then gaining an understanding of what to say and how to say it is critical to your success.

IT'S A GAME OF FOUR DIMENSIONAL CHESS

The concept of language doesn't have to be a hard thing to figure out, but oftentimes we make it that way. And at first glance the transgender and non-binary community may seem like we talk about ourselves and to each other in a language that may seem to the uninitiated like it is a cross between Greek and Gaelic. There was a time that I felt that, as a community, we were drowning in a sea of our own labels. Each faction trying to outdo the other in gaining recognition for their own unique slice of the community's language. But now, I feel very strongly that it's their right to claim that place and the language that accompanies it.

The language we use in the trans community has roots just like any other language. It defines how we present our gender, but more than that, it's a direct reflection of how we *see each other* and *how we want society to see us*. In our struggle to be *seen* as equals in society we also need to be *heard*.

And language helps us do that. It helps me do that. It's the means by which I have forged every relationship I have made since I came out; relationships built on respect and understanding. And it all starts with these four components:

◊　Birth sex
◊　Gender expression
◊　Sexual orientation
◊　Gender identity

I wish I knew about these when I was growing up and wandering through my life too scared to know the truth about who I really was. They can explain a lot about how you feel about yourself. But here's the thing. These aren't just for trans folks. Each one of these exists within every one of us—and in different combinations.

I'd like to impart a little advice that has been shared with me on more than one occasion by my spiritual director, Sister Luisa, when we are talking about a particular issue that I am grappling with. She always tells me to "hold it gently." In other words, don't try too hard to grasp all of this at once. If you've never had to familiarize yourself with any of these concepts before, just recognize the fact that you are starting from zero. And that's okay. There's a lot of pieces to the puzzle and sometimes you have to just sit with them for a while to see how they all interact with one another to create someone like me. And someone like you.

You may have already heard about the "gender binary" and how it is the prevailing wisdom in society with regard to gender. All that means is that in that very black-and-white view of gender "men are men" and "women are women." Two choices, that's it! Hence the use of the word "binary." That construct simply fails to reflect what society looks like today. Think about how *limiting* that is.

What helped me better understand the world of gender that I was living in was to think of gender as more of a *continuum*, with multiple places where one could reside and on any given day. Because that's the reality for many trans and non-binary people. That's how they *experience* their gender.

Think of gender as a subway line in a major city. It winds its way from the suburbs through the business district and inner city neighborhoods before it ends in another suburban area on the other side of the city. It has multiple station stops along the way and it goes in both directions. Now how useful would that subway line be if all it had were two stations—one at either end, nothing in the middle, and only went in one direction? It would be useless!

And that's precisely what the gender binary version of that train line is. It is much more useful and serves society in a much greater capacity when it stops at all the stations and goes both ways. That's what the gender continuum version looks like.

And that's why we need language to describe each of the places along the line where people live.

BIRTH SEX

So when I was born, the doctor more than likely smacked me on the butt, took a look at what was between my legs, and proclaimed to my mom and everyone else who may have been in the room, "It's a boy!" How nice. How *tidy*. If he only knew. What he really should have said was something like, "well, it *appears* to be a boy. We'll see."

Whatever my genitals, or for that matter *anyone's* genitals, looked like should never be the sole determining factor of gender. It's a starting point at best. It is most certainly not the end-all-be-all of gender. Unfortunately, for decades and decades that is how society viewed it and that to a large degree is how we wound up with the gender binary in the first place. Two sizes fit all. Not exactly.

GENDER EXPRESSION

My own journey—and it is most definitely a journey—with the concept of gender expression has been fraught with many twists and turns. For a long time it had everything to do with what I thought the world was expecting me to look like, as I had yet to connect with the soul of who I really am. The textbook definition on the surface is very straightforward; gender expression is the external manifestation of one's gender. In other words, it is what you choose as the outward representation of *you* to the world every day. It's things like the clothes you choose to wear, the hairstyle you choose, and your mannerisms, just to name a few.

And therein lies the rub, at least it did for me. As I began my transition I was still in the process of forging a deeper connection with my truest inner self and it was reflected in how I *expressed* my sense of who I was to the outside world. For a time, I fell back on hold habits of fashioning my appearance around what I thought others expected of me. It's not like I ever left the house looking like a train wreck or anything, it's just that I didn't have that internal compass guiding my decisions. That connection came with time and with me feeling more comfortable with myself.

Case in point: my hair. In the beginning of my journey, it was never long enough. I felt like it just didn't make me look feminine enough. Never mind the fact that millions of women wear their hair short. I couldn't possibly be seen in public without wearing a wig. And what wig did I wear? It was shoulder length, straight with just a little flip at the end, and dark auburn in color. It's what I wore on my first day and for months thereafter. But the thing is that it became the hallmark of my developing my own sense of style. From there, elements of my style, like makeup and wardrobe, began to fall into place with how I *felt* about them. I became much more confident in the choices I was making in presenting myself to society because they were emanating from inside of me. It gave me permission to embrace my own unique gender expression.

SEXUAL ORIENTATION AND GENDER IDENTITY

If it seems like I have been on a journey with each of these dimensions you would be correct. And sexual orientation is no different. Of all these dimensions, sexual orientation may be the one that most people *think* they understand the best. And so did I. It's simply a matter of who you are *attracted* to. You're either straight or you're gay. Not so fast.

As I moved along on my journey it became very apparent that I didn't really understand it at all. I discovered that there's more to it than just the *binary* explanation. For example, I had the pleasure of meeting people who identified as *bisexual*—and were attracted to both sexes. And there are others that I'll leave to the glossary to explain.

For me, I needed a little help from my therapist Margie to really understand what sexual orientation meant to me and, most important, how *gender identity*—my internal sense of my gender—*didn't* play a role in it. We were in session right around the time that I met my wife Mari and somehow the conversation came around to attraction. I guess I was confusing myself because I clearly had feelings for Mari, who identified as a lesbian, but I had been in a variety of past relationships which led me to thinking that perhaps, maybe, I was bisexual. Margie sensed the need to level-set with me. The enlightening conversation went something like this:

> *Margie: "So, back in the day if you saw a handsome guy across the street did it do anything for you, sexually?*
> *Me: "Definitely not."*
> *Margie: "How about when you saw an attractive woman?"*
> *Me: "Oh yes, absolutely!"*
> *Margie: "So let's fast forward to now. You see that same guy across the street. Do you feel anything?*
> *Me: "Maybe a little stirring."*
> *Margie: "Okay, what about the woman?"*
> *Me: "Oh, absolutely—most definitely feeling something for her."*

And that is precisely when the light bulb went on over my head! Margie had just illustrated for me two hugely important things. First, it was pretty clear that I have always been attracted to women (my sexual orientation) and second, in my experience, it didn't change from when I was living as a man to after I transitioned and was living as a woman. In other words, my gender identity, which was always female—hadn't changed.

But here's the thing. Society labeled me *differently*. In society's eyes I went from being a straight male to a gay woman (that is, lesbian) after I transitioned. It was a seminal moment in the timeline of my journey. For the first time I understood how the interplay between gender identity and sexual orientation worked in my own experience.

Over time, as I became more confident in my presentation, I most definitely embraced a decidedly *feminine* gender expression. Thanks to my therapist's intervention, I now have a better understanding of who I am physically and emotionally attracted to—other people who identify as female—and how that really remained the same even as my journey to my authentic self, guided by my internal compass—my gender identity, evolved. As I like to say, I can only do "me" one way, and I have finally arrived at a place where I know what that means.

And that's how all of the variables have played out for me. So far. There exists a certain amount of *fluidity* to much of this. But for me I have reached a stop on the train line where I am very comfortable in my own skin. And I had to get there. I am by no means an overnight sensation.

Gender identity and sexual orientation are *independent variables* of the framework of gender. Just because I'm trans doesn't mean that I'm automatically gay. There are plenty of trans people who consider themselves as something other than having a homosexual sexual orientation.

This one simple phrase should help you out in a pinch:

Gender Identity Is *Who I Am*
Sexual Orientation Is *Who I Love*

DOING THE RIGHT THING

"It's not what you say, but how you say it."

I'm not exactly sure who originally said that, but it really speaks volumes (ouch!) about the underlying truth of how we as humans communicate with each other. On some level we all have heard, in one way or another, about how the majority of communication is non-verbal. I have been in situations where people were saying the correct words, but were delivering them in ways that clearly sent messages to me that they were somewhat less than supportive of who I am.

There have been times where I have been confronted by people who practically spit out the word "transgender" at me, with their bodies posed to lash out at me physically as their faces twisted with rage. Or even worse perhaps, are the times when I have had people who I thought were family or friends deliver that word about who I am in a mocking and sarcastic tone—as if I was just making this all up to attract attention to myself. Right word perhaps, but the delivery was clearly hurtful and *invalidating.*

These examples may seem a bit extreme, but they actually happened. And I hope they bring the point home about how potentially discordant and harmful the verbal and the non-verbal elements can be when delivered this way.

What's even worse, perhaps, is when people do this unconsciously. They are totally unaware of how their delivery of language reveals their internal bias against trans and non-binary people. I've heard stories of my trans sisters and brothers being treated that way in job interviews, where according to one person, "The recruiter seemed to be going through the motions. She knew she had to talk to me. But her body language and her overall attitude made it clear to me that she was just doing this so she could say that they met some sort of quota. She didn't care at all and she sure as hell wasn't about to hire me."

This story just infuriates me. The recruiter, and the company she works for, clearly couldn't care less about treating trans people fairly in the interview process. But what's worse is they are probably telling the world that they are an LGBTQ-inclusive workplace. What's authentic about that? Nothing!

That's why it all comes down to a matter of authenticity. As the examples illustrate, *intent* matters—and it matters a lot. And that starts with being thoughtful and believing in what you are about to say. Using the correct words and non-verbal cues mean little if you are not intentional and believe in your heart what you are about to say.

It's about putting the "Platinum Rule" into action. Coined by Dr. Tony Alessandra in his book, *The Platinum Rule,* it's a different take on the "Golden Rule":

"Treat others the way they would like to be treated."

To put it another way, if you really do want to do the right thing from the start, then set that positive intention in your head and in your heart.

There's a lot to process here, especially if you are trying to wrap your head around all of this for the first time. And as we'll see in the next chapter, your company's culture can play a role in encouraging or inhibiting this, but if all else fails, let your own personal sense of integrity, respect, and grace be your guide.

These points on your moral compass more often than not will always steer you to your true north.

To always doing the right thing.

CHAPTER THIRTEEN
FOR THE CULTURE

". . . people will forget what you said,
people will forget what you did,
but people will never forget how you made them feel."
~ Dr. Maya Angelou

"YOU KNOW, STEPH, I WASN'T REALLY TOO SURE IF I had made the right decision when I first came here. This place seemed very bureaucratic and uptight. But then I saw you, and how you were going about your work, very out, very . . . you. That's when I knew that perhaps I read the company incorrectly and that I would be happy here."

These were the words spoken to me by a cisgender woman who I worked closely with who eventually became my boss for the last two years or so of my corporate life at New York Life. Actually, she shared this story with me twice. The first time, she just came right out and told me when she and I first met at one of the offsite meetings we were working at. She reiterated it when she became my boss and we had our first face-to-face meeting in our new roles.

It really had an impact on me each time she recounted it. It certainly wasn't the first time someone had pulled me aside to have an honest conversation with me about how they supported me. And it certainly wasn't the first time a colleague told me that by just being who I was and being as out as I was, I had made an impact far greater than I could ever realize.

It's not like I went around every day thinking about what I could specifically do to change the culture at the company. Sure, all of the work we did at NYLPride created cultural change, but when I got back to the "day job," it was the furthest thing from my mind.

But this felt different. It really hit home with me because, perhaps for the first time, I was seeing up close and personal what "making a difference" really meant to someone and on such a critical decision in their life.

But to get the whole culture story, I have to take you back to those days before my coming out day when I was in the throes of my planning and my plate spinning. To put it mildly, the culture at New York Life had everything to do with how my transition played out. Sure, there may have been other factors at play, like how I took a proactive approach in its planning, for instance. But even with that consideration, how the company reacted to my coming out and in turn how they worked with me every step of the way had everything to do with its culture. It's unavoidable. Because a company's culture is *everywhere* and it serves as the backdrop for *everything* that takes place there. And here's the craziest part: you may not even be all that aware of its *presence* to begin with. In the beginning, I certainly wasn't.

It isn't invisible, although some parts of it are less tangible than others. And it's not something you necessarily think about every day, either. Especially if you've been at your company for a while. The way I first became aware of the culture at New York Life was when I realized how dramatically different it was from AT&T's.

During the time I was there, AT&T seemed very progressive to me. I'm sure some of my former colleagues that were there then might laugh at that notion. But that's how I *experienced* it. The battle for long-distance market share was raging when I joined the company. From the moment I got there I could feel the pulse of what was happening around me. It was electric, challenging, exciting, and the pace was fast. Suits and ties Monday through Thursday and casual Fridays, which usually concluded at one of the many bars scattered around the area. It was "work hard, play hard" and twelve to fifteen hour days were very often the norm.

I began traveling nationally and internationally on business trips with vendors and advertising agencies. For the first time I had my own corporate card and managed my own calendar and expenses. I loved all of my internal clients and they loved me. I was impressing them and my superiors at every turn. It was intoxicating. I felt like I had jumped aboard a bullet train from a standing start. It was quite a rush. And what cemented it all for me was that I got to work in this amazingly palatial building that looked like it was teleported from the future. And it had a waterfall inside! It was like working on a Hollywood movie set every day.

What I really was experiencing was its culture, from the pace to the physical space that I worked in. All of it represented a vastly upgraded experience from my days in the world of banking. First of all, the banks in Delaware were starting out from scratch culture-wise. Everyone who worked there, with the exception of the executives and senior managers who were transplanted from corporate headquarters, were brand new. Whatever staid and antiseptic culture was present, it was imported from someplace else. So whatever may have been happening with the inner workings of office politics, I was most certainly oblivious to it. Primarily because I hated where I was working and I was too lazy to do anything about it.

It did improve dramatically once I returned home to New Jersey, but banking is banking. In my experience, it was not the most dynamic and progressive of cultures. Quite the contrary. It was very traditional and very male-dominated. The big difference was I was happy. I had a great job, a great boss, and I made that culture work for me. Regardless of how traditionally structured it may have been.

Before I ever arrived at AT&T, how I functioned within that culture taught me the value of proactively managing one's career. Until it didn't anymore.

So when I came to New York Life I did so with that *history* and a mistaken expectation that elements of AT&T's culture existed there as well—including the one about career progression. From the very start it shaped how I interacted with my new work environment. And how I mentally prepared for my transition which was to come five and a half years later.

Hints at the culture were there from the very beginning, such as the building's architecture. It's beautiful, iconic, a masterpiece of neo-Gothic architecture and designated as a New York City landmark. It's everything you need to know about the company in some respects. It stands as a powerful and significant symbol of the company's lasting stability, and as a central figure of its culture, even if it doesn't have a waterfall inside. And anyone I talked to about it in those first few years embraced that significance. It didn't take me long to drink the Kool-Aid, either. I soon viewed our "home office" with the same amount of reverence as my colleagues—and did so for the balance of my twenty-year career there.

Another element of the culture that played into my pre-transition thinking was the "speed" of the decision-making that I encountered. Or more precisely, the lack thereof. Of all the cultural differences I experienced between my former employer and my new one this one provided the starkest difference. AT&T made decisions relatively quickly, which wasn't easy for a company of its vast size. But the ultra-competitive marketplace called for it. New York Life's approach seemed much more methodical, much more cautious. And I wasn't the first person to notice its glacial pace of reaching decisions.

Turns out my coworkers had been dealing with it for years. In more than one meeting I can recall telling my colleagues about my frustration with how long it took a plan or even a memo to the executives to be approved. They would just shrug their shoulders and say "join the club. It's been like that for as long as I've been here." I can remember thinking, "how do they ever get anything *done* around here?" Turns out there was a method to the madness.

What I know now that I didn't realize then is that it's a direct by-product of the company's DNA. Life insurance, by definition, is bought with the long term in mind. So it should come as no surprise that decisions are reached in a very thoughtful and, to some, a protracted manner.

And then there's the whole *old-boy network* aspect of the culture. For those who might be new to the term, the exact Merriam-Webster definition states: "an informal system in which wealthy men with the same social and educational background help each other." And that may have been how it started ages ago, but the version I saw had more to do with a preponderance of men occupying the majority—not all—but the majority of senior level positions throughout the company.

Before my transition, I was actually a part of that network and didn't think that much about the fact that it included me. Of course I recognized it. How could I not? It jumped out at me along with all of the other differences I was noticing between my new company and where I had been. The group I was hired into was small, but there was only one woman in it: my boss' administrative assistant. Post-transition it became more of a real eye-roller for me. Primarily because I was amazed that this artifact of culture from a time gone by still existed in corporate America.

Actually, there was another woman who joined our little "men's club" a number of months after I came on board. Kate was hired sometime after me to oversee the company's fledgling—at the time—intranet. Kate was a generation younger than I, smart, and not afraid to express her opinion. All of which did not sit very well with our boss, Chuck, who seemed to dislike her from the start, which made me wonder why he even hired her in the first place. She was the only woman in our group and nobody seemed inclined to give her the time of day about the plans and ideas she had devised for developing our intranet further. I didn't realize it then, but Kate's experience was providing a glimpse of what I would be dealing with one day on the other side of my transition, which was still four years away.

The only one who really gave her any time and really listened to her was me. We had many lunches and numerous cups of coffee where she would tell me how every time she put a proposal or idea out there it was met with grudging acceptance at best and completely ignored at worst. I really felt a strong sense of empathy for what she was going through because I was in the strange position of hearing the other side of it.

When all of the men were together in another meeting it was clear that there were those who saw Kate as a thorn in their side. I do recall hearing the word *bitch* mentioned from time to time. And how classically old school behavior is that? It was like I had suddenly been teleported into a scene from the show *Mad Men*. Misogyny ruled the day, but I was not going to play. I had my own challenges with getting my internet marketing plan over the line. And besides, I viewed Kate as a friend and I wasn't going to violate that trust.

No one, as far as I could tell, stopped to even consider how bright she was and the new ideas she was bringing to the table. Okay, so maybe she was very direct in her approach, but that she was immediately tagged as a bitch and somebody who was difficult to work with was unconscionable. If a man behaved as she did, he would have been called ambitious.

And what's even worse is that the company—in the form our boss—couldn't get past that to see how talented she was. All he could see was a challenge to the status quo and his own standing in the organization.

He could not see beyond the fact that he would be judged by how well he was able to rein her in, too steeped in the old, but yet to be completely worn out, notion that "that's not how we do things around here" to listen to her. As a result, the company lost that talent when Kate, completely fed up with the entirety of the situation, left and was immediately snatched up by another financial services firm downtown. And in the end, they lost a very talented individual who could have made a difference if she hadn't been subjected to a culture that wasn't prepared to assist her and promote her ideas. What a shame.

WHAT COULD POSSIBLY GO WRONG?

Such as it was, this was my frame of reference as I began to think about what I might be up against transitioning at work. It caused me a lot of anxiety, because any scenario I could think of didn't end well. And it was all a direct result of how I had internalized the company's culture—with a dash of self-consciousness thrown in for good measure. I found that I was at odds with myself *and* my environment.

If I had stopped all of the negative self talk for just a minute, I might have been able to allow the possibility of a much more positive outcome to emerge. Many positive elements of the company culture were staring me right in the face, but I just couldn't see them because my mind was already made up. This was going to be excruciating and I was going to go through with it come hell or high water.

What was lost in all my overthinking was that I worked with an amazingly *collegial* group of people. And it wasn't just the work groups I was a part of. It was everywhere. The fact that somehow escaped my thinking, was that I worked with genuinely nice people. For many of them they saw New York Life as a *family*. And as my tenure at the company increased I, too, felt like I was a part of something bigger than myself. But that fact didn't make me feel any less concerned about the outcome that I just *knew* I was facing.

The other big piece of company culture that somehow eluded me was something the company called its "operating principles." This was certainly not new or innovative. Many companies have them as a way of telling their customers, employees, and potential recruits what they stand for. And in many respects, this collegiality was a direct outgrowth of them. There are three, which formed the pillars of its culture: humanity, integrity, and financial strength. These principles have guided the behaviors of everyone who ever worked at New York Life from its inception in 1845. If I had ever stopped to consider the possibility that they could have a profound effect on how people would react to my coming out perhaps I would have been a little less stressed.

I had already seen these principles in action before. The most telling example being on 9/11 when our chairman at the time, Sy Sternberg, declared our building a "safe haven" and openly encouraged all employees to direct any family members or friends who might have been in lower Manhattan on that terrible day to come and take refuge in our building. The cafeteria, he was quick to point out, would stay open to serve all free of charge for as long as it had to.

And what's more, the very nature of our business was all about humanity and integrity. We insure lives. We protect families. We help people in their time of need—it was in the DNA of the company all along. So when the initial reaction to my coming out was, and I quote, "How can we make this transition as smooth as we can for you?," I should not have been so surprised!

But my *interpretation* of the company's culture or, in other words, how I *internalized* it over the first four years of my tenure is what led me to conclude the only outcome to my coming out would be the worst one. And that's the moral of the story: company culture is a multi-faceted, complex thing. But it's also a two-way street of sorts. You can *choose* how you deal with it, how you interact with it. For example, you can see the culture as limiting your growth or one that is rife with opportunities. And for me it turned out that I viewed it as a little bit of both.

Never give a sword to a woman who can't dance —Confucius

Even though I took the liberty of changing the gender on his quote, Confucius had written the perfect metaphor for how I dealt with the culture over the course of my career at New York Life—minus the sword. There were days when I felt like I was a dancer in a Broadway musical company darting around the culture freestyle and then with it as my partner, riding the crest of the wave of change that I played a part in. And then there were days, many days, where I just felt mired in it, unable to move, like I had two left feet.

My frame of reference had done a complete one-eighty. I was now interacting with the culture as a woman. And that simple fact made a huge difference in how the culture began to push back at me. I saw it and felt it in how I was being treated by some of my male colleagues. How I was always being challenged and sometimes, second-guessed, as if I suddenly lost my abilities of critical reasoning and strategic thinking.

Some just ignored me. In a meeting they would act like I wasn't even there. I was talking, but they were someplace else, as if they could be bothered by my mere existence. I think those instances bothered me the most. I would think to myself "how can you just ignore what I have to say? I worked hard to prepare this, you transphobic asshole!" And that's where I always went first: "They aren't paying attention because they don't want to even deal with me—because I'm trans."

I never thought for a second that it had anything to do with the fact that they saw me as just another woman. And that's on me because I was trying to work through my own feelings of self-doubt and self-consciousness. It wasn't until a bit later in that I realized I was now getting a glimpse at what many of my cisgender female colleagues had been facing for years. It's what made me realize how much culture has to do with the thickness of the glass ceiling.

And I would characterize how I experienced that thickness as more of a cumulative experience in different dimensions. It was one thing to have to deal with the head-to-head challenges and the second-guessing by some of my male counterparts in more meetings than I can count, but it was quite another to see my career come to a standstill. Over time I came to understand that any shot I had at career progression had vanished with my transition. A big part of that was how the culture took its shape in the form of the company organizational chart. There were lots of people at my level and a lot fewer people at the next rung of the ladder; more people fighting for markedly fewer positions.

It was a classic example of the corporate pyramid. The higher up you go, the fewer positions are available. And from what I could tell, it became a game of "who you know" and it looked like mostly men were playing it. I had done that so many times in my career before that I could see it happening from a mile away. I swear I could even smell it. And I was just so tired of it all. I was forty-six years old. Certainly not an old timer, but younger, high flyers eager to impress were beginning to show up in meetings more and more. When I would see how they would twist themselves in a pretzel just to make a point to score points with their boss, and it happened a lot, I would just kind of chuckle to myself and think "I was that person once." I had expended so much emotional and mental energy by keeping my coming out plates from falling to the floor that I had precious little capacity left for the office politics that the culture required.

And in those early post-transition months I didn't really mind because I was so thankful that I was still gainfully employed. I knew what the job market looked like outside the hallowed halls of New York Life, and it wasn't pretty, especially for trans people. I had a young son who would eventually be going to college and I was responsible for paying three-quarters of the bill. I had to provide for him before anything else. I was, for all intents and purposes, a single parent. So I sucked up all of the office crap and tried, sometimes in vain, to keep my chin up and my head held high, rooted in the notion that above all else that was going on around me, I had remained true to myself.

I was also concerned that whatever wave of twenty-first century workplace innovation that had happened passed the company by. There were days when it seemed like I was being teleported back to the '60s or '70s. That's how out of step the culture felt to me. What seemed almost quaint to me as a male in this culture did not seem even remotely acceptable to me now. "Was anybody at all aware of this?" I thought to myself on several occasions. If they were, I didn't see anybody speaking up about it.

And it was interesting to see how my cis female colleagues did their own dancing, too. It seemed to vary based on their rank and longevity. Those at levels lower than mine and with many more years of service than me seemed to take it all in stride. It looked to me like they had become calloused to the behavior of some of the men in charge. By contrast, some of the younger women who had only been at the company for a few years seemed to be much less at ease with the culture. I sensed a lot of frustration about how decisions were reached and how long that took. Generally it seemed like the answers these women gave were all too frequently "by too many men" and "too long." Eyes rolled noticeably in many meetings. Their unease, depending on the particular situation, could be quite palpable.

There were more than a few times I found some of the newer generation of women in the ladies' room crying tears of frustration over not being heard in a meeting or of having their ideas rejected. And sometimes it was women who were much closer in age to me. I felt their pain—as much as I could. The fact is I was a "new" woman in the world of work and was only just starting to see what the landscape was like on the other side of the glass. All of these women had been dealing with this brand of discrimination for years. And the culture allowed it to happen. Some, but not all, of the managers were men and whether it was a conscious thing for them or not, they knew they could get away with their aggressive and abusive tactics.

I often wondered back then, "Where the heck is human resources on this?" I can remember trying to console one female colleague in particular by suggesting that she should go directly to HR and tell them how she was treated. She quickly composed herself and looked at me somewhat bewildered and said flatly, "That's a complete waste of time, they won't do anything." I had no come back for that one.

I had heard through the grapevine and saw in company emails that that area of the company had gone through multiple changes in leadership and structure in a relatively short amount of time, but I always thought that they were the first line of defense in situations like this. But I guess they weren't. At least not yet. And they certainly weren't seen that way by my emotionally wounded colleague. It made me wonder what recourse is there for these women. Or for me, for that matter. At this particular stage of my history at the company, the culture didn't seem to allow for it. As time passed, and our HR area solidified with new personnel and new leadership, I sensed that a greater level of responsiveness existed with processes put in place that gave employees a way to express their concerns or grievances. It was one of the first indicators that told me the culture was shifting—and in a good way.

STEPHANIE BATTAGLINO

These experiences taught me a lot about how culture works inside the walls of a company. How quickly or slowly it moves and what its boundaries are. Or, to put it more succinctly, how far you can push it before it pushes back. And that's where the dancing comes in. If you want to transform something as embedded as culture, it's about how you *maneuver* with it to create the change you seek. Any movement that you believe in requires persistence and a healthy dose of fortitude to keep you moving forward when it seems like there is no light at the end of the tunnel.

My transition taught me that. I just reached a point where I realized I had spent enough of my precious mental, physical, and emotional energy on simply surviving and it was high time to grab the proverbial bull by the horns and start living my life, on my terms. That's what got me out of the muck and mire of being *frightened* by the prospect of my future and instead *relishing* the possibilities that future held for me.

So that was my thinking at the time as it pertained to changing the culture. In the beginning, I wasn't something that I did in a premeditated or purposeful way. I just bought my true self to work every day. It wasn't like I wore a sign taped to my forehead that said "transgender" on it or anything, but I tried as hard as I could to show up and be fully present as "me" every day. If that had some unseen impact on the company culture then so be it.

And that's really how NYLPride was founded.

And that was just the beginning. From adding gender identity to the company's non-discrimination policy, to the executive support we received in the formation of NYLPride, for the first time in its history the company was embracing LGBTQ inclusion in a very visible way. To be sure, we had support from some key executives who embraced the notion that it was time for this to happen there. And we ran with it.

We staged a coming out event of sorts to announce the launch of the group which took place adjacent to the executive suite on the same floor where the chairman's office was. We had low expectations for the turn-out. Really low. But as it turned out, nearly seventy-five people showed up and filled the room. We were floored. Our chairman spoke and said wonderful things about how it was time for a group such as NYLPride to be formed at the company.

Then each one of the founding members took turns speaking to the assembled group, which included many, if not all, of our senior executives. When it was my turn I made a remark about how I thought we'd be talking to ourselves and perhaps some crickets in the back of the room, which got a few laughs. I thanked the senior leadership for their outward show of support and what that meant to me personally. I tried not to cry, but I think the magnitude of the moment was a bit too much for me and I got a little choked up. How could I not? We had all just made history. By creating what we did it sent a powerful message throughout the company to those employees who were not out at work—and there were many—that they were supported and affirmed by the company.

Soon after the meeting, we were marching under the company banner in the New York City Pride March. There may have been only a dozen or so people at that first one, but it was a very emotional day for all of us who thought that we'd never, ever see that day. There's a point on the parade route where you can actually see the New York Life building and as it came into view that first time people, including me, openly wept.

All of us were so proud of what we'd accomplished while at the same time being pretty shocked at how quickly it all seemed to fall into place. From there, we went on to achieve a lot of other accomplishments that helped shape the policies and markets for the company. For example, NYLPride had a hand in the launching of the first-ever LGBTQ target market in the company's history. For years we had known that there were both LGBTQ-identified and straight agents who actively worked with the LGBTQ community and had any number of LGBTQ clients. But the company didn't support their efforts from a headquarters perspective until the target market was launched which allocated funding to helping our agents get a larger slice of the LGBTQ market.

Over the years we added the establishment of domestic partner benefits and transgender-inclusive benefits, which was a journey unto itself. But even beyond that, the one thing that the group did that shocked and delighted me all at the same time was when we got the company to agree to sign on to the amicus brief that was filed with the Supreme Court in support of same-sex marriage in 2015. I didn't think it would pass muster. It meant that New York Life would have to really put its name out there on a document for the entire country and every one of our agents and customers to see. I wasn't sure we had quite gotten there yet. I thought that perhaps we had stretched the cultural envelope about as far as we could by that time. But I was wrong. And I'm so glad I was.

But that's the thing: You never know how close to the tipping point of change you might be until you start to push the envelope. That was the moral of the story for me. You can accept things as they are, or you can seek to make a difference. I am forever blessed to have played a part in all of it and to have experienced it firsthand.

Over the course of my fifteen post-transition years, I had several conversations with colleagues who told me how I was making an impact on those around me and, more broadly, at the company. The thought that I was changing hearts and minds by just being comfortable in my own skin was a real eye-opener for me. Even though I had become very active outside of the company with my trans workplace inclusion activism, when it came to my day job I was always very focused on the tasks at hand. I tried very hard to always keep the two separated. My last role with the company, for the last ten years or so, had its very visible moments, but I never really dwelled on how others were *seeing* me. I was too busy doing my job. So when people would actually stop me and take the time to tell me the difference I was making to them, and to a lot of other people as well, it was very gratifying and humbling all at once. I was making a difference by simply being me. And if it was moving the culture at the same time then I saw that as a bonus.

When I first began in this very outward-facing role, which involved the staging of the company's incentive business meetings for its high-performing agents and field managers, I made it a point to have a conversation with a gentleman who was retiring after many highly successful years with the company. He was the go-to guy responsible for making sure every single aspect, every detail, of these well-received gatherings went off without a hitch. And he did it with a level of class and style that made it seem so effortless.

We were sharing a cocktail at the staff party at his final meeting and I simply asked him, "Jerry, as I begin this job if there is just one thing you could share with me, one piece of advice, what would it be?" He just looked at me, smiled and said, "Just make them feel special, Stephanie." He could have told me many things, I suppose, regarding operational details and perhaps which people to watch out for, but that wasn't his way.

But I knew exactly what he meant and I also knew that my personality was more than up to the task. I took those words to heart at every meeting that I was involved in from that moment on, treating it as if it was a celebration that I was throwing and that every agent and every manager I touched would know how genuinely happy I was for them. It created an energy inside of me that told me it was more than okay to just be myself, to let my light shine. And if the visibility that created moved the culture to be more open and inclusive then that's a consequence I can live with.

I have had my struggles with New York Life's culture. It never moved as quickly as I wanted it to. But, with time, it got there. It has a lot to do with being "patiently persistent." Sure, there were times when I thought I had reached the end of my rope, but I never stopped believing that change could be achieved. If that ever happened I might as well have folded up my tent and gone home.

But through some sage advice, finding and then tapping into my own light, I found the power to just keep on going. I didn't have any other choice. I had reached the point in my own life's journey where most of the spinning plates were no longer teetering above my head anymore It gave me the space to embrace the vision of what a more inclusive culture could look like—and how I factored into its creation.

I held that desired outcome firmly in my mind so much that I actually could visualize what it looked like. It became real because in my mind I had given it life. And it's that vision that kept me going during those times when I thought I was the only one around that truly got it.

"So, you're going to have the surgery, right?"

If I had a dollar for every time I had to deal with the question of surgery, I would most definitely be an extraordinarily rich woman by now. Many—and I do mean *many*—well-meaning and supportive colleagues asked me that in the months after my coming out day. They thought they were being supportive by exhibiting enough interest in my well-being and my future that it just made sense to ask. But however well-intentioned they might have thought they were being, it always landed with a thud and made me wince inside and out.

Depending on how close I was to the person asking, I usually said something like this: "I really appreciate you taking an interest, but it's kind of inappropriate that you ask me that."

Many were shocked at my response. That gave me the perfect opportunity to go right into "teachable moment mode" and tell them that anything that I might be contemplating medically was really none of their business, "I would never walk up to you and ask you if you were going to have gallbladder surgery or if you were planning to have a hysterectomy. I don't think you'd appreciate that very much."

At this point the person who asked the question would practically fall over themselves apologizing. Recognizing that I had made my point, I would say how I understood it wasn't meant maliciously and that it was an "honest mistake" and then move on with the conversation.

It happened enough that it became sort of a reflex action for me. As soon as somebody asked, it was like a switch was flipped in my brain and out came all of the corrective language. In the beginning, as I was still getting comfortable with myself, I would do it rather sheepishly because I didn't want to offend anyone. I was worried that somehow my accepting colleague would turn their back on me if my response was seen as too abrupt. But after a while, my inside voice was like: "Screw that. No one else is going to stick up for me but me, and if people don't like getting corrected then that's too bad."

But it's not like I never had conversations with them about many other things beyond work matters like sports, fashion, and the weather, for example. I always knew when a colleague was really interested in wanting to get to know me better, because they were comfortable enough to ask me about what was going on in the transgender and, more broadly, LGBTQ community. They had a genuine interest in wanting to better understand the issues that my community was faced with. And that opened the door to some very meaningful conversations about how they affected me and what my journey to my true self was all about. And that's a perfect example of what allyship looks like too.

YET ANOTHER PLATE TO SPIN

And a big part of that journey for me was having my gender reassignment surgery, commonly referred to as GRS, at least it was back in

2006 when I had my procedure. In the years since, even the acceptance of that term has changed.

When I first became familiar with what was being used to describe the procedure known in medical circles as vaginoplasty, it was actually called "sex reassignment surgery" or by the acronym SRS. But after a while the community came to view this term, and its derivatives, "sex change surgery," or simply "sex change," as offensive. The term "gender affirmation surgery," is now widely seen as acceptable. That said, the more generic "bottom surgery" is also preferred as well.

But remember: it is never cool to ask! It's none of your business!

So, yes, I added yet another spinning plate to the mix. As if I didn't have enough challenges already. But the truth is that putting *that* plate in the air was something I knew was going to happen all along. I told my ex back in the fall of 2004 that the only way I could do this was to go all the way—which meant GRS.

So it became a matter of *when*, and as it turned out, *how* I could make it happen. For starters, I knew I would have to wait until at least after I came out at work. And back in the fall of 2004 I really had no idea exactly when that might be. So, as with most of the big transition milestones I planned for in my mind back then, I just kept trying to tell myself that it would all work itself out. I convinced myself that I would know when the timing was right to address each milestone, each plate. and move on with my journey.

And as I predicted, the day did come when it was time for me to address planning for my surgery. It wasn't long after my coming out day that I found myself on the phone with my surgeon, Dr. Marci Bowers, discussing potential dates for "my new birthday." Being my usual pragmatic self, I knew that I would need to allow enough time for me to heal and it seemed that the following summer would be the best time for that to happen. My son was going to be away at camp, too, so that made it the logical choice. The date we arrived at was July 7, 2006.

Just like I did in planning when to discuss my transition with my closest colleagues, I created a countdown in my day planner so I could check off each day as my surgery date drew closer. Yet another countdown! And this one began on Day 230! How I lived each one of those days was shaped, to a large degree, by the policies and unique culture of my workplace.

A BRIDGE TOO FAR

As each page of my day planner was torn out, all of the logistics of my trip to Trinidad, Colorado, which is where Dr. Bowers was practicing at the time, fell into place. My flights, car rental, where to stay after I got out of the hospital, all of it. Except one very important thing: how to pay for the procedure and the hospital stay. You see, back in early 2006, the vast majority of companies in the United States *did not* have transgender-inclusive health benefits. And New York Life was no different. But I didn't know that yet.

I was blissfully unaware that my GRS was *not* covered, as in I would have to pay the approximately $20,000 price tag out of my own pocket somehow. I actually just assumed that with all of the positive movement that was happening within the company on the LGBTQ front that surely there were already provisions in place in our company health benefits to pay for it. I could not have been more wrong.

I came face-to-face with that reality one day in the spring of that year. I had gotten a visit from our department's budget and administration officer, George. He was actually just stopping by my office for a chat. As we often did, we talked about our kids and any number of other random subjects. The conversation found its way to the topic of my surgery. It had become common knowledge around the office, as I had told my management months earlier what my plans were so they could make plans for coverage while I was away recovering.

As we talked about my travel plans I casually asked him, "Do you happen to know if my procedure is covered in our benefits?" He thought for a minute and said, "You know, I really have no idea. Why don't we take a look on the company intranet. It should be listed somewhere in the benefits section.' As we sifted through the pages together I couldn't find it mentioned anywhere, and any searches that I tried came up empty. I started to get more than a little nervous. Finally, I found the list of excluded procedures in our benefit plan.

I had heard from other trans folks that it is there where the "rubber meets the road." If *gender reassignment surgery* or similar words to that effect appeared there that meant it was not covered and you were out of luck and on your own. My heart raced as I clicked open the document. It didn't take long for me to find it, as big as life, included in the same paragraph with other "elective" procedures like breast augmentation and "cosmetic" plastic surgeries like nose jobs. I stared at the screen in horror as my heart sank. My inside voice screamed, "This isn't an elective procedure!" I looked up at George as tears started to well up and run down my cheeks and muttered, "It's not covered. Oh my God, it's not covered!"

My mind started racing and I was suddenly panic-stricken. Tears really started flowing and I began to sob uncontrollably. The notion that, after all of this planning, I wouldn't be able to have the surgery was completely freaking me out. The reality that this was not going to happen slapped me in the face. My dream was crashing and burning right before my very eyes! As I tried in vain to pull myself together I felt so bad for George. He had just stopped by to shoot the breeze and now he had a front-row seat to this major meltdown I was having. I kept apologizing to him as he tried to console me and fumbled for the tissue box that was on my desk. After apologizing profusely (after all, it wasn't *his* fault that the company didn't cover the surgery!) he made sure that I had sufficiently composed myself before heading back to his office to finish out what had turned into an unexpectedly bizarre day for him I am sure.

In the days that followed I frantically scrambled for a solution to my problem. As it turned out, I had options that I was completely unaware of. One was an old life insurance policy that I had completely forgotten about that I had taken out on myself when I was married. It turns out I could take out all of the money that had built up in it. My sister is the one who deserves the credit for bringing that one to my attention—and talking me off the ledge in the process.

The second source was my 401k. A friend at work who had just done it told me I could take out a loan against a portion of the balance and then pay it back over time. The paperwork for both was pretty straightforward, and within a few weeks the funds to pay for everything were in my bank account. Crisis averted.

But here's the thing: Being a white trans woman of privilege, even as clueless as I was to their availability at first, I was in a position to take advantage of these options to solve my funding dilemma. The reality for *most* trans people is that they *never* have access to these options, because they are either unemployed or under-employed in a job at a company that does not offer them health coverage or benefits that cover gender-affirming procedures. And you can't have access to a 401k or have enough discretionary income lying around to pay for a life insurance policy when you don't have a job.

Among many other things that have to change for the transgender and non-binary community, this is pretty damn close to the top of the list.

A LIVING AND BREATHING PARADOX

New York Life's culture presented quite a conundrum to me from the time when I came out to the days leading up to my last day in the office before my surgery. On one hand, the company could not have reacted to my transition with more compassion. If the culture was at all different than what it was, I could have easily found myself out on the street in the blink of an eye. "We want to make this transition as comfortable as we can" could have very easily turned into "pack up your things and get out" if it were not for the humanity of its culture.

Everyone who I worked with in my department for the most part, were very supportive. And in many ways, that didn't surprise me either. The collegiality of the culture was something I marveled at from the very beginning of my time there. Many times during those first few years I would often say to myself, "Why are these people all so nice?" Turns out, I consider myself very fortunate that they were. I've heard too many horror stories from other trans people that were exactly the opposite, where they had to deal with openly hostile and verbally abusive colleagues

Many of them seemed to be artifacts of the cultural setting. For instance, there was one trans woman who worked on an assembly line in a tractor factory who had to endure insults from her fellow employees on the line at every turn. That doesn't come as a big surprise given the "macho" environment—and culture—that surrounded her on the factory floor. It wasn't until she filed a grievance with her union that they finally stepped in to call a meeting and essentially read the riot act to all of the employees on her shift. The union, of course, had to work in concert with the company's HR representatives, but somehow they made it work and the message was received loud and clear. The taunting stopped and over time she was able to create a positive connection with her coworkers.

But on the other hand, the policy side of things, which as far as I was concerned was also a reflection of the culture, troubled me. The lack of trans-inclusive health benefits was a big red flag. It seemed so antithetical to all of the outwardly supportive behaviors that I had experienced. I tried to reason it away by saying that their policies had not yet caught up to their culture. But the reality was these policies were a *byproduct* of that culture. As a result I was confused and more than a bit frustrated. It stuck out to me as a real disconnect between the two.

Apparently it was a bridge too far. And it remained that way for several years after I had my procedure. I learned that sometimes, after all of the "pushing of the cultural envelope," that the culture can push back. And do so in ways that can be infuriating. And that was a battle that I had to put aside for the time being, as my upcoming surgery needed my full attention.

In the days and weeks leading up to my surgery this cultural puzzle became even more contradictory. But, I must confess, in a way that worked to my benefit. That piece involved my getting short-term disability to cover the eight weeks that I would be out of the office recovering. To make sure that did not become a problem, I called in a favor. I placed a call to Ann, the HR VP who had handled the bulk of my transition to tell her that I "just wanted to make sure that I didn't hit any unexpected snags" with receiving my benefit. She assured me she would facilitate everything and for my entire time out of the office I never missed a paycheck.

That's another area where trans folks can get screwed by their "supportive" employer. The company will be happy to give them time to recover, but they have to use whatever vacation and personal time they have accumulated to do so. And that means that in most cases the person having surgery has to come back to work far too early to allow for a proper recovery. My experience, which only required me to make one phone call, taught me a valuable lesson in the importance of advocating for myself. My wife Mari, had a similar experience after her surgery, but it involved an unexpected twist. Before she left the office, she had checked with her employer to make sure that her recovery time would be covered by short term disability. She was assured that, yes, she had nothing to worry about.

Fast forward to two weeks after her procedure. She was at her mom's house recovering and out of the blue received a call from her short term disability provider informing her that she was not covered! She immediately went into self-advocacy mode and would not let the representative off the phone before getting a commitment that—yes—she *was* covered and that whatever paperwork from her surgeon was needed would be sent over right away. She did not hang up the phone without first getting a commitment from the provider that she would be receiving her benefit. In the end, she did get it, but not without having to grab the proverbial bull by the horns to make it so.

A CELEBRATION FOR EVERY OCCASION

As the days on my day planner dwindled down to the single digits, I found myself very involved with contacting all of my internal clients and putting the finishing touches on my back-up coverage plan. It made my last day in the office somewhat anticlimactic because I had everything in place beforehand. I made the rounds and touched base with a number of my colleagues for what I thought was one final time before heading out. Turns out, there was a surprise birthday celebration that everyone in my department and I were invited to. This was just another example of the culture at New York Life.

We celebrated everything—bridal showers, baby showers, birthdays, anniversaries—with cake, ice cream, pizza, you name it. We even had a "send off" celebration in appreciation for a number of individuals who were part of a large layoff that occurred while I was there. I remembered it as being more than a surreal experience. I had never experienced anything like that before. These were not voluntary. People were given severance packages and given a last date of employment and that was it. But such was the culture at New York Life, and I embraced it wholeheartedly.

So one day we all assembled in one of our conference rooms for a coworker's big surprise birthday party—but there was also a surprise for me! I was more than flabbergasted, and just a bit embarrassed. Our administrative assistant, Sophia, a longtime employee at the company, the amazing organizer of all of these celebrations, a huge ally of mine, and the embodiment of what the New York Life culture was all about, decided to include a "good luck with your surgery" element to the party. I even had my own cake. Everyone was so sweet. They all wished me the best with hugs and well wishes. I was overwhelmed by all of the heartfelt sentiment for me. And, of course, I cried.

Less than a week later I was in Trinidad, Colorado with my dear friend Diana, who came out from her home in Ohio to be with me. In the years before I met my wife Mari, and for a time thereafter, Diana was the closest person to me in the entire world even though we lived ten hours by car away from each other. She was my spiritual companion and best friend, which is what I referred to her as in the documentary that chronicled the entire affair.

I was the subject of the second episode of an unfortunately-titled documentary series called *Sex Change Hospital*. It aired in the United Kingdom and the United States on the Women's Entertainment ("We") network in 2007, and in re-runs for a few years after that. It just kind of happened, really. My surgeon told me that there were going to be some "media interests" in town when I was scheduled for surgery, and if it was okay, she'd have them get in touch with me. From that rather understated introduction what followed were a couple of months of me videotaping my life before I left for Colorado.

Upon my arrival and then again after I finished my recovery, I was followed around by a film crew. It was invasive to some degree, but they were great guys and I honestly felt like telling my story in this way would help others who were contemplating a similar journey. In the end it turned out really well. I never thought it was exploitive in any way, just my story, honestly told. I even had a screening party at my home for a large group of friends to celebrate its release.

Once I got back to New Jersey my recovery time went pretty smoothly for the most part. My sister insisted that I stay with her for a couple of weeks before heading back to my own home. She wanted to make sure she was there to look after me if anything unforeseen happened. Very "big sisterly" of her and I was more than grateful.

It was during this time that the NYL culture made an appearance in my surgery timeline again. I told my department head that I would check in with her at some point after I got home to let her know how I was doing. After we caught up, I mentioned to her that I was on track to come back to the office during the last week of August.

She replied, "Just stay out for another week. We are all going to be out of the office at off-site agent meetings, so come back after Labor Day." Gee, an extra week of just hanging out and getting better? Sure! Collegiality was at work once again.

I did eventually get back to work and my re-entry back to the daily grind was pretty uneventful—except for one very important thing. As was stipulated in my agreement with the HR VPs, I could now use the women's bathroom! Yippee! Actually, it was pretty uneventful the first time I went there, no news flashes across my department or anything. I just went there to do what every other woman has done in the ladies' bathroom for centuries—go to the bathroom. Not hugely exciting, but no less liberating for me.

I was only back at work for a few days when I found myself—surprise—in the bathroom when something happened to me that has stayed with me ever since. I was washing my hands somewhat absentmindedly when another woman who I had never seen before walked in and before she went into the stall, she just stopped, looked me in the eye and said, "You are so brave." I was not, in any way, anticipating that. But I could just feel how sincere her words were. For one of the few times in my life, I was at a loss for words. All I could muster was a thank you. And we went our separate ways.

Maybe it was the personification of the culture on display right before my eyes. Or maybe she was the physical manifestation of the divine sent in to reassure me that I was going to be okay and that I could face anything head on and triumph over it. The reality is I'll never really know for sure. At first glance, it might seem like a small, insignificant event in my timeline, but I can assure it is everything *but* that. It became a source of strength for me that I drew on for years afterward. And if that's what culture can do then I am down for it all—every bit of it.

CHAPTER FOURTEEN
THE SIMPLE TRUTH

I always wondered, 'Why somebody doesn't do something about that?' Then I realized I was somebody."

~ Lily Tomlin

THERE JUST AREN'T THAT MANY TRANSGENDER PEO-ple out there in the United States. We need all of the allies we can get. And that journey begins with my lesbian, gay, and bisexual brothers and sisters. All of us who reside under the LGBTQ umbrella have an obliga-tion to support each other, because support and respect for each other's journeys should begin in our own community. And if you are thinking that is some sort of slam dunk you'd be sadly mistaken.

Unfortunately, I have encountered my own share of resistance and at times outright hostility from gay men, for example. It's really kind of strange. It's like there's no middle ground. In my life experience, some of my dearest friends and closest confidantes have been gay men For many of them, I was the first transgender person they ever met and they sincerely wanted to know more about what my life, and my decision to transition, was like. They were part of my support structure and they wanted to learn so that they could be a better friend to me and an ally to all transgender people.

Recently, I attended a gala for a large California-centric non-profit in Palm Springs. Hundreds of people were in attendance. It was quite the affair. My "date" for the evening was my dear friend Tobi who, it just so happens, is a trans man. He and I were a part of a small but mighty contingent of trans people in attendance. As Tobi and I made our way around the cocktail reception meeting people and visiting with friends—some of whom were super supportive gay men—it was fascinating to see the looks I was getting from many of the other gay men. Narrow gazes, furrowed brows, and outright stares were common. Not exactly what you would call welcoming non-verbal cues. I doubt that Tobi, who has lived in the area for years and is more than familiar with the local LGBTQ scene, even noticed.

I'll never know what is going on in their heads when they do that, and I don't ever want to know. I suppose for some they think it's their community and trans people have no place in it. The trans community, for my money, has always been seen as the outlier, the proverbial "red-headed stepchild" who is always picked last on the playground. Are we somehow just too weird, too "out there" for their sensibilities? It infuriates me.

I am who I am, and if for some reason it causes that reaction in you then perhaps I wouldn't want you as a friend, or ally, to begin with. Over the years, I have engaged in debate with some of my gay friends over how our coming out stories have many similarities. Like making the life changing decision to leave the closet behind, to embrace our truest self; it is something we all share, but somehow, for some, they either don't recognize it or don't care to.

The need for understanding who transgender people are and the challenges they face—both inside the LGBTQ community and in society—is as great, if not greater, than it has ever been. As younger and younger generations of trans people emerge, the greater the need to understand their journeys and really listen to their stories. And it's not like it's hard—it's a mouse click away on the internet.

I have had many instances with my colleagues where they have sent me articles they have found that they thought I might be interested in reading. I love that. One of my colleagues and friends, Alex, was particularly adept at doing this. It seemed like every few weeks, or when a particular hot-button issue for the trans community was being discussed in the media, an email from Alex with a link to the story would show up in my inbox. He would always attach a little note to go along with the story link like, "Hey, I found this the other day and I wanted to make sure you saw it," "This is really important!," "Wow, I didn't know this was going on with transgender people," or perhaps the one I liked getting the most—"Can we talk about this?" Alex was one of my biggest allies for years and what I loved about getting these stories was that it not only showed he cared, but that he was open to learning more.

And what's more, when I thanked him for sending it to me we would actually sit for a few minutes and talk about whatever the topic was. Most times these were quick on-the-run conversations because we were both busy, but he made the time to engage with me and that's really the point. He probably doesn't think much about these short talks we had, let alone remember them, but they meant the world to me. In his own way, Alex was putting his vulnerability on display to me. And that takes a lot of character to do that as far as I'm concerned.

And many times that vulnerability means admitting that this is all new and that you need—and want—to learn. That happened with one of the executive sponsors we had for NYLPride. He never sponsored an LGBTQ employee resource group before, and when he sat down with us for the very first time he let his vulnerability lead the conversation.

"Look, I'm a straight white guy. I have no idea what any of you have been through in your lives, but I want to learn. I want you to teach me, so that I can better advocate for you and for the group inside and outside of the company."

We all looked at each other somewhat dumbfounded by his candor. But he was sincere and we knew it. There's an element of courage in that display of vulnerability. And trust. He trusted us enough to be completely candid with his lack of knowledge and genuine intent. There is a valuable lesson in that story for anyone who wants to be an ally to the transgender community. It's okay to take the risk, because we, more than anyone, know what that feels like.

He went on to be an amazing sponsor and ally to the group and to me personally. I would often interact with him and his wife at large company incentive business meetings I was involved in later on in my career. Their very public show of support of me meant more than they could ever realize.

And I quickly realized I could not expect that level of engagement from senior management or every one of my coworkers, for that matter. Because at the end of the day, we all have our jobs to do. That's why we are all there in the first place. My being transgender was not the lead story. It may have been for a few weeks after my coming out day, but that faded fairly quickly. And a big part of that was how I carried my "transness" into my workplace. It's not what I led with because, quite frankly, it was secondary to the work. I showed up as "me" every day. I didn't have to walk in the door every morning with the trans flag wrapped around me for people to know who I was. They had no doubt heard a version of my story by then. And that was enough for me.

SO I'M AN ALLY ALREADY?

I think people are of the opinion that becoming an ally is some arduous task. That you have to really work hard to become worthy of the term "ally." If that was your expectation, I'm sorry to disappoint you. There is no six-week training course. There are no final exams. You don't have to write an essay and submit it to the National Transgender Ally Association (NTAA) to become certified. Spoiler alert: there actually is no such organization.

It simply starts with you and your willingness to be vulnerable and to be human; to be comfortable with the fact that you don't know everything. And by the way, who does? And most important, it's about realizing—and taking comfort in—the fact that there isn't just one way to be an ally. It's not like you have to put on some sort of uniform that magically transforms you into an ally. Make it work for you. Let your ally journey carve out its own path. And if the uniform idea still seems like a good idea, then go for it.

For example, take one of my dearest friends at work, Jim. I couldn't ask for a more supportive and honest ally. In the entire time we worked together he never once hesitated to ask me a question about how an issue the trans community was facing was affecting me. Or in wanting to sincerely better understand what my journey was like. He was always my friend, before he ever became an ally.

It wasn't until one day while Jim and I were having one of our frequent impromptu chats in his cubicle that I realized this. I was talking about an upcoming event that NYLPride was having when it hit me. In the middle of the conversation I just stopped and said to him, "You know, Jim, you are an *ally* to the transgender community."

To which he responded, "What's an ally?" So for the next ten minutes or so I explained to him what it meant to be an ally of the community and that everything he was doing supported that. He was a bit dumbfounded by all of that. I was going on about what an awesome ally he was and he really had no idea that he was in the first place. He thought he was just being my friend. Which I explained was amazing, but that there's another element to it that he hadn't even thought of.

That's when I asked him if he wanted to join NYLPride, the LGBTQ employee resource group. His response didn't surprise me. "But I can't, I'm not gay." That's when I explained that we actually have more straight allies in the group that we have LGBTQ persons. And that it's like that for many other ERGs in other companies, too. At that point he said, "Sure, sign me up!" And after that he proudly displayed a small rainbow flag and assorted other NYLPride paraphernalia in his cubicle.

There's a couple of things happening in this conversation that are important. The whole point of being a straight ally is the most obvious one: you don't have to be gay or trans to be one. The root of being a straight ally is that you are, of course, straight to begin with. Second, he displayed his allyship to everyone around him by having the rainbow flag on his desk. I have encountered many people who will swear up and down that they are allies of trans and LGTQ people but if you looked in their office, you'd never know. This, of course, begs the question "So are you really an ally if you are in the closet about it?" To my way of thinking, that answer is a resounding "no."

We, as in myself and my fellow NYLPriders, found out that some straight colleagues were hesitant to express their visual support at some of the initial events that we had because they didn't want the public to think they were LGBTQ-identified. As we approached our first New York City Pride March as a group we all knew that since the membership of NYLPride was still in its infant stages, we would need a robust showing from our straight allies. But how to defuse the concern about being seen as gay?

I'm really not sure who came up with the idea, but it was nothing short of brilliant: buttons that read "straight but not narrow." And it worked! And it stuck around for years thereafter because it gave our allies a way to identify themselves as straight, and at the same time visibly proclaim their support for their LGBTQ colleagues. It was a creative way to disarm the fear.

And all of this begs the question, "Are you an ally with a small 'a' or an ally with a capital 'A'?" In other words, how committed are you to standing with me—or any other trans person for that matter—arm-in-arm, in solidarity, to ensure that together we move the needle for trans equality and inclusion? How willing are you to put yourself on the front line and stand up for what's right for trans people everywhere? I can't make that decision for you. All I can do is present the facts and the reasoning behind them. The rest is up to you. And I understand this might all seem like a serious commitment, a heavy lift, for you. That's because it is. Anything worth fighting for usually is.

And it all boils down to "teaching moments." I don't know when they will happen, or where, but I can assure you they will. These are the moments when you will be faced with a situation that will require you to step up and be seen and heard as an *Ally*. How the situation presents itself to you is irrelevant. How you deal with it is everything.

Before speaking at a client company event I was having lunch with the leaders of the LGBTQ employee resource group that sponsored my talk. As we ate and talked the conversation came around to allies and that's when I was told a story about a manager at their company who displayed serious *Capital A* Ally behavior. One of his employees had recently transitioned and was experiencing an "issue" with one of her male colleagues. Evidently, he was not being very respectful: misgendering her and saying disparaging things about her to other employees. The manager got wind of this from one the other workers in the unit and quickly pounced. He brought the guilty party into his office and made it very clear to him that there was a policy prohibiting his behavior and that it would not be tolerated.

And here's the kicker: as soon as he was finished dressing him down he asked the trans woman to come to his office so that her colleague could apologize in person. Now I get it that this person was a manager, and by virtue of his job description was handling a situation that required his immediate attention. But the message that his actions sent to the rest of his group might very well be the larger story. The ERG folks told me he is now a member of the group—he wasn't when all of this happened—and proudly displays a rainbow flag on his desk and marches with the group along with his wife at their local Pride march.

Just think for a minute if that situation that the manager addressed turned out completely different. Imagine for a moment if, despite the company policy specifically prohibiting this behavior, the manager did nothing and allowed the abusive behavior to continue. And what if that happened and he still claimed to be an ally and a member of the company's LGBTQ ERG? That's beyond hypocritical, that's dangerous. Specifically, it's dangerous to his trans employee who faces the possibility of having to deal with a toxic work environment. His failure to take a stand, to do his job, sends a horrible message to all his employees that it's okay to be disrespectful and perhaps even threatening to a coworker that simply makes you feel uncomfortable. As one of my old bosses used to say, "silence condones." Or, As Dr. Martin Luther King, Jr. once famously said, "In the end, we will remember not the words of our enemies, but the silence of our friends."

I was told another story at another company that reinforced my faith in our allies. This one was about how a colleague came to the defense of one of her transgender team members that she happened to be friends with. It seems as though someone from another department came into their group to "see what all the fuss was about with the new 'company transvestite.'" He continued by using just about every inappropriate word that is out there to describe how he felt about this person.

Her friend was outraged and lept to her defense. As the story goes she got up in his face and made it very clear to him that this behavior and language would not be tolerated—that it was wrong and offensive and that he needed to "get himself right." She was pissed. And angry. And promptly reported him to HR after she escorted him out of that area of the building. If that's not *Capital A* behavior then I do not know what is. In each of these instances, people who called themselves allies of the trans community moved up to Advocate status. Each of these people, in their own way, made a clear choice. They made themselves be *heard*— loudly and proudly—without any prompting. They simply reacted with a level of personal integrity that took them from *Ally* to *Advocate*. By their words and by their actions they stood with their trans colleague—and the entire transgender community to creating positive change and make a piece of the trans equality narrative wholly their own.

CREATING RIPPLES

I have learned that by doing all of these things these advocates are reinforcing what is perhaps the biggest point of advocacy work in the first place: *our voices make a difference.*

When we raise up our voices we raise up the voices of those who we stand for and stand with. And when we do that we create new and vibrant narratives. Suddenly, our collective voice has grown and can now be heard in places it may never have been heard before. And that's how change happens. Sure, there may be push back, there often is. But that's what happens when you stir up, as the late congressman John Lewis called, "good trouble."

Think of it this way. You are on a lake out in the country and it is very still and quiet. There is no wind. The lake resembles a sheet of glass. Suddenly, it begins to rain very gently over the lake. As each individual raindrop falls and hits the placid water a ripple extends out from its center.

Think of that as your voice.

As more raindrops—more voices—hit the water, more ripples roll out over the water. As the number of raindrops multiply, so do the number of voices and the ripples they create begin to intersect in a crosshatch pattern that covers the entire lake. All of these *ripples*, telling their own unique tales of how they stand with the trans community as agents of change form a collective voice that is much larger than the sum of its parts. This voice has the power to reach more ears and change more hearts and minds than the trans community could ever reach by itself. That's how movements begin.

And that's how we achieve the change we seek in the world—*together.*

EPILOGUE

*I may not have gone where I intended to go, but I think I have ended up
where I intended to be.*
~Douglas Adams

IT HAS BEEN QUITE A RIDE.

I have made it to the other side of what I believe I set out to do when
I spun that very first plate into the air fifteen years ago: to find my truest
self. Everything else that has happened to me in my professional life as
well as my personal life has flowed from that first flash of authenticity.
Whatever success I have had or goal I have achieved since then can be
traced back to that moment when I—finally—began to believe in myself and live my life on my own terms, not what I thought someone else
wanted me to be.

Like so many of my trans brothers and sisters, when I took that
first step toward authenticity I knew that I was embarking on a journey,
but I had no idea what the finish line looked like. Being somewhat of a
pragmatist, all I could see were the many real and imagined barriers that
stood in the way of my happiness. And they were mountainous in size.
I had no idea how to climb them or get around them. But I knew I still
had to *confront* them. If I had any hope of surmounting them I had to

first *embrace* them. So I did. And with a lot of help from a lot of people who cared about me, I found my way.

With nose pressed firmly to the grindstone, I soldiered on solely focused on the tasks ahead of me, blind to the bigger picture of the progress I was making toward my goal. The internal motor that God put inside of me may have slowed from time to time, but it never once stopped as I pursued—without reservation—my authentic self. It's like I was climbing a mountain in the fog. I couldn't see how far up I was until I stopped long enough to notice, in the momentary break in the clouds, the valley below disappearing from my view. And there were certainly enough times when I lost my footing on the climb, but somehow— through my own perseverance and the support of those around me, I avoided falling all the way down.

A funny thing happened along the way. I found a whole new group of sisters that embraced me for who I am and in so doing enlisted me in their quest for equal and fair treatment in the workplace. The experiences we have shared, together and separately, have deepened my understanding of their struggle and have forever bonded me to their cause. It is an honor and a privilege to stand in solidarity with them.

And I found my happy place too. I suppose leaving the corporate world after four decades and moving across the country has a lot to do with that, but it also has everything to do with finding love and companionship. I am beginning a new chapter of my life that is rooted in the type of happiness that can only come from finding love and companionship. Thank you for that, Mari. And I have learned that I have just as much of a right to that happiness as anyone else, especially my trans and non-binary brothers and sisters.

New chapters mean new beginnings and everyone has a right to experience that if they so choose. That's how you discover things about yourself that you never knew existed. Like being an author, for instance.

I always knew I had something to say, some would even tell you that I have never been at a loss for words, but I wasn't ever sure I had enough to span the pages of a book. Apparently, it turns out I was wrong.

There is more work to be done, and so I have only just begun. There are so many stories and so many voices inside and outside of the workplace that need to be raised up. There can never be *too many* voices speaking truth to power, challenging those government, business, and religious institutions that seek to compartmentalize and marginalize communities of people just because they are different.

The sky is truly the limit. I can say without a hint of hesitation that, despite the roller coaster ride, I loved my time in corporate America. It enabled me to grow as a professional and it shaped the human being that I am today. I am living my authentic life. I am ready for the next chapter of my life and the chapter after that—whatever they look like. I am excited for what lies waiting for me just around the corner from where I am right now. And I'm taking you along with me—because it's no fun if you can't share it.

ACKNOWLEDGMENTS

Writing a book is hard. Writing a book during a global pandemic makes it even harder. Writing a book is also a journey, at least it was for me. It was a journey that began shortly after the Pulse massacre in June of 2016. The book I set out to write back then is most definitely not the book you have in your hands right now. So much in my life and in our world has changed since then. As I have evolved so has what I have chosen to write about.

Making sense of all of it and being my trusted guide throughout the entire journey has been my coach, my publisher and my friend, John Peragine. He and his wife Kate Schantz Peragine have always believed in me as a person first and an author second and for that I am eternally thankful. Your belief, your perseverance, and your friendship have made me a better writer and for that I am forever grateful.

My wife Mari has quite simply been my rock throughout this entire project. Her thoughtful perspective and her uncanny ability to get me out of my own head is beyond a blessing. Thank you, babe, I love you.

And a very special thank you:

To my son, Andrew, words can hardly express my love for you and my admiration of your courage and strength in walking this journey with me. You will always be my hero. I love you, pal.

To my sister, Betty, whose steadfast love and support has never wavered. You are the best big sister ever. I love you.

To my spiritual director and friend, Sister Luis Derouen, whose calling to serve the transgender community has taught me so much about faith and my relationship with God. Bless you, Sister.

To my therapist and friend, Margie Nichols, PhD and all of the terrific staff at the Institute for Personal Growth, you were there for every plate I insisted on spinning and every meltdown. The journey to my true self would not have happened if it weren't for the path you helped me create.

To my dear friend and brother Michael Todd, you were one of just a handful of people that saw firsthand the butterfly emerge from its cocoon. Thank you for helping me navigate me.

To my colleague and partner in crime at New York Life, Bill Flanagan, you had a front row seat to a lot of what I have written about—the highs, the lows, the hard times, and fun times too numerous to mention. You are more than just a friend and an unflinching ally, you're part of the family. I love you, man.

I want to thank every cis woman that I ever worked with. Your friendship and camaraderie meant the world to me. I learned more from each of you and our conversations than you can possibly realize. It's an honor to be counted among you.

To Scotty, Shawn, and Jenna, thank you for trusting me with your own coming out stories. Your individual acts of courage are inspiring. I am beyond grateful for being given the privilege of including your words in this book.

My heartfelt thanks go out to every LGBTQ non-profit I have had the privilege of serving as a board member: The Center in New York City and the Transgender Legal Defense and Education Fund (TLDEF). I would especially like to thank PFLAG National, our amazing executive director Brian Bond, and my entire PFLAG family. Each of you has made me see the reward that comes with being a part of something much bigger than myself.

And, finally, to the people that have left this world while I wrote this book: My *older* brother Jimy (he gets the joke), my mother-in-law, Ruthann, my brother-in-law, Bill, and my dear friend Diana, who was the first person to recognize my writing ability and who showed me what the true meaning of friendship looks like; each of you forever occupy your own special place in my heart. I miss you and I love you.

www.ingramcontent.com/pod-product-compliance
Lightning Source LLC
Chambersburg PA
CBHW030406130626
46549CB00004B/1651